REA: THE LEADER IN CLEP® TEST PREP

CLEP® HUMAN GROWTH AND DEVELOPMENT

Norman Rose, Ph.D.

Research & Education Association
Visit our website at: www.rea.com

Research & Education Association
258 Prospect Plains Road
Cranbury, New Jersey 08512
Email: info@rea.com

CLEP® Human Growth and Development with Online Practice Exams, 10th Edition

Printed in the United States of America

Library of Congress Control Number: 2019930821

ISBN-13: 978-0-7386-1252-2
ISBN-10: 0-7386-1252-9

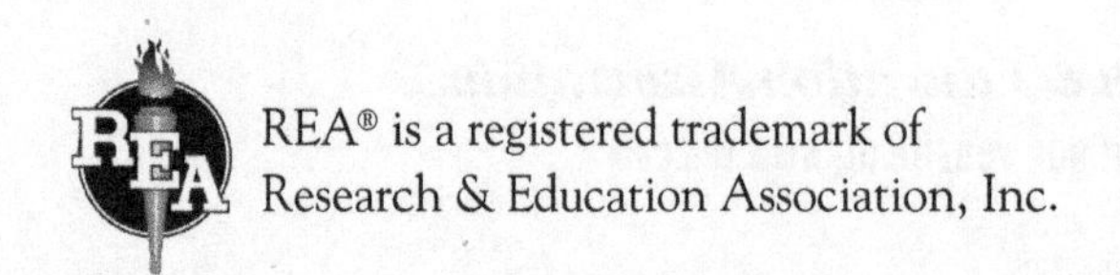

F19

CONTENTS

CHAPTER 3

CHAPTER 4

CHAPTER 5

CHAPTER 6

CHAPTER 7

CHAPTER 8

CHAPTER 9

CHAPTER 10

CHAPTER 13

CHAPTER 14

ABOUT OUR AUTHOR

Dr. Norman Rose is an instructor and online course development expert in the areas of education, psychology, and computer applications. His 25 years of teaching runs the gamut from early elementary to university-level teacher preparation programs.

Dr. Rose has developed online courses offered by Modern States Education Alliance, a nonprofit advocate for college access, for both CLEP Human Growth and Development and CLEP Introduction to Educational Psychology. He is the author of *The Design of Life: Human Development from a Natural Perspective* (Westphalia Press, 2016), published under the aegis of the Washington-based Policy Studies Organization. He has written numerous article, papers, and books on education, human development, and psychology.

Dr. Rose holds degrees in elementary education, psychology, sociology, and music from Washington University in St. Louis. He earned his doctorate in curriculum and instruction from the University of North Texas, Denton.

ABOUT REA

Founded in 1959, Research & Education Association (REA) is dedicated to publishing the finest and most effective educational materials—including study guides and test preps—for students of all ages.

Today, REA's wide-ranging catalog is a leading resource for students, teachers, and other professionals. Visit *www.rea.com* to see a complete listing of all our titles.

ACKNOWLEDGMENTS

We would like to thank Pam Weston, Publisher, for setting the quality standards for production integrity and managing the publication to completion; John Paul Cording, Technology Director, for coordinating the design and development of the online REA Study Center; Larry B. Kling, Editorial Director, for supervision of revisions and overall direction; Alice

Leonard, Senior Editor, for coordinating development of this edition; and Transcend Creative Services for typesetting this edition.

In addition, we extend our thanks to Jessica Flitter, AP Psychology teacher at West Bend East High School, West Bend, Wisconsin, for technically reviewing the manuscript; Diane Goldschmidt, Managing Editor, for editorial review; Karen Lamoreux for copyediting; Ellen Gong for proofreading; and Jennifer Calhoun for file management.

CHAPTER 1

PASSING THE CLEP HUMAN GROWTH AND DEVELOPMENT EXAM

Congratulations! You're joining the millions of people who have discovered the value and educational advantage offered by the College Board's College-Level Examination Program, or CLEP. This test prep focuses on what you need to know to succeed on the CLEP Human Growth and Development exam, and will help you earn the college credit you deserve while reducing your tuition costs.

GETTING STARTED

There are many different ways to prepare for a CLEP exam. What's best for you depends on how much time you have to study and how comfortable you are with the subject matter. To score your highest, you need a system that can be customized to fit you: your schedule, your learning style, and your current level of knowledge.

This book, and the online tools that come with it, allow you to create a personalized study plan through three simple steps: assessment of your knowledge, targeted review of exam content, and reinforcement in the areas where you need the most help.

Let's get started and see how this system works.

Test Yourself and Get Feedback	Assess your strengths and weaknesses. The score report from your online diagnostic exam gives you a fast way to pinpoint what you already know and where you need to spend more time studying.
Review with the Book	Armed with your diagnostic score report, review the parts of the book where you're weak and study the answer explanations for the test questions you answered incorrectly.
Ensure You're Ready for Test Day	After you've finished reviewing with the book, take our full-length practice tests. Review your score reports and re-study any topics you missed. We give you two full-length practice tests to ensure you're confident and ready for test day.

THE REA STUDY CENTER

The best way to personalize your study plan is to get feedback on what you know and what you don't know. At the online REA Study Center *(www.rea.com/studycenter)*, you can access two types of assessment: a diagnostic exam and full-length practice exams. Each of these tools provides true-to-format questions and delivers a detailed score report that follows the topics set by the College Board.

Diagnostic Exam

Before you begin your review with the book, take the online diagnostic exam. Use your score report to help evaluate your overall understanding of the subject, so you can focus your study on the topics where you need the most review.

Full-Length Practice Exams

Our full-length practice tests give you the most complete picture of your strengths and weaknesses. After you've finished reviewing with the book, test what you've learned by taking the first of the two online practice exams. Review your score report, then go back and study any topics you missed. Take the second practice test to ensure you have mastered the material and are ready for test day.

If you're studying and don't have Internet access, you can take the printed tests in the book. These are the same practice tests offered at the REA Study Center, but without the added benefits of timed testing conditions and diagnostic score reports. Because the actual exam is Internet-based, we recommend you take at least one practice test online to simulate test-day conditions.

AN OVERVIEW OF THE EXAM

The CLEP Human Growth and Development exam consists of approximately 90 multiple-choice questions, each with five possible answer choices, to be answered in 90 minutes.

The exam covers the material one would find in a college-level introductory course in developmental psychology or human development course. The exam stresses basic facts and principles, as well as general theoretical approaches used by psychologists.

The approximate breakdown of topics is as follows:

10%	Theoretical Perspectives
6%	Research Strategies and Methodology
12%	Biological Development Throughout the Life Span
6%	Perceptual Development Throughout the Life Span
12%	Cognitive Development Throughout the Life Span
8%	Language Development
6%	Intelligence Throughout the Life Span
12%	Social Development Throughout the Life Span
8%	Family, Home, and Society Throughout the Life Span
8%	Personality and Emotion
6%	Schooling, Work, and Interventions
6%	Developmental Psychopathology

CLEP and Technology-Enhanced Questions

While most of the questions you will find on your CLEP exam will be standard multiple-choice questions, the College Board is now incorporating some technology-enhanced questions. These new question types include: filling in a numeric answer; shading areas of an object; or putting items in the correct order. In addition, several exams now have an optional essay section.

If you're familiar with basic computer skills, you'll have no trouble handling these question types if you encounter them on your exam.

ALL ABOUT THE CLEP PROGRAM

What Is CLEP?

More adult learners use CLEP than any other credit-by-examination program in the United States. The CLEP program's 33 exams span five subject areas. The exams assess the material commonly required in an introductory-level college course. Based on recommendations from the American Council on Education, a passing score can earn you at least three credits per exam at more than 2,900 colleges and universities in the U.S. and abroad. Policies vary, so check with your school on the exams it accepts and the scores it requires. For a complete list of the CLEP subject examinations offered, visit the College Board website: *www.collegeboard.org/clep*.

Who Takes CLEP Exams?

CLEP exams are typically taken by people who have acquired knowledge outside the classroom and wish to bypass certain college courses and earn college credit. The CLEP program is designed to reward examinees for prior learning—no matter where or how that knowledge was acquired.

CLEP appeals to a wide spectrum of candidates, including home-schooled and high school students, adults returning to college, traditional-age college students, military personnel, veterans, and international students. There are no prerequisites, such as age or educational status, for taking CLEP examinations. However, because policies on granting credits vary among colleges, you should contact the particular institution from which you wish to receive CLEP credit.

How Is My CLEP Score Determined?

Your CLEP score is based on two calculations. First, your CLEP raw score is figured; this is just the total number of test items you answer correctly. After the test is administered, your raw score is converted to a scaled score through a process called *equating*. Equating adjusts for minor variations in difficulty across test forms and among test items, and ensures that your score accurately represents your performance on the exam regardless of when or where you take it, or on how well others perform on the same test form.

Your scaled score is the number your college will use to determine if you've performed well enough to earn college credit. Scaled scores for the CLEP exams are delivered on a 20–80 scale. Institutions can set their own scores for granting college credit, but a good passing estimate (based on recommendations from the American Council on Education) is generally a scaled score of 50, which usually requires getting roughly 66% of the questions correct.

For more information on scoring, contact the institution where you wish to be awarded the credit.

Who Administers the Exam?

CLEP exams are developed by the College Board, administered by Educational Testing Service (ETS), and involve the assistance of educators from throughout the United States. The test development process is designed and implemented to ensure that the content and difficulty level of the test are appropriate.

When and Where Is the Exam Given?

CLEP exams are administered year-round at more than 2,000 test centers in the United States and abroad. To find the test center nearest you and to register for the exam, contact the CLEP Program:

CLEP Services
P.O. Box 6600
Princeton, NJ 08541-6600
Phone: (800) 257-9558 (8 a.m. to 6 p.m. ET)
Fax: (610) 628-3726
Website: *www.collegeboard.org/clep*

The CLEP iBT Platform

To improve the testing experience for both institutions and test-takers, the College Board's CLEP Program has transitioned its 33 exams from the eCBT platform to an Internet-based testing (iBT) platform. All CLEP test-takers may now register for exams and manage their personal account information through the "My Account" feature on the CLEP website. This new feature simplifies the registration process and automatically downloads all pertinent information about the test session, making for a more streamlined check-in.

OPTIONS FOR MILITARY PERSONNEL AND VETERANS

CLEP exams are available free of charge to eligible military personnel as well as eligible civilian employees. All the CLEP exams are available at test centers on college campuses and military bases. Contact your Educational Services Officer or Navy College Education Specialist for more information. Visit the DANTES or College Board websites for details about CLEP opportunities for military personnel.

Eligible U.S. veterans may apply for reimbursement of CLEP exam fees pursuant to provisions of the Harry W. Colmery Veterans Educational Assistance Act of 2017, commonly called the "Forever GI Bill." For details on eligibility and how to apply for reimbursement, visit the U.S. Department of Veterans Affairs website at *www.gibill.va.gov*.

SSD ACCOMMODATIONS FOR CANDIDATES WITH DISABILITIES

Many test candidates qualify for special accommodations when taking CLEP exams. Accommodations include, among other things, extra time, screen magnification, modifiable screen colors, and untimed rest breaks that don't cut into test time. You must make arrangements for these accommodations in advance. For information, contact:

College Board SSD Program

P.O. Box 7504

London, KY 40742-7504

Phone: (866) 360-0114 (toll free) (Monday through Friday, 8 a.m. to 6 p.m. ET)

TTY: (609) 882-4118

Fax: (866) 360-0114

Email: *ssd@info.collegeboard.org*

Website: *www.collegeboard.org/students-with-disabilities*

6-WEEK STUDY PLAN

Be sure to set aside enough time—at least two hours each day—to study. The more time you spend studying, the more prepared and relaxed you will feel on the day of the exam.

Week	Activity
1	Take the Diagnostic Exam at the online REA Study Center. The score report will identify topics where you need the most review.
2–4	Study the review focusing on the topics you missed (or were unsure of) on the Diagnostic Exam.
5	Take Practice Test 1 at the REA Study Center. Review your score report and re-study any topics you missed.
6	Take Practice Test 2 at the REA Study Center to see how much your score has improved. If you still got a few questions wrong, go back to the review and study any topics you may have missed.

TEST-TAKING TIPS

Know the format of the test. Familiarize yourself with the CLEP computer screen beforehand by logging on to the College Board website. Waiting until test day to see what it looks like in the pretest tutorial risks injecting needless anxiety into your testing experience. Also, familiarizing yourself with the directions and format of the exam will save you valuable time on the day of the actual test.

Read all the questions—completely. Make sure you understand each question before looking for the right answer. Reread the question if it doesn't make sense.

Read all of the answers to a question. Just because you think you found the correct response right away, do not assume that it's the best answer. The last answer choice might be the correct answer.

Use the process of elimination. Stumped by a question? Don't make a random guess. Eliminate as many of the answer choices as possible. By eliminating just two answer choices, you give yourself a better chance of getting the item correct, since there will only be three choices left from which to make your guess. Remember, your score is based only on the number of questions you answer correctly.

Don't waste time! Don't spend too much time on any one question. Your time is limited, so pacing yourself is very important. Work on the easier questions first. Skip the difficult questions and go back to them if you have the time. Taking our timed practice tests online will help you learn how to budget your time.

Look for clues to answers in other questions. If you skip a question you don't know the answer to, you might find a clue to the answer elsewhere on the test.

Be sure that your answer registers before you go to the next item. Look at the screen to see that your mouse-click causes the pointer to darken the proper oval. If your answer doesn't register, you won't get credit for that question.

THE DAY OF THE EXAM

On test day, you should wake up early (after a good night's rest, of course) and have breakfast. Dress comfortably so you are not distracted by being too hot or too cold while taking the test. (Note that "hoodies" are not allowed.) Arrive at the test center early. This will allow you to collect your thoughts and relax before the test, and it will also spare you the anxiety that comes with being late.

Before you leave for the test center, make sure you have your admission form and another form of identification, which must contain a recent photograph, your name, and signature (i.e., driver's license, student identification card, or current alien registration card). You may not wear a digital watch (wrist or pocket), alarm watch, or wristwatch camera. In addition, no cell phones, dictionaries, textbooks, notebooks, briefcases, or packages will be permitted, and drinking, smoking, and eating are prohibited.

Good luck on the CLEP Human Growth and Development exam!

CHAPTER 2

THEORIES OF DEVELOPMENT

This chapter will examine the major theories that psychologists use to describe and explain human development. Later in this book, you will be introduced to numerous lesser theories within each of these. However, first it is important to understand some of the basic issues that all theories grapple with.

CONTROVERSIAL ISSUES REGARDING DEVELOPMENT

Nature versus Nurture

The **nature-versus-nurture controversy** is an old argument in philosophy and psychology. The question posed in this debate is whether our development is influenced more by the genetic makeup we inherit from our biological parents (nature) or by the experiences we have (nurture).

According to the nature view, development is an unfolding process guided by preprogrammed, genetic information. Development is seen as a predictable, predetermined unfolding of inherited traits and abilities. "Nature" emphasizes these areas:

- how the body and brain develop
- how initial personality can be genetically determined
- how disease or abnormality can be predicted

According to the nurture side, at birth the human mind is like a blank slate, or **tabula rasa**, and experience writes upon it. It is argued that we are shaped by the quality of nurturing and care we receive, as well as environmental influences that impact us. "Nurture" is especially important in these areas:

- how thinking and learning develop
- how personality develops
- how culture and environment affect various aspects of development

Theories of human development tend to emphasize either the "nature" or the "nurture" influence on development, but most theorists agree that it is unlikely for either one to be the sole influence on our growth and development. Both nature and nurture interact from conception forward. The goal of research in human development today is to understand the relative influence of each factor in the development of particular traits or abilities. For instance, researchers might try to discover what proportion of one's level of intelligence is the product of environment and experience, and what proportion is controlled by genes.

Patterns of Development

Theories differ in how they describe development. **Discontinuity** or **stage theories** argue that development progresses through a series of distinct, discrete phases. Each phase or stage is seen as involving a specific set of traits and tasks. Once the defining biological process or psychological task is accomplished (fully or enough), the individual moves on to the next stage. The developing person is viewed as changing qualitatively, not just maturing quantitatively or sequentially.

Continuity theories, on the other hand, suggest development is best described as a steady growth process. Developmental change is described as occurring in small steps or increments. Skills and behavior improve, but the person does not change qualitatively. An 11-year-old, for example, can remember more information compared to an 8-year-old, but does not go about remembering the information in a qualitatively different way.

Child Development versus Life Span Perspective

Some theories of development argue that psychological and cognitive development is complete by the onset of adulthood. **Sigmund Freud** and **Jean Piaget** are two examples of theorists who argued that development was complete once one reached or completed adolescence. However, life span theories of development argue that growth and change continue to occur throughout the entire life span. **Erik Erikson** is a theorist who took a **life span perspective**.

Universality versus Context-Specific Development

Some developmentalists search for universals of development. These theorists underscore the similarities in development across cultures and historical time periods. Piaget is an example of the former approach. He argued that all children progress through the same stages of cognitive development in the same order and at the same approximate ages. Hence, for Piaget there was a **universality** of cognitive development.

Other developmentalists emphasize the role that the environment plays in development. **Urie Bronfenbrenner** is an example of this approach. Bronfenbrenner created an ecological systems theory of development that describes various social contexts in which development takes place, such as home and school. Development is affected as the child forms relationships within those contexts. The quality of conditions and relations in one context can affect relations in other contexts. To prove their point, psychologists who argue for **context-specific** development point out that there are differences in development between people from **collectivist cultures** and those who are from **individualistic cultures**. A collectivist culture places greater value on the common good than individual achievement. An individualistic culture values individual achievement and the pursuit of individual goals. Individuals from those two kinds of culture develop different personality and social traits due to the differences in cultural outlook.

With these issues and debates in mind, it is time to examine the major theories and perspectives in human development.

THEORETICAL PERSPECTIVES

The following paragraphs provide an overview of the various types of theories on human development. You will see that within each theoretical perspective, there are variations on its main theme. This has come about due to experimentation and theorizing carried out by a progression of scientists who study or practice within each perspective.

Because these are just overviews, be aware that each of these perspectives shows up in future chapters where they are discussed in greater detail. Applications of these theories will also be presented later. It is to your advantage to learn to identify which theory supports any particular real-world application or practice, such as used in schools.

Also note that some of these theories originated before there could be scientific research to verify them. Modern studies in such sciences as genome-typing and brain scanning have led to confirmation as well as modification of the major theories.

Evolutionary Theory

Ethology and evolutionary psychology are theoretical perspectives on development that grew out of **Charles Darwin's Theory of Evolution**. The main characteristics of Darwin's theory are:

(1) there are never enough resources in the environment for all members of a species to survive, so there is a constant struggle for existence among members of a species;

(2) there are variations in traits and abilities among members of a species that are the product of chance combinations of inherited traits from their ancestors;

(3) some chance variations in traits will better enable members of a species to adapt and survive in the environment in which they live; and

(4) those members who do survive will reproduce, passing on the chance variations they inherited into the gene pool.

Therefore, though this process is called **natural selection**, traits of a species evolve very gradually over time. Chance variations that increase chances of survival are passed down to offspring. Chance variations that do not increase chances of survival pass out of the gene pool. Darwin also argued that there is continuity between species, and that humans evolved from related animal species.

Both ethology and evolutionary psychology see human development within the framework of Darwin's theory of evolution. Both attempt to identify the historical roots of human traits and behaviors, and to understand their adaptive value, i.e., how traits contributed to survival in the past, even if they are not so helpful now. **Ethologists** conduct comparative studies of humans and other animal species such as the chimpanzee. An important finding of ethologists is that there are **critical periods** in development. A critical period is a narrow span of time within which a trait or behavior must develop, or it will never appear. An example of a behavior that has a critical period for development is imprinting in ducklings, i.e., following a mother duck. Ducklings will imprint when they are a few days old if they are exposed to their mother, but they will never imprint if this exposure does not take place during a critical window of time. When applying this phenomenon to humans, psychologists prefer the term **sensitive period** to critical period. There may be a window of time that is the most conducive for the development of a human behavior or skill, such as language, but humans can still acquire such behavior to some degree beyond this time.

Evolutionary scientists view human development in the womb as recapitulating (repeating) the evolution of species: progressing in appearance from fish to amphibian to reptile to mammal. Likewise, these psychologists view human development over the life span as recapitulating the evolution of lower species and our own. They focus on discovering the adaptive, survival value of specific animal and human behaviors. Traits and behaviors in the newborn, for example, are viewed as residuals of the behavior coming out of our most primitive ancestors. **Konrad Lorenz** and **John Bowlby** are among the more influential theorists within this perspective. Both Bowlby and Lorenz studied the mother-infant relationship in animals. Their work is discussed in more detail in Chapter 10: Social Development throughout the Life Span.

Biological Theory

From a biological perspective, much of human development is dependent on inborn patterns and traits. At the most basic level, the structure and content of DNA seems to determine everything from hair color to temperament to the tendency or certainty of contracting a disease. In physiological function, body chemistry seems to use hormones in the brain and other parts of the body to dictate our responses or reactions to stimuli.

For these reasons, the work of biological researchers is important to our understanding of how humans behave and develop over the life span. Some of that research gives us data about what is typical or normal for human growth. But much of the research centers around what can thwart natural processes and cycles of development. For instance, there can be

- aberrations in the DNA or in the chromosomes of individuals that cause structural or cognitive defects
- pharmaceutical or environmental substances that cause developmental problems
- nutritional excesses or deficiencies that affect development

These topics will be discussed mainly in Chapter 4: Biological Development throughout the Life Span, and Chapter 5: Perceptual Development throughout the Life Span. But it is important to recognize that biology is a strong influence in all the topics in each of the other chapters.

Cognitive Developmental Theory

Piaget: Pioneer of cognitive developmental theory

Until his death in 1980, **Jean Piaget** was a predominant figure in the field of cognitive psychology. It is safe to suggest that perhaps no other single individual has had greater influence on modern educational practices than Piaget.

Piaget, through observations of his own children, developed a theory about how learning takes place through a series of processes. **Adaptation** involves the complementary processes of **assimilation** and **accommodation** to create each mental category or **schema** (plural **schemata**) in the developing mind.

Piaget also postulated that there are four distinct life stages of cognitive development. In other words, he maintained that thinking actually changes qualitatively over several years of life. The infant begins learning through direct interaction with the environment—looking, touching, moving, hearing. Later, the toddler or young child is characterized by rigid, semi-logical, and egocentric reasoning. The elementary-aged child can think more concretely, is less egocentric, and can group, sort, and sequence—making it possible to read and do basic math. Finally, the older child and adolescent can engage in abstract thought, including logic and scientific reasoning.

You will find more on Piaget in several of the following chapters, due to his influence in the fields of cognition and education.

Information processing

A newer approach to studying cognitive development is the **information-processing approach**. This theoretical perspective uses the computer as a metaphor for the human mind and studies how the human mind processes information. Information-processing theorists examine how information (learning) is stored and retrieved, and how those processes change in capacity and speed as individuals mature.

Information processing will be discussed further in Chapter 7: Cognitive Development throughout the Life Span, and Chapter 13: Schooling, Work, and Interventions.

Moral development

Lawrence Kohlberg extended Piaget's model of cognitive development to the study of the development of moral reasoning. His stage model of moral reasoning is discussed in Chapter 10: Social Development throughout the Life Span.

Psychodynamic Theory

Psychodynamic theories of personality developed from Sigmund Freud's original **psychoanalytic theory**. For most psychodynamic theorists, personality is mainly unconscious. That is, it is outside of one's awareness. To understand someone's personality and its development (or one's own), the symbolic meanings of behavior and hidden inner workings of the mind must be investigated. Early life experiences are considered most important in the development of personality, with primary focus on how parents' actions and attitudes shape personalities.

Freud's Theory

Sigmund Freud (1856–1939) was a medical doctor from Vienna, Austria, who specialized in neurology. His psychoanalytic approach to personality developed from his work with adult patients who had psychiatric and emotional problems. Freud's theory emphasized three main points: the formative early childhood years that affect adult function, the presence and power of the unconscious mind, and the influence of unconscious conflicts on human behavior.

To explain how unconscious feelings and urges influence a person's daily behavior, Freud constructed a model of personality, consisting of three components: an **animalistic id**, a **socially responsible ego**, and a **moralistic superego**. According to Freud, behavior is the result of ongoing inner conflicts among those three personality components. These conflicts occur because primitive sexual and aggressive impulses are not socially acceptable and must be discouraged. So the mind finds ways to deal with these conflicts that may or may not result in healthy or socially appropriate behavior.

Freud considered personality to be like an iceberg, with the mind repressing undesirable thoughts and conflicts down into the unseen unconscious mind. This causes anxiety, which the mind assuages by creating defense mechanisms. However, defense mechanisms can lead to personality distortions ranging from quirky to dangerous.

There is much more to Freud's theory of personality, and it will be discussed in greater detail in Chapter 12: Personality and Emotions. The more severe personality distortions that he and his followers have noted will be discussed in Chapter 14: Developmental Psychopathology.

Erikson's Psychosocial Stages of Development

Another psychodynamic theory of personality development was offered by **Erik Erikson**, who was trained in Freudian psychoanalytic theory and practice. Erikson's theory, however, was very different from Freud's. For instance, Erikson believed that personality continues to develop over the entire life span (not just through childhood). Also, Erikson emphasized innate urges or challenges at each stage, rather than id-driven motives or desires. The degree of success in meeting the challenges of each stage would determine later social and emotional development.

Erikson considered his construct to be a **psychosocial theory**, because it was based on emotional and social adjustment, as opposed to psychosexual adjustment. While Freud described development as the resolution of conflicts arising between instinctual drives and social expectations, Erikson argued that the developing individual is faced with social-emotional tasks that progressively enable the individual to function in the social world. According to Erikson, at each stage the ego either strengthens by mastering a psychosocial crisis or task, or else weakens by failing in the task. Mastery or failure will influence how the individual will be able to cope with the challenges of the next stage.

This theory will be discussed in detail in Chapter 10: Social Development throughout the Life Span, and Chapter 12: Personality and Emotions.

Ecological and Sociocultural Theory

The sociocultural theory of development argues that there is a bidirectional relationship between the child and the sociocultural environment, such that a child influences the people and the environments he or she interacts with, as much as those people and environments influence the child's development. This is known as **reciprocal determinism**.

Lev Vygotsky offered a sociocultural theory of cognitive development. His theory offers an alternative to Piaget's approach. Vygotsky was critical of Piaget because he believed Piaget had not taken into consideration the social influences on cognition. He noted that a child interacts with peers and adults, not just with objects in the environment. Vygotsky believed a great deal of cognitive growth comes from these social interactions. He observed that societies have particular and culturally specific ways of understanding the world. These understandings are transmitted through the members of the culture through cooperative dialogue among peers and especially between children and adults. Older children and adults provide what Vygotsky called **scaffolding**, which is cognitive support provided to a younger thinker by a more advanced thinker. In this theory, the young thinker can only function at the lowest level of his or her **zone of proximal development (ZPD)** when trying to learn a skill. An older thinker helps the younger one function at the highest level of the ZPD, and that social mediation accelerates the learning process. Vygotsky also studied the role of language in the development of cognition. You will find his ideas discussed in Chapter 7: Cognitive Development throughout the Life Span, and Chapter 9: Language Development, as well as in Chapter 13: Schooling, Work, and Interventions.

Urie Bronfenbrenner developed an **ecological systems theory** of development, also called the bioecological approach. He emphasized the influence of sociocultural contexts on development. His bioecological approach describes development as taking place within various systems that the child participates in or is affected by. He studied how the psychological and biological changes within the child influence his or her environment and, in turn, how various environmental systems influence the child's development. According to Bronfenbrenner, a child's development is affected by several contexts or systems, starting with the home and family and expanding outward into school and culture. Development is also influenced by contexts that the child does not participate in directly, such as parents' work. Bronfenbrenner's theory is discussed further in Chapter 11: Family, Home, and Society throughout the Life Span.

Learning Theory

Learning theory, or the **behaviorist perspective**, describes developmental change as the product of learning. These theorists fall more heavily on the nurture side of the nature-versus-nurture debate and are continuity theorists who define learning as changes in observable behavior. In 1913, John Watson founded a school of psychology called Behaviorism (or Behavioral Psychology) as the basis for learning theory. Important figures in this theoretical perspective include Pavlov, Watson, Thorndike, and Skinner.

Learning theory suggests that behavior is controlled by actions or reactions to stimuli in the environment. **Ivan Pavlov** conditioned dogs to salivate at the sound of a bell because they learned to associate the bell with the arrival of food. This proved that learning could take place when reflexive or automatic behavior comes under the control of a novel stimulus. This process is known as **classical conditioning**.

John Watson extended classical conditioning by focusing on changing emotional responses in children. From his experiments, he argued that we learn to associate new environmental stimuli with reflexive emotional responses. This work served as the foundation for the classical conditioning theory of phobias or irrational fears (to be covered in Chapter 14: Developmental Psychopathology).

Edward Thorndike conducted animal experiments that led to his **Law of Effect**. This law states that behavior that leads to pleasant consequences will likely be repeated, while behavior that leads to unpleasant consequences will not likely be repeated. **B.F. Skinner** further developed the learning principles of **operant conditioning** by demonstrating that behavior is shaped by the reinforcing or punishing consequences that follow it.

Note: Learning theory is a continuity theory, as opposed to a discontinuity or stage theory. It assumes that all learning takes place by the same processes at all times. As one matures, one carries lessons learned into the next learning experience, but the same processes of associations, rewards, and punishments will still define all future learning. It is not a "developmental" perspective in the sense of describing changes through the life span. So, learning theory has to be treated differently from other theories. A fuller explanation of learning theory and how it is applied appears in Chapter 9: Language Development, and Chapter 13: Schooling, Work, and Interventions.

Social Cognitive Theory

Albert Bandura created a major shift in thinking about learning in the late 1960s with a **social-cognitive theory** of learning (also called **social learning theory**). He introduced the idea that changes in behavior are acquired not only through the processes of conditioning, but also through **observational learning**. The process of **modeling** is observing the behavior of a model and then later imitating that behavior. Bandura observed that people can exhibit a new behavior in its complete form after simply watching someone else perform that behavior. In short, we can learn by observation. Bandura went on to study the factors that control modeling, including what influences one's choice of a model and the underlying cognitive processes required for modeling, such as self-efficacy beliefs.

This theory and the behaviorists will be discussed in greater detail in Chapter 6: Learning through Behavioral Change. It is covered there since it describes a type of mostly instinctive shaping of behavior, and because it does not predict or describe changes throughout the life span. Even if a person matures and switches role models, the process of observing and imitating stays the same.

Humanistic Psychology Theory

Humanistic psychology is the newest of all the theories presented here. It is based on the work of **Abraham Maslow** and was furthered by the therapeutic practices of **Carl Rogers**. Unlike psychodynamic psychology, it emphasizes what is positive about human development, rather than focusing on what can go wrong. In other words, it attempts to outline what contributes to an individual's maximum potential for happiness, well-being, and social functioning. It is associated with psychological and social phenomena such as the human potential movement and positive psychology.

Maslow was interested in living and historical figures who exhibited fine character qualities, such as compassion, creativity, and wisdom. He traced the origins and processes that led to their exemplary abilities and traits. As a result, he theorized that human potential was closely tied to a **hierarchy of needs**. He represented that hierarchy with a pyramid diagram. The diagram is meant to show the steps or levels that individuals must go through to reach their maximum potential cognitively, emotionally, and socially.

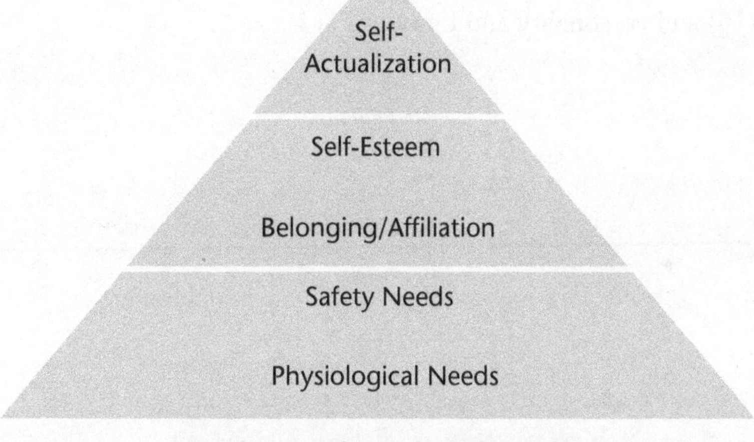

Maslow's Hierarchy of Needs

When the lowest needs are met, the individual will begin to feel new and higher needs arise. For instance, once basic needs of food, water, and safety are met, a person begins to desire social connections and intimacy. When that has been met, a person feels the urge to attain recognition and self-esteem through learning or achievement. And when that has been met, the person feels the need to function optimally, with assurance, wisdom, and courage. Maslow later added a level above self-actualization, which he called self-transcendence. This level is marked by selflessness in all aspects of thought and living.

Of course, some exceptional people do not seem to respect the hierarchy. They rise above their lack of basic provisions and safety to achieve great things despite hardships. We can think of certain writers, artists, and social activists in this regard.

According to this theory, self-actualization does not occur very often, as adults find themselves stressed to meet family and career demands. So they do not tend to achieve high levels of happiness or wisdom or strength of character. Most adults just "get by" as they cope with their complex lives. It takes deliberate steps to reach that top-most level, which might include therapy, self-reflection, or other activities that "free up" the individual to be the best version of themselves.

Is humanistic psychology a developmental theory? If so, is it a discontinuity or stage theory? In some ways, the answer is yes. In our society, children are usually born into a setting in which physiological and safety needs are met on a regular basis. By school age, most are ready to pursue affiliation and self-esteem needs, which expand and progress into adulthood. Thus, the hierarchy of needs does seem to define a stage progression of development. You will find applications of humanistic psychology theory in the chapters on Social Development (10) and Personality and Emotions (12).

CHAPTER 3

RESEARCH STRATEGIES AND METHODOLOGY

One or more individuals used experimentation to create each theory discussed in the last chapter. Once each new theory was proposed and accepted in the scientific community, it then became essential for others to verify the theory and to discern the limits, implications, and applications of each theory. Those tasks define the role of researchers. Research is essential for determining the validity, extent, and limits of theories.

Psychological research is based on the scientific method. The scientific method consists of five steps:

(1) defining a research problem;

(2) proposing a hypothesis and making predictions;

(3) designing and conducting a research study;

(4) analyzing the data;

(5) communicating the results, and building or revising theories.

When researching some aspect of development, it is obvious that entire populations cannot be interviewed or observed. (You could not study all 7-year-olds if you wanted to find out what social skills were possible at that age.) A **sample** is a subset of a **population** selected to participate in the study. All the participants in a research study make up the sample. A population includes all members of a class or set from which a smaller sample may be drawn and about whom the researcher wants to draw conclusions.

A **random sample** is one in which every member of the population being studied has an equal chance of being picked for inclusion in the study. A **biased sample** occurs when every member of a population does not have an equal chance of being chosen. Researchers are better able to generalize their findings to an entire population if a random sample is used. This seems obvious and easy, but it is not. For instance, getting a truly random sample of 7-year-olds to study social skills would require making sure every ethnic, economic, religious, and geographical group had equal opportunity to be represented. Since this is not possible, follow-up studies can use different sampling methods to test the same hypothesis. For instance, research that studied children in schools in one city might be followed by a similar study involving children in a city located in a different region of the country or in a rural or suburban area.

THE EXPERIMENT

Psychologists use the **experimental design** to determine cause-and-effect relationships. An **experiment** requires that the researcher systematically manipulate and control one or more variables and then observe how the research subjects or participants respond to this manipulation. The variable that is manipulated is called the **independent variable**. The response that is measured after the manipulation (or intervention) of the independent variable is known as the **dependent variable**.

An experiment consists of at least two groups of participants. The **experimental group** is the group that is exposed to the manipulation of the independent variable. Some experiments have more than one experimental group, meaning there are several different manipulations of the independent variable. The **control group** of an experiment is not exposed to the independent variable. The responses of participants in the control group are compared to the responses of participants in the experimental group(s) to determine whether the independent variable(s) had any effect on the dependent variable.

Participants usually are assigned to experimental groups based on random assignment, which ensures that each participant has an equal chance of being assigned to any one of the groups. Random assignment helps guarantee that the groups are similar to one another with respect to important characteristics before the manipulation of the independent variable. When participants are not randomly assigned to groups, the study is referred to as a **quasi-experiment**. A study is called a **field experiment** if it is conducted in the participants' natural setting rather than in a laboratory. This is the preferred method when a researcher is concerned that the artificiality of the laboratory setting might affect the experimental outcome.

Example of an Experiment
Research question: Does praising or rewarding middle school students' helping behavior cause an increase of helping behavior? (field experiment)
Population: Students in 6th grade
Sampling: 6th grade students in three classrooms in an ethnically diverse middle school
Independent variable A: Teacher A will give out verbal praise for helping behavior. **Independent variable B**: Teacher B will give out small rewards for helping behavior. **Control group**: Teacher C will give neither praise nor rewards for helping behavior.
Dependent variable: Helping behaviors by students as tabulated by observers each day for 2 weeks.

A **single-subject experiment** involves the participation of only one subject. The independent variable is systematically changed over time, and the subject's behavior at one time is compared with the same subject's behavior at another time. In this case, time is used as the control. For instance, a 20-year-old might be given different treatments for depression in 1-month trials. Both observed and self-reported results for each treatment would be compared at the end of all the trials.

Subject bias occurs when research participants' behavior changes because they know they are being studied or because of their expectations. Here are two examples of this:

- If subjects change behavior because they know they are being observed—even if they are in the control group that is not getting any manipulation or intervention—it is called the **Hawthorne effect**. In the example above, some middle school students might exhibit behaviors different from usual just because they see that someone is observing them.
- A **placebo effect** occurs when participants believe they are experiencing a change due to a drug they have been given, when in fact they have been given a placebo with no medical effect.

Observer or **researcher bias** occurs when the expectations of the researcher influence what is recorded or measured. To control both subject and observer biases, a double-blind technique is used. In the **double-blind technique**, neither the participants nor the researcher who is measuring the dependent variable knows who is assigned to which group in an experiment. In the example of observing middle school students, such bias might occur if an observer knows the students or talks with them after class time, or if the observer knows which intervention the class is getting.

CORRELATIONAL RESEARCH

Nonexperimental methods of research do not include the systematic manipulation of variables by the researcher and thus cannot be used to define cause-and-effect relationships.

Correlational research involves measuring two (or more) variables to determine whether they are related. If the value of one variable increases as the other variable also increases in value, or if one decreases as the other decreases, this is known as a positive correlation. A negative correlation occurs when there is an inverse relationship between the variables measured; that is, as the value of one increases, the value of the other decreases.

A **correlation coefficient** is a calculated number that represents the statistical strength of the relationship between the variables measured. A correlation coefficient can range in value from −1 to 1. A correlation coefficient of 1 indicates a perfect positive relationship between the two variables, while a coefficient of −1 indicates a perfect negative correlation. With 1 or −1, you can predict one variable exactly by knowing the value of the other. Therefore, the closer a correlation coefficient is to plus or minus 1, the stronger the relationship between the variables measured. A correlation coefficient of 0 indicates no relationship between the variables measured. So the closer a correlation coefficient is to 0, the weaker the relationship.

Even if a strong correlational relationship is found, however, cause-and-effect conclusions *cannot* be made because there is no systematic manipulation by the researcher. For instance, you might find that during a 1-year period, a population's ice cream consumption has a positive correlation with the number of drownings in that population. You cannot conclude that increased consumption of ice cream causes an increase in drownings. Obviously, they are both caused by something else, namely seasonal changes in temperature.

OBSERVATIONAL RESEARCH

Descriptive or **observational research** methods are used to obtain accurate records of behavior without manipulating or controlling any variables. **Naturalistic observation** is a type of descriptive research study that occurs in a natural setting that has not been manipulated or altered by the researcher. The researcher systematically observes and records what occurs in an unobtrusive manner. This is done so that the behavior of the participants being observed is typical for them. Sometimes it is useful to employ more than one observer. **Inter-observer** reliability is the calculated amount of agreement between two (or more) observers who simultaneously observe the same event.

Survey research is another descriptive method that requires the researcher to ask a group of people about behaviors, thoughts, or opinions. Data is collected through interviews or questionnaires. The **interview** has the advantage over a questionnaire in that the interviewer can see the reactions of the person being interviewed and may also be able to ask follow-up questions. The disadvantage is that a person being interviewed face-to-face with an interviewer may not provide complete or truthful information. Responding to questions in a way that is perceived to be more acceptable to the interviewer is called social desirability.

Questionnaires have the advantage of being able to reach a very large and geographically diverse sample of a population. They have the disadvantage of potentially having a low rate of response—in other words, there might not be enough people responding to make the data analysis reliable. Or there might be a disproportionate number of responses from one type of person over other types. For instance, if a questionnaire is sent out to teachers, perhaps not enough will respond, or perhaps mostly only younger teachers will respond.

CASE STUDY

A **case study** is a descriptive research method that is an in-depth study of a single subject or specific group of subjects. It can include interviews, observations, and test results. It is particularly useful to study some unusual trait or circumstance. For instance, one could do a case study on a refugee child's adaptation to school in a new country. The results of this study could be reported as a narrative supported by observational (qualitative) data as well as quantitative data such as test scores and attendance records. All the data can be analyzed, and conclusions can be drawn. Such a report could help professionals relate this child's situation to children in similar situations, through the process of inductive reasoning.

CROSS-SECTIONAL RESEARCH DESIGN

The **cross-sectional research design** is used to examine subjects, or differences between different-aged subjects, at one point in time. A single sample of subjects is studied if the researcher just wants to know something about that group—like a snapshot of that group at one point in its life span. For instance, a researcher might ask a cross-section of high school juniors their opinions regarding curfews.

If the researcher wants to compare some trait at different ages, more than one group of subjects is chosen. In this case, the researcher recruits two or more samples of participants of differing ages and measures them on some variable. For example, a researcher interested in age differences in short-term memory capacity could administer the same memory test to thirty 10-year-olds and thirty 50-year-olds. One weakness of this design is that if the younger group performs better than the older group on the memory test, the group difference could be due to either differences in age or because they are from two different generations, or birth cohorts. Perhaps one generation had more need for or experience with short-term memory tasks than the other one. So the researcher cannot conclude that memory capacity declines with age. However, the strength of this approach is that it is a quick and easy way to collect information on how different age groups differ at one point in time.

LONGITUDINAL RESEARCH DESIGN

In the previous example, there was a problem with comparing two different age groups at the same time, since each group was not only at a different life stage, but also had different generational experiences. The **longitudinal research design** measures changes on a variable in the *same* group of participants at several points in their lives. For example, a psychologist interested in the development of memory capacity could recruit 30 participants who are currently 10 years old, and measure their memory skills, labeling this as Time 1; then measure again when they are 20 years old, calling it Time 2; and finally again when they are 30 years old, labeled Time 3.

A strength of this approach is that differences in performance can be interpreted as indicating changes that occur with age. One weakness is that it is time consuming and expensive to carry out. In addition, subject mortality (dropout) is a problem with this design. Findings may be biased if subject dropout has occurred. The participants who complete the study may differ in significant ways from those participants who have dropped out. The participants who complete the memory study described above may be healthier or have better memory ability compared to those who dropped out.

CROSS-SEQUENTIAL RESEARCH DESIGN

It is obvious that both the cross-sectional and the longitudinal designs can be difficult to carry out or to interpret. The **sequential (or cross-sequential) research design** was created by **Klaus Warner Schaie** in his research on developmental changes in intelligence over time. Schaie was concerned that there are significant differences in intelligence between birth cohorts or generations.

He designed this methodology, which combines the cross-sectional and longitudinal designs, to examine cohort differences. You can think of it as staggered layering or staggered timing.

Example: At Time 1 in the year 2000, a sample of 10-year-olds and a sample of 20-year-olds are both tested for reaction times to identify camouflaged animals in pictures. At Time 2, 10 years later in 2010, both samples come back to be tested. Also, a new sample of 10-year-olds is tested then. (So now there are 3 samples in the study.) At Time 3 in 2020, all three groups are tested again, 10 years later. With this design, time has been "compacted"—being able to get results on 10-, 20-, 30-, and 40-year-olds within a space of 20 years. And with this design there are both longitudinal and cross-sectional results for comparison. Researchers have been able to quantify or account for **birth cohort effects** using this design.

The following chart compares the various research methods discussed in this chapter.

Comparing Research Models

Method	Strengths	Weaknesses
Experiment	Can test cause-and-effect relationships. Researcher has control.	Sampling errors. Can be hard to generalize to the real world.
Correlation	Can study real-world behavior. Can determine relationships.	Cannot determine cause-and-effect.
Naturalistic Observation	Can gather information in its usual setting as it naturally occurs.	Cannot determine cause-and-effect. Observer or subject bias possible.
Case Study	Intensive information can be gathered about individuals.	Cannot determine cause-and-effect. Expensive and time-consuming. May not be able to generalize information gathered. Biased sample possible. Researcher bias possible.

(continued)

Comparing Research Models (continued)

Method	Strengths	Weaknesses
Survey or Interview	Large amounts of information can be gathered from many people in a relatively short period of time.	Cannot determine cause-and-effect. Biased sample possible. Response bias possible. Questions might not be reliable or valid.
Cross-sectional	Data show differences between different-aged people at one point in time. Relatively quick and inexpensive.	Cannot show changes that occur with age. Findings may be subject to birth cohort effects.
Longitudinal	Data show how a sample of people change as they age.	Time-consuming and expensive. May not be able to generalize the findings to other birth cohorts. May have the problem of subject dropout.
Sequential (Cross-sequential)	Has the strengths of both the cross-sectional and longitudinal methods and can also measure birth cohort effects.	Time-consuming and expensive. May have the problem of subject dropout.

CHAPTER 4

BIOLOGICAL DEVELOPMENT THROUGHOUT THE LIFE SPAN

Psychologists studying development make a distinction between developmental changes that are the result of learning versus changes due to **maturation**, which is genetically programmed biological development. (This is the nature-versus-nurture debate.) Biological development is an area controlled substantially by maturation (nature) but is still affected to some degree by environmental influences. Other facets of development—cognitive and psychosocial, for instance—differ in the degree to which they are controlled by experience versus maturation.

HEREDITY, GENETICS, AND GENETIC TESTING

Evolutionary psychologists study heredity, that is, the traits and behaviors that are common in all humans. For example, all healthy neonates (newborns) are born equipped with the same set of motor reflexes. Psychologists also study individual inheritance to understand individual differences in traits and abilities. Both types of inheritance are controlled by information carried in the thousands of **genes** on the 46 **chromosomes** found in the nucleus of each cell in the human body.

Chromosomes are arranged in pairs. Twenty-two of these pairs are called **autosomes** and carry genetic material that controls all our characteristics except for biological sex. These 22 pairs of chromosomes are the same in males and females. The two chromosomes of the 23rd pair are called the **allosomes,** or **sex chromosomes**. In normal females, the sex chromosome pair is XX and normal males inherit an XY pair. (The X and Y relate to the shape of the chromosome, as seen in powerful magnification.) Biological parents pass on one set (not pairs) of 23 chromosomes in each **sperm** cell or **ovum**. The mother can only pass on an X sex chromosome since she has an XX pair, but the father can pass on either an X or a Y chromosome in each sperm cell. The biological father's sperm cell therefore determines the sex of the offspring.

When a sperm cell of the biological father penetrates and fertilizes an ovum from the biological mother, conception occurs, and the new cell that is formed is called a **zygote**. This process of fertilization normally takes place in the fallopian tube of the mother. The zygote then travels down the tube to the uterus and embeds in the uterine wall. The zygote contains 23 newly paired chromosomes that control its development. The zygote will develop into a female unless there is a Y sex chromosome present. A gene on the Y chromosome causes the fertilized cell to differentiate into a male.

Dominant-Recessive Principle of Inheritance

Chromosomes are composed of genes. Some of the genes controlling our characteristics are dominant while others are recessive. (Think of inherited traits such as color of hair or eyes.) A **dominant gene** is the more powerful of the two types. A **recessive gene** will not be able to exert any influence on a characteristic if it is paired with a dominant gene. Gene pairs can be:

- dominant-dominant
- dominant-recessive
- recessive-recessive

A trait carried on a dominant gene is called a dominant trait, and a trait that is carried on a recessive gene is called a recessive trait. A trait carried on a dominant gene will always be expressed regardless of what type of gene it is paired with. A recessive trait can only be expressed as a characteristic of the individual if the individual inherits a recessive-recessive gene pair. Someone who inherits a dominant-recessive gene pair is called a carrier of the recessive trait. Carriers can pass on a dominant gene or a recessive gene to their offspring. **Genotype** is the term used to describe all the traits carried in a person's genetic material, including recessive traits, but the characteristics that are expressed are referred to as an individual's **phenotype**.

The dominant-recessive principle becomes very important when studying genetic diseases. Some diseases are inherited because the program for the disease is carried in a gene or set of genes. There are genetic diseases carried by dominant genes and diseases carried by recessive genes. **Genetic testing** can be done in couples considering having children to determine whether either person is a carrier of a genetic disease. **Genetic counseling** is available to help couples make decisions about childbearing by calculating their chances of passing on a genetic disease or abnormality to their offspring.

GENETIC DISORDERS

Some developmental abnormalities have a genetic basis, but there are several different mechanisms of inheritance that produce normal traits as well as abnormalities. **Single gene-pair inheritance** describes a trait or abnormality controlled by just one gene pair. (Recall that single gene-pair inheritance follows the dominant-recessive principle.) These are some examples of single gene-pair abnormalities:

Sickle cell anemia is caused by two recessive genes. People with this disease have abnormally shaped red blood cells that carry less oxygen than normal through the circulatory system. People with this disease have trouble breathing when they exert themselves and often die of kidney failure by adolescence. There are more carriers of sickle cell among the African-American population than the general population.

Huntington's disease is genetically transmitted via a dominant gene on chromosome four. This gene causes nervous system deterioration and is fatal. Since it is a dominant gene trait, a child who inherits the gene from just one parent will have the disease.

Phenylketonuria (**PKU**) is caused by a pair of recessive genes which cause a child to be unable to metabolize phenylalanine, an amino acid found naturally in protein foods and put into artificial sweeteners. This disease is typically managed with a diet free of phenylalanine, but without this controlled diet, a buildup of phenylalanine in the system will cause intellectual disability and hyperactivity.

Tay-Sachs disease, like Huntington's disease, causes nervous system degeneration and is fatal. Unlike Huntington's, Tay-Sachs is carried by a pair of recessive genes.

Cystic fibrosis is also caused by a pair of recessive genes and is a disease that causes a build-up of mucous in the lungs and is eventually fatal.

Sickle cell anemia, cystic fibrosis, phenylketonuria (PKU), Huntington's disease, and Tay-Sachs disease are all caused by an inheritance from a single gene-pair. All of them are recessive traits, except for Huntington's disease which is carried on a dominant gene.

It is also important to know what traits are related to the sex of an individual. **Autosomal** traits are related to the 22 autosomes, while **allosomal** traits are related to the 23rd chromosome pair, the sex chromosome. **Sex-linked inheritance** occurs when a trait or disease is carried by a gene on the sex chromosome pair (XX for female, XY for male). For instance, **color blindness** is carried on a recessive gene on the X chromosome and is therefore called a **sex-linked recessive**

trait. A male who inherits this recessive gene will be color-blind because it is impossible for him to also have a dominant gene on a second X chromosome to repress the recessive trait. Females who are color-blind have a recessive-recessive gene pair. **Hemophilia** is also carried the same way as color blindness. There are also **sex-linked dominant disorders**, although they are relatively rare.

Abnormalities can also be caused by chromosomal irregularities and genetic mutations in the fetus. A genetic mutation is a change to the structure of inherited genetic material that occurs spontaneously or is the result of environmental toxins. Chromosomal abnormalities occur if a child has inherited too few, too many, or abnormal chromosomes.

Down syndrome, or trisomy 21, is caused by having three rather than two chromosomes at the 21st chromosome position. This condition causes intellectual disability, distinctive facial features, and stubby limbs.

Turner syndrome occurs when a female is born with only one X chromosome (X0). **Klinefelter syndrome** occurs when a male is born with an extra X chromosome (XXY).

Some abnormalities show up in certain families or bloodlines. Some show up mostly or exclusively in certain gene pools or cultures. Still others show up due to a parent's exposure to chromosome-altering factors, such as x-rays or other forms of radiation. Parents who are aware of potential risks for their unborn child can request genetic testing.

There are several prenatal tests available to screen for abnormalities during development. While an ultrasound can be used to detect the number of fetuses in the uterus and may detect some visible defects, better assessment techniques include **amniocentesis** and **chorionic villus sampling**. Amniocentesis involves testing fetal cells in amniotic fluid removed from the amniotic sac in the uterus for indicators of genetic abnormalities. The disadvantage of this technique is that it cannot be done until the 16th week of pregnancy.

Chorionic villus sampling (CVS) can be done as early as the sixth week of pregnancy. In CVS, tiny hair cells of a membrane surrounding the fetus (called the chorion) are extracted via a small tube inserted into the vagina. The hair cells contain fetal genetic material which can be analyzed. These tests can give physicians and parents information about such conditions as Down syndrome, blood-type mismatch, and neural-tube defects such as spinal bifida.

Some of these abnormalities and syndromes are discussed at greater length in Chapter 14: Developmental Psychopathology.

DEVELOPMENT OF THE BRAIN AND NERVOUS SYSTEM

During gestation, the brain and spinal cord emerge in weeks 4 and 5. From that time, neurons migrate to specific areas to form the complex structure of the brain.

The **nervous system** is made up of the brain and the spinal cord (the central nervous system) and the neural circuitry of the peripheral nervous system. The complex circuitry of the nervous system contains billions of single cells, called **neurons**, connected by **synapses**. The human brain has a great deal of plasticity, meaning that its neural circuits change over time as a result of stimulation, i.e., experience and learning. New circuits are formed, and unused or faulty circuits are lost through a process called **pruning**. For the first two years after birth, there is a brain growth spurt involving both the production of neurons and neural circuits, as well as this pruning. The brain is the most developed part of the body at birth but still must develop further. It is 75 percent of adult weight at age 2 and 90 percent of its adult weight by the age of 5.

The brain, through the process of evolution, has developed in parts. More primitive organisms do not have all the parts that humans have. The uppermost and most recent portion (in evolutionary terms), the **cerebral cortex**, is divided into two hemispheres. In adults, each hemisphere is somewhat specialized to do different tasks. In most people, the left hemisphere controls the right side of the body and the right hemisphere controls the left side. The left hemisphere generally controls language processing, while the right hemisphere controls spatial processing, although this is an oversimplification. The specialization of the hemispheres is called **brain lateralization**. Even newborns show brain lateralization. For instance, most newborns show a preference for grasping objects with their right hand rather than their left. However, lateralization strengthens with age. The presence of handedness in newborns has led some people to suggest that handedness is genetically controlled.

PRENATAL INFLUENCES ON DEVELOPMENT

Prenatal development refers to the period of development from conception to birth and is divided into three stages or trimesters. The **first trimester** includes the first brief germinal period, the entire stage of the **embryo**, and the beginning of the fetal stage. It lasts for the first 13 weeks of pregnancy. The **second trimester** lasts from the 14th to the 27th week and includes the stage of the **fetus**. The **third trimester** completes the fetal stage and lasts from the 28th week until birth. The average pregnancy lasts 270 days, or 40 weeks. The chart below shows the development of these growth stages.

First Trimester	Second Trimester	Third Trimester
Weeks 1-13	**Weeks 14-27**	**Weeks 28-40**
Germinal →		
Embryonic →		
	Fetal →	→

After conception, the fertilized zygote repeatedly divides as it travels down the fallopian tube to the uterus, where it becomes attached to the uterine wall. If a mother is carrying multiples (twins, triplets, etc.), it is due to one of several possibilities. There are two types of twin pairs, **monozygotic** (identical twins) and **dizygotic** (fraternal twins). Monozygotic twins occur when the fertilized ovum divides abnormally, creating two developing zygotes. Both zygotes embed into the uterine wall and develop separately. Monozygotic twins have identical genetic endowments. They are frequently studied by researchers interested in the nature-versus-nurture controversy since they share the same genes but can have different environmental influences. This research will be discussed in greater detail in the chapter on Intelligence.

Dizygotic twins are the result of two ova being fertilized by two different sperm cells at the same time. Triplets or larger sets of multiple births are produced this same way. Fertility drugs meant to stimulate the release of ova during ovulation often cause multiple births.

There are reproductive technologies available to help infertile couples conceive. **Artificial insemination** involves injecting sperm from the father into the uterus of his partner. **In vitro fertilization** is a process in which a sperm cell fertilizes an ovum outside the mother's body. The fertilized ovum is then implanted in the uterus. These procedures can be done with the couple's reproductive cells or with donor cells.

Stages of Prenatal Development

The three stages of prenatal development are outlined below.

Germinal Typically the first 10 days after conception. The zygote is a microscopic mass of multiplying cells. It travels down the fallopian tube and implants itself on the wall of the uterus. The **placenta** begins to form. This structure will allow nourishment and waste to be exchanged with the mother's body through the **umbilical cord.** Thin membranes keep fetal and maternal bloodstreams separate.

Embryo Second to eighth week after conception. The fluid-filled amniotic sac surrounds the embryo to protect and provide a constant temperature. The embryo differentiates into three layers for further development: endoderm, mesoderm, and ectoderm. Most vital organs and bodily systems begin to form. The brain and spinal cord develop. The embryo is only about one inch long by the end of this stage. Major birth defects are often caused by problems that occur during this stage.

Fetus From two months after conception until birth. Muscles and bones form. Vital organs continue to grow and begin to function. During the last three months, the brain develops rapidly.

Below is an outline of *what* develops *when* during the prenatal period.

Approximate prenatal week	Development
2nd week	Implantation on uterine wall.
3rd–4th week	Heart begins to pump.
4th week	Digestive system begins to form. Eyes begin to form. Brain and spinal cord form.
5th week	Ears begin to form.
6th week	Arms and legs first begin to appear.
7th–8th week	Male sex organs form. Fingers form.
8th week	Bones begin to form. Legs and arms move. Toes form.
10th–11th week	Female sex organs form.
12th week	Fetus weighs about one ounce. Fetal movement can occur. Fingerprints form.
20th week	Mother feels movement. Reflexes—sucking, swallowing, and hiccupping—appear. Nails, sweat glands, and soft hair developing.
27th week	Fetus weighs about two pounds.
38th week	Fetus weighs about seven pounds.
40th week	Full-term baby born.

Factors that Influence Prenatal Development

There are several factors that influence the success of a pregnancy. Prenatal development is most successful if the mother

- is between the ages of 16 and 35.
- has good prenatal medical care.
- is in good physical health.
- has good mental health and avoids prolonged stress that would alter hormone levels.
- has good nutrition.
- does not expose the fetus to the harmful effects of **teratogens.**

The last three items on this list will be discussed below.

HORMONAL INFLUENCES ON DEVELOPMENT

During pregnancy, the mother's **endocrine glands** secrete **hormones** for specialized purposes, most importantly preparation of the womb for pregnancy, sex determination, and preparation for lactation.

There is also a relationship between the mother's hormone secretions and stress. Under stressful conditions, the body secretes stress hormones **adrenalin** and **cortisol** that control the body's **fight-or-flight response**. Evolutionary theory suggests that this was highly adaptive in our species' past, when individuals had to mobilize quickly for fighting or fleeing. In this hormonal process, blood flow shifts from the core of the body to the extremities. There is a decrease in blood pressure and an increase in heart rate. All these autonomic reactions get the body ready for action. Unfortunately, the body responds the same way to emotional stress as it does to a real physical threat. Research suggests that the long-term effect of high cortisol levels in the blood is reduced immune response.

During pregnancy, stress is debilitative because it draws blood flow away from the fetus and to the muscles of the mother. This deprives the fetus of oxygen. Adrenalin and cortisol also can pass through the semi-permeable placenta and cause an increase in fetal heart rate. Long-term stress can cause stunted prenatal growth, low birth weight, and birth complications. Studies suggest that infants born to mothers who were stressed during pregnancy have a heightened reactivity to stress in their own life and a reduced physiological ability to manage stressful conditions. Furthermore, studies have shown that emotional stress during pregnancy can predict anxiety, aggression, anger, and overactivity among school-aged children. These effects appear even after controlling for factors such as smoking during pregnancy, low birth weight, postnatal maternal anxiety, and low socioeconomic class.

After birth, the child's endocrine system begins to work, causing growth and other functions. The **pituitary gland** (embedded within the brain) is called the master gland because it causes other glands to secrete hormones. It is controlled by the hypothalamus of the brain. The pituitary also secretes its own **growth hormone (GH)** which stimulates physical growth and development. Without GH, children do not grow taller than four feet. Hormones secreted from the pituitary gland also stimulate the adolescent growth spurt.

The thyroid gland in the neck also controls physical growth and development as well as development of the nervous system. It secretes the hormone thyroxine. Inadequate levels of thyroxine cause cognitive deficits. Early treatment is effective. Children who develop a thyroxine deficiency after brain maturation is completed have stunted physical growth but no intellectual disability.

Males and females have differing levels of sex hormones in the body. Sex hormones called **androgens** control the development of sex organs as well as secondary sex characteristics. At conception, the fertilized egg cell has either of two sex chromosome pairs, XX or XY. During the 7th and 8th week of fetal development, a gene on the Y chromosome triggers the development of male reproductive organs. This process begins with the development of the testes. The testes secrete the male hormone **testosterone**, which stimulates the development of male reproductive organs in the fetus and inhibits the development of the female reproductive organs. In the third month of prenatal development, the penis and scrotum appear in the male, and female genitalia appear in the female. In females, the ovaries are the organs that control sexual maturation, as they also function as glands. Ovaries produce the hormones **estrogen** and **progesterone**.

NUTRITIONAL INFLUENCES

The expectant mother needs extra nutrients to nourish her unborn child and to avoid low birth weight. But it is not enough for an expectant mother to "eat for two" as the saying goes. Good nutrition during pregnancy involves giving the child vital substances that are essential for normal and healthy development. Extra amounts of these nutrients need to be consumed. Often, supplementation is advocated, prescribed or not.

- Folic acid (a B vitamin) and iodine are important for neural support as the brain and nervous system develop.
- Vitamin D is important for bone development.
- Iron is important for healthy blood in both mother and child.

After birth, an infant needs nutrients to thrive outside the womb. Breast milk is ideal, since it contains all the nutrients that are needed, plus antibodies to start the infant's immune system. Once solid foods are started, the child is subject to family and cultural preferences and food availability.

TERATOGENS

Teratogens are any substances that may cross the placental barrier from mother to embryo or fetus, causing stunted growth, malformation, or death. Possible teratogens include:

- exposure to x-rays.
- environmental toxins in air and water.
- some drugs, including alcohol and nicotine—to be discussed in the next section: "Influences of Drugs."
- maternal diseases (see paragraph below).

Several diseases can be transferred from the mother to the fetus during prenatal development. For a disease to infect the fetus, it must be capable of passing through the semi-permeable placenta into the fetal bloodstream. **Rubella** (**German measles**) is a disease that passes through this membrane and causes birth defects in 60 to 85 percent of infants if they are infected during the first eight weeks of pregnancy. Defects include vision and hearing loss, heart defects, cerebral palsy, and intellectual disability. **Syphilis** can be passed this way as well and can lead to miscarriage or birth defects, depending on the timing of exposure. Syphilis is more damaging in the middle and late stages of pregnancy. **AIDS** can be passed on to the fetus through the placenta, but this is less likely if the mother is taking AIDS medication. AIDS can also be transmitted during the birthing process if there is an exchange of blood between the mother and baby or through breastfeeding. Both of these two means of transmission are prevented today through the use of medications during birth and through bottle feeding. **Genital herpes** passes the placental barrier and can cause brain damage or death if the fetus is exposed in the first trimester. A baby can also be infected with herpes by a vaginal delivery. Mothers with genital herpes usually have cesarean deliveries to avoid infecting the child.

Another prenatal teratogen has to do with the **Rh factor** in blood. People either have or do not have an Rh factor in their blood. Those who do not are called Rh– (negative) and those who do are Rh+ (positive). In the past, one common cause of intellectual disability was an Rh incompatibility between the mother and her fetus. An Rh– mother's immune system would attack the cells of an Rh+ fetus. This is prevented today by an inoculation given to the mother that prohibits this immune system response.

What abnormalities occur from teratogens depend on the timing of exposure, what is developing in the womb during the exposure, as well as what the harmful agent is. The fetus is generally not affected by a teratogen if exposure occurs during the first or third trimester. Because so many vital organs and body parts are developing during the embryo stage, harmful agents are especially dangerous during this prenatal period. This is often referred to as a critical period in prenatal development. A critical period is any time that some developmental process must occur, or it never will. For example, if something interferes with legs developing or forming during the critical period for that process, they will not develop or be formed later.

It is also important to note that males are more susceptible to the effects of teratogens than females. The reason for this has not been identified.

INFLUENCES OF DRUGS

Drugs taken by the expectant mother can have serious effects on the unborn child. For this reason, it is important for a woman to confirm her pregnancy as soon as possible, so she can take precautions regarding drug usage. As for prescription drugs, it is important to let physicians know about the pregnancy, so they can prescribe or continue prescriptions that are known to be safe. Usually, prescription drugs offer more benefit than risk, but there are exceptions. For instance, in the 1950s, many pregnant women were given the prescription drug **thalidomide** to control nausea. Unfortunately, the drug caused birth defects. Many children born to these women had defective limbs, feet, hands, and ears, or were born without limbs.

Nicotine can cause low birth weight, preterm delivery, and even sudden infant death. Alcohol consumption during pregnancy can cause **fetal alcohol syndrome**, resulting in a short nose, thin upper lip, widely spaced eyes, small head, and intellectual disability. Some refer to this condition as a spectrum, since a wide range of severity is possible.

Other recreational drugs are equally risky during pregnancy. Heavy use of marijuana can lead to brain damage. Cocaine can cause low birth weight, stillbirth, and spontaneous abortion. Heroin users can pass their addiction through the placenta to the child.

PERINATAL INFLUENCES

For the mother, the **perinatal period** is a critical time. This spans the last three months of pregnancy through the first week after birth. Birth preparations are one part of this period, and post-delivery factors are another part.

Parents need to choose a birthing option and location, with an understanding of the benefits and risks of each. This will also determine what professionals will be present and what other individuals might be allowed. Most deliveries in the United States take place in a hospital setting, where a variety of birthing options might be available with full medical staffing. Birthing centers, which are not in hospital settings, may offer other options. Home births utilize the services of midwives, with hospitals on-call in case of complications.

Many couples prepare for the birth of a child using the **Lamaze** or prepared childbirth method. This method teaches a pregnant woman and her partner how to use breathing and other relaxation techniques to reduce the experience of pain and stress during labor and delivery.

The birth process involves several stages, including labor, delivery of the fetus, and delivery of the placenta. Certain conditions during the birthing process can be harmful to the neonate. **Anoxia** (oxygen deprivation) is a condition caused by reduced oxygen flow to the fetus during birth. It can be caused by a build-up of mucous in the throat of the baby or a crimp in the umbilical cord. The harm to the baby from anoxia depends on the degree and length of time that oxygen flow is hampered. If anoxia is prolonged, the baby may develop **cerebral palsy**. Cerebral palsy is a neurological disorder that is characterized by a lack of muscle control and coordination. Medications taken by the mother to reduce pain during labor and delivery can have harmful effects. They generally slow down the birth process and can also increase the risk of harm to the fetus.

Normal delivery is vaginal, in which the baby is pushed through the vaginal canal by the mother. **Caesarian section** is an alternative birthing method in which the fetus is surgically removed from the uterus of the mother.

At delivery, the **Apgar scale** is used to assess the overall condition of the **neonate** immediately after birth and again 5 minutes after the birth. The results of these simple tests on reflexes and vital signs will give practitioners quick information about the overall health of the child. Although created and named by **Virginia Apgar**, her last name became an acronym for the checklist that is included in the test: **A**ppearance, **P**ulse, **G**rimace (reflex), **A**ctivity, and **R**espiration.

There are further risks for both mother and newborn after delivery. **Postpartum depression** should be monitored, as this can be debilitating for the mother and a risk for the child. Symptoms can include sadness, fatigue, and/or anxiety about caring for or harming the child. If symptoms become severe, the child would be at risk. Sometimes a doula is employed to help with the new mother's stresses and routines.

Some infants are neglected or abused; some have protracted separations from attachment figures, such as when newborns are given long-term interventions to alleviate birth complications (e.g., an incubator). Any of these situations may result in a syndrome called **failure to thrive**. Such infants do not develop normally, become grossly underweight, and show signs of depression. Most infants born under such difficult circumstances rebound once situations are corrected, but some never grow to normal size and suffer social and cognitive deficits.

MOTOR DEVELOPMENT IN INFANTS

Several **reflexes** (involuntary responses to stimuli) can be elicited in newborn infants. All healthy newborns exhibit them, and many of these reflexes will disappear with age. For example, healthy newborn infants will blink when a light shines in their eyes and will suck on an object placed in their mouth. These reflexes do not disappear with time. But other reflexes will disappear over the course of the first year of life, such as these:

- **Moro** (extension of arms when an infant feels a loss of support)
- **Babinski** (big toe flexes up when the sole of foot is stroked—abnormal after age 2)
- **Palmar/grasping** (squeezing any object placed in the hand)
- **Rooting** (turning toward an object brushing the cheek and sucking)
- **Walking** (making walking motions when body held upright with toes touching surface)

Evolutionary psychologists consider these newborn reflexes to be remnants of behaviors that were adaptive during earlier times in our species' evolution but no longer contribute to survival. Clearly, the **sucking reflex** and the **eye blink reflex**, which protects the eye from injury, have survival value.

The **proximodistal principle** of development describes the center-outward direction of motor development. For instance, children gain control of their torso before their extremities; they can sit independently before they can stand. The **cephalocaudal principle** describes the head-to-foot direction of motor development. That is, children tend to gain control over the upper portions of their bodies before the lower part. For example, they can hold their heads up and reach and grasp before they can stand and walk. Children generally master **gross motor skills**, such as standing and walking, before mastering **fine motor skills** such as finger dexterity. Gross motor skills require the coordination of large parts of the body, while fine motor skills involve small, coordinated movements of muscles in the hands, fingers, or toes. Infants show a fairly well-developed fine motor skill of manipulating objects with their fingers by about 9 to 12 months of age.

The developmental norms or average age of achievement for gross motor development are as follows:

Age	Behavior
1 month	While prone (on stomach), can lift head.
2 months	While prone, can hold chest up. Can roll from side to back.
3 months	Can roll over. Will reach for objects.
6–7 months	Sits without support. Stands holding on to objects.
8–10 months	Crawls.
8–12 months	Pulls self up to stand.
11–12 months	"Cruises"—walks by holding on to objects.
12–18 months	Walks alone.

PHYSICAL GROWTH, MATURATION, AND AGING

Early Physical Growth

The average newborn is 20 inches long and weighs between 7 and 7½ pounds. Infants may reach about half of their adult height by the age of 2. This indicates that infancy is a period of rapid physical growth called a **growth spurt**. Of course, nature and nurture interact here. While a child's mature physical size is preprogrammed in his or her genotype, the child may not reach that size. Environmental or nutritional influences can stunt physical growth, as can hormonal abnormalities. There is also a possibility of **failure to thrive**, as discussed previously, but with no obvious cause. Biological and environmental factors need to be identified to counteract this.

Childhood Brain and Nervous System Development

During childhood, and throughout the rest of life, the neural circuitry of the brain continues to change and develop. In childhood, brain lateralization becomes stronger as parts of the cortex take over different functions. The process of **myelination** continues from birth, putting a fatty coating (myelin) around each neuron's axon. Myelination speeds up the transmission of neural messages. This process continues for several years, and it may be what is responsible for quicker reaction time in older compared to younger children.

Childhood Motor Development and Physical Growth

Development of motor skills is slow but steady during childhood compared to the spurts of development in infancy. The muscles of the body get stronger and parts of the body get closer to adults in relative size and proportion. Fine motor and gross motor coordination continue to improve during this period and reaction time speeds up.

Adolescent Brain and Nervous System Development

The part of the cerebral cortex called the **prefrontal cortex** (immediately behind the forehead) matures during adolescence. This is the newest area of the cortex in evolutionary terms, and it is responsible for higher-order thinking and processing of complex information. The maturation of this area may be responsible for improved attention-focusing capacity in the adolescent compared to the younger child. Myelination continues during adolescence and into adulthood. The full weight of the brain is achieved by late adolescence.

Adolescent Physical Growth and Sexual Maturation

There is a rapid period of growth in adolescence. The adolescent growth spurt in males is triggered by the testes secreting large amounts of testosterone and other male sex hormones. The increase in androgen levels in the blood causes a rapid growth spurt. GH (growth hormone) and thyroxine are also secreted in larger quantities. In females, the ovaries secrete an increased amount of estrogen which in turn triggers the production of GH and leads to the female adolescent growth spurt. Females reach their full height by around the age of 16, four years or so ahead of males.

Along with the adolescent growth spurt comes **puberty**, achieving full sexual maturity. In females, ovaries start producing large amounts of estrogen and progesterone, which causes maturation of the ovaries, uterus, and vagina—primary sex features. This causes the onset of **menarche** (the first menstrual cycle), although some girls may not be able to reproduce for several years after menarche. The average age of menarche is 12½ years but can range from ages 11 to 15, and it has been occurring at younger ages than in previous generations due to increased nutrients and fats consumed by society. Also, hormones produce secondary female sex features during this time—breasts and enlarged hips—and trigger an increase in fat storage.

Males will start producing large amounts of testosterone at about age 13. This causes enlargement of the penis and testicles and the beginning of puberty. Males will experience their first ejaculation, but that does not necessarily mean sperm are viable enough to reproduce. Hormones also cause the appearance of secondary sex features, including an enlarged Adam's apple, voice change, and facial hair.

Both males and females will experience other features at the onset of puberty: pubic and underarm hair growth and a change in sweat glands that cause odor.

There is a growing concern in our country about the rising rates of **obesity** in children and adolescents. Obesity is defined as having a Body Mass Index (BMI) of 30 or greater, where BMI is calculated as a ratio between weight and height. Obesity correlates with increased risk of cardiovascular disease, high blood pressure, diabetes, and liver and kidney problems. Adolescents have a greater risk of obesity than children because their metabolism rates start to decline. This risk continues to climb in adulthood as metabolism continues to slow down.

Adult Brain and Nervous System Development

The brain continues to show plasticity, developing and pruning neural circuits throughout adulthood. However, along with this growth there are declines that are the result of normal biological aging. It is important not to confuse the effects of biological aging with the effects of diseases that occur with increasing risk in old age. Normal changes in the brain include a slowing of the transmission of neural messages, decreased blood flow to the brain, loss of neurons, loss of brain weight, and a decrease in neurotransmitters—the chemicals that neurons emit as they connect with other neurons at the synapses. Hence, there is a slowing of neural processing associated with normal aging and a loss of brain mass, but new neural circuits can continue to be formed to replace those lost.

Adult Physical Growth

The body reaches full adult size at the end of adolescence. Most of the physical functions of the body are at peak levels of performance in early adulthood and then begin a slow, but steady, decline. Researchers studying aging generally agree that there is an inevitable process of **biological aging** that eventually would cause death even in the absence of disease. Evidence for this view is that there appears to be a maximum length of life for humans. There are few records of people living beyond 110 years or so. Maximum length of life is different from **life expectancy**. Life expectancy is the average length of life expected for members of a birth cohort. This average is a calculation that includes all members of a cohort, even the predicted number of those who will die prematurely due to injury or early disease. (This is why life expectancy a thousand years ago was very low, although individuals could live about as long as in modern times if they could stay healthy and avoid injury.)

Researchers disagree on the nature and cause of biological aging. One theory, the wear-and-tear theory, suggests that the human body, like a machine, eventually wears out from normal use. However, continued physical activity in adulthood has been shown to correlate with both physical as well as mental health, not more deterioration.

Other researchers argue that biological aging is in part due to the gradual failure of the endocrine system. The gradual decrease in GH that occurs with age is associated with loss of muscle and bone mass, an increase in body fat, thinning of the skin, and a decrease in cardiovascular functioning. Diet and physical exercise have been found to partially mitigate these effects. A decrease in secretions from the thymus is also correlated with age. Secretions from the thymus aid in the body's immune response. Stress hormones discussed earlier also decrease the body's immune response. There is also a theory that aging is caused at least partially by the buildup of cell damage caused by free radicals (unstable molecules) rampaging through the body.

Loss of bone mass in the aging process is due to decreased levels of calcium and GH in the body. Loss of bone density can lead to a bone disease called **osteoporosis** in which bones are very brittle and may spontaneously fracture. Post-menopausal women have a higher risk for osteoporosis. Physical activity and calcium supplements have been found to help prevent or mitigate this bone disease.

While changes in glandular activity are primary causes of aging, there are some common secondary causes. In our society, these conditions often contribute to the aging process:

- Arthritis
- Diabetes
- Hypertension (high blood pressure)
- Heart disease (related to conditions of heart valves, heart rhythm, or arteries)

Hormones also control the **climacteric** or **menopause** in females. The climacteric is the cessation of a female's reproductive capacity. The climacteric typically spans a 10-year period and usually begins in a woman's early fifties, triggered by a drop in estrogen level. Lower estrogen in the body causes changes in the female's sex organs. Organs shrink, and genitals react more slowly to stimulation. The vagina secretes fewer lubricants during arousal. The body also loses the protections afforded by estrogen, such as protection against plaque build-up on the walls of arteries and protection against loss of bone mass density. Lowered levels of estrogen are also associated with mood fluctuations, hot flashes, and night sweats. Hormone therapies have been developed to combat these side effects of menopause. These treatments include estrogen replacement therapy (ERT), which is normally used only with women who have had hysterectomies, or hormone replacement therapy (HRT) in which both estrogen and progesterone are given. There is ongoing controversy about the risks associated with ERT and HRT. If administered late in menopause, HRT may increase the patient's risk for developing Alzheimer's disease, but if started earlier, may reduce this risk. ERT has been shown in some studies to increase the risk of breast cancer and blood clots.

The male climacteric is caused by decreasing amounts of testosterone, but it is a more gradual, less obvious process compared to the female climacteric. Some men may never lose their reproductive capacity. It is difficult to determine whether changes in males' sexual activity or sexual arousal is due to hormone levels or other factors.

CHAPTER 5

PERCEPTUAL DEVELOPMENT THROUGHOUT THE LIFE SPAN

This chapter deals with the development of perception. **Perception** is the way our brains give meaning to stimuli in the environment. Our sense organs receive stimuli all the time—sights, sounds, smells, etc. But we do not perceive all the stimuli, and for good reason, because we would be overwhelmed and unable to act on all the incoming messages. So our brains select what will be perceived and acted on. The following paragraphs will outline the mechanisms and development of perception, as well as factors that can impair it.

Sensation is the process of registering stimuli and transmitting that information to cortical brain centers. **Perception** is the process of assigning meaning to a sensation.

Sensitivity to a perceptual stimulus is measured by the **absolute threshold**. The absolute threshold is the minimal intensity of a stimulus an observer can detect. For instance, a newborn's absolute threshold for vision and hearing is higher than a normal adult's, but rapidly decreases. Young infants do not hear very soft whispers that adults with normal hearing can.

It is important to note that while the perceptual development in each modality will be discussed separately, perception is really **intermodal**. That is, sensory systems coordinate and communicate with each other. If we feel something while unable to see it, we can identify the object by sight when we are finally able to see it among a group of other objects. This is even true for infants.

Also, the sensory perceptual experiences we have are associated in memory. For example, we associate a face with a particular voice. **Andrew Meltzoff** and **Richard Borton** reported evidence of intermodal perception regarding sight and touch in one-month-old infants. Infants in the study looked longer at a picture of a smooth nipple if they had previously sucked on, but could not see, a smooth nipple. Other infants in the study showed the same pattern with a bumpy nipple.

Before examining the development of perception through the life span, it is important to understand three facets of perception that have been researched over the years: sensitive periods, habituation, and sensory deprivation. These three terms will appear throughout this and other chapters.

SENSITIVE PERIODS

A **sensitive period** is a time when certain experiences are ideal or necessary for development. There are sensitive periods in gestation, when the fetus is developing particular body parts. And there are sensitive periods in infancy and early childhood. For example, there is a "window" that represents the best times for learning language, and for scooting, crawling, and walking. There are sensitive periods for sense development as well. If there is a disruption or lack of opportunity during a sensitive period, development will be hampered, sometimes permanently.

HABITUATION

Habituation is a mechanism by which the brain "programs" itself to ignore certain stimuli after they have been introduced. The brain accepts (and thrives on) novelty, and repetition of a stimulus is no longer novel. So the brain tends to filter out—no longer perceive—familiar stimuli in favor of new ones. In evolutionary terms, this is highly adaptive, since it is new information that needs attention in order to survive. In modern times, habituation is a helpful coping mechanism, as it helps us to notice and adapt to changes in settings and circumstances.

Many experiments in infant perception take advantage of the fact that newborns exhibit habituation. For instance, when newborns are shown a new picture, they look at it and scan it. However, over time they look away. When this picture is presented side by side with a new one, newborns look longer at the new picture. This tells us that the infant has habituated the familiar, old stimulus in favor of a new, unfamiliar stimulus. Young infants can also be trained using Skinner's operant conditioning techniques. For instance, an infant can learn to respond a certain way (for example, look left when a certain tone is presented) to receive a reinforcement. In this way, a researcher can study an infant's ability to discriminate different sounds.

Sensory Deprivation

Sensory deprivation is anything that keeps a person from using one or more senses. In research, this has been done intentionally with laboratory animals. But it has also happened unintentionally in humans, and psychologists have studied those unfortunate incidents. Sensory deprivation is most impactful when it happens during a sensitive period related to the sense being deprived.

Sensory deprivation has been studied in infants, especially in the areas of congenital visual/auditory problems and lack of tactile (touch) sensation from caregivers. We have learned that sensory deprivation during critical sensitive periods cannot only lead to sensory difficulties later, but they can also have impacts on other areas of development, such as personality and social skills. We have two sources for evidence of this:

- Harlow's experiment with monkeys (discussed at length in Chapter 10: Social Development throughout the Life Span) demonstrated that depriving infants of touch (i.e., being able to feel the mother or a soft surrogate) caused psychological and social development problems.
- Eastern European infant orphanages in the 1990s were overcrowded and understaffed. Children were rarely touched and were given only the most essential care, such as diaper changes. Follow-up research showed psychological and social problems as these children grew into adolescence.

SENSORIMOTOR ACTIVITIES

Perceptual Functioning in the Newborn/Infant

Infants take full advantage of the intermodal nature of their sensory organs. They explore and learn from their environment using eyes, ears, hand touching, and even their mouths.

The five sensory perceptual systems, although not fully developed, are all functional at birth. Furthermore, perception researchers have discovered that there are **neonate preferences** and perceptual abilities regarding vision, taste, and hearing.

As the newborn receives sensory stimulation, his or her perceptual abilities improve and the neural circuits in the brain centers that control each sensory perceptual function are strengthened. Sensory deprivation research with animals indicates that there are sensitive periods for being able to receive and process sensory stimulation. In other words, there seem to be short time periods when it is ideal to have experiences to develop certain kinds of sensory functions or abilities. For instance, some chimpanzees raised in the dark have permanently impaired vision due to the degeneration of the optic nerve—the nerve that transmits visual information to the cortical vision center. However, if the deprivation lasts no longer than seven months, the damage is reversible. Human infants born blind due to **cataracts** (clouding on the lens of the eye) sometimes do not fully recover normal visual acuity. This is why it is recommended that cataracts be removed before 2 months of age to prevent permanent vision problems.

Vision

Vision occurs when light waves enter the opening of the eye (the pupil) and are focused by the lens onto the retina in the back of the eye. An image forms on the retina that will vary in size depending on the distance and size of the visual object. But the retina does not "see." Rod and cone cells of the retina are designed to respond to light energy and begin a process of transforming light information into neural impulses. These visual receptor cells transmit signals to the vision center in the occipital lobe of the brain. This is where we "see," i.e., perceive, what has been transmitted from the eye.

At birth, neonates can see, although their **visual acuity** is poor. Visual acuity is the ability to see fine gradations or details in a visual stimulus. Perfect acuity is quantified as 20/20. Newborn visual acuity ranges from about 20/400 to 20/800. What this means is that a newborn can see something as clearly at 20 feet as a person with normal vision could see clearly at 400 to 800 feet. Newborn infants can see objects clearly that are about nine inches away. The poor acuity in newborns is caused by weakness in the muscles that control the lens, the part of the eye that focuses light onto the retina. Visual acuity improves rapidly over the first four months of life. Newborns are also capable of **tracking** a moving object, although their tracking movements are not very smooth or coordinated. They track by moving the entire head rather than just the eyes.

Depth perception involves the interpretation of visual cues to determine how far away objects are. There is currently a debate as to whether depth perception is an inborn ability or a learned response from experience (nature versus nurture). By the time infants can crawl, they indicate that they have depth perception by refusing to crawl across the deep side of a **visual cliff**. Gibson and Walk (1960) developed this apparatus to measure depth perception in infants and toddlers. The visual cliff consists of an elevated glass platform divided into two sections. One section has a surface that is textured with a checkerboard pattern of tile, while the other has a clear glass surface with a checkerboard pattern several feet below it so it looks like the floor drops off. Gibson and Walk hypothesized that if infants can perceive depth, they should remain on the "shallow" side of the platform and avoid the "cliff" side, even if coaxed to come across by parents. When they tested infants from 6 to 14 months of age, Gibson and Walk found that infants would crawl or walk to their mothers when the mothers were on the "shallow" side of the platform, but they would refuse to cross the "deep" side, even with their mothers' encouragements to cross. The results of this and other visual cliff studies still do not prove that depth perception is innate because, before infants can be tested, they must be able to crawl and may have already learned to avoid drop-offs.

Another important characteristic of visual perception is the **perceptual constancy**, or stability, of the shape, size, brightness, and color of objects in our visual fields. We can recognize the same objects at a variety of angles, at various distances, and even under different colored lighting because of perceptual constancies. The four perceptual constancies are as follows:

- **Size Constancy**—Objects we are familiar with seem to appear the same size despite changes in the distance between us and the objects.
- **Shape Constancy**—Objects appear to be the same shape despite changes in their orientation toward the viewer.
- **Brightness or Lightness Constancy**—Objects appear to stay the same brightness despite changes in the amount of light falling on them.
- **Color Constancy**—The hue of an object appears to stay the same despite changes in background lighting.

Newborns have been shown to have size constancy. In a clever experiment, newborns were shown to habituate to a particular-sized cube even though the cube was presented at different distances from the newborn. After habituation, the newborns preferred to look at a different-sized cube even when it projected the same sized image on the retina as the training cube.

Studies of color perception using the habituation phenomenon report that very young infants see color and have a mature ability to perceive color by two to three months of age.

Newborns and infants also have visual preferences. They prefer to look at faces and other visual stimuli that have contour, contrast, complexity, and movement. Some 2-day-old infants are even capable of discriminating their mother's face from a stranger's face. By 3 months of age, almost all infants can do this. At 6–7 months old, infants will show surprise when shown a face with jumbled parts.

Young infants show **selective looking**. They will scan the borders and edges of objects in a visual stimulus while older infants will scan inside the edges. This difference may be due to the fact that young infants are still learning to pick out objects in a scene which older infants can accomplish very quickly. The older infant has more time to scan inside the contours of an object for details.

Discovering whether or how infants visually perceive a whole scene or a whole object is a part of research on the development of **Gestalt principles**. These principles include the perceptions of proximity, similarity, continuity, closure, and connectedness—perceptions that help us make sense of our surroundings, especially in new situations. Research indicates that different Gestalt principles may become functional at different times during development. For instance, infants can recognize that all the pieces of an object are part of a unified whole, but only after they see all the parts moving in unison.

Hearing

Infants can hear prior to birth. They can hear many sounds in the womb, including the sound of their mother's voice. Shortly after birth, newborn infants can discriminate between sounds of different duration, loudness, and pitch. Newborns also appear to prefer the sound of a human voice to other sounds and prefer to hear complex sounds over pure tones. Young infants will listen longer to the sound of a person speaking than non-speech sounds. At birth, infants will suck more on a nipple to hear their mother's voice compared to a stranger's voice, and to hear their native language as compared to a foreign language. By 6 months of age, infants can discriminate between any two basic vocal sounds, called phonemes, used in all the world's languages. In fact, they can make discriminations between phonemes that older children and adults can no longer make. These findings have led many psycholinguists—psychologists who study language—to argue that humans are innately prepared to acquire a language.

Smell

The sense of smell is also well-developed in the newborn. The fetus is exposed to many odors as well as sounds in the womb. By 6 weeks of age, infants can smell the difference between their mother and a stranger. Four-day-old, breast-fed infants prefer the smell of their own mother's breast compared to that of an unfamiliar woman who is also breastfeeding them.

Taste

Infants' ability to discriminate tastes has been studied by observing changes in infants' facial expressions after different flavored liquids are placed on the tongue. Infants respond differently to the five basic tastes (sweet, sour, salty, bitter, and umami, or savory), and they show a clear preference for sweet-flavored liquids. There is even evidence that sugar water has a soothing effect on newborns, particularly if the infant is experiencing pain.

Touch, Temperature, and Pain

Infants are also very responsive to touch. Touch is one of the best-developed senses at birth and the earliest sensory perceptual systems to develop prenatally. Some research has shown that female infants may be more sensitive to touch than males. Swaddling infants, i.e., wrapping them tightly in cloth, has a soothing effect on infants perhaps because of the stimulating effect swaddling has on the sense of touch. Gentle massaging has also been found to improve the development of premature infants. At birth, infants are also highly sensitive to pain and are sensitive to warm and cold temperatures.

SENSORY ACUITY

Perceptual Development in Childhood and Adolescence

Sensory acuity reaches its maximum during childhood and adolescence. Vision is most acute from about age 8 to age 18. Hearing is most acute between about 10 and 15 years. Acuity of the senses starts to decline very slowly after that.

An important part of perceptual development in childhood and adolescence is the development of **attention**. As children age they acquire more control of perception. Attention is the process of focusing on particular aspects of the sensory world. Between 4 and 10 years of age, visual search of a stimulus becomes more controlled and systematic. Attention spans increase from 18 minutes in 2- to 3-year-olds to more than an hour in 6-year-olds. Learning to read requires these attentional capacities and is probably the most significant perceptual challenge for children.

Perceptual Development in Adulthood

Absolute thresholds for sensory stimuli rise with age in adulthood. This means that adults gradually lose some sensitivity for sights, sounds, flavors, and odors. In addition, there is a slowing of the processing of sensory stimulation. For example, older adults may have trouble understanding rapid speech. However, training or necessity can enhance acuity for those adults who need a high level of perception in one or more senses. This can be seen in the performances of adult athletes and musicians.

Vision

There are changes to the eye that occur with aging. The lens of the eye gradually loses flexibility and therefore cannot change its shape to refract light as well as it did at an earlier age. This condition is called **presbyopia** and is present in most people after the mid-to-late 40s. Presbyopia is corrected with lenses that help focus images from near objects onto the retina.

The lens of the eye can also develop deposits called **cataracts**. Cataracts can be surgically removed, or lenses can be removed and replaced with artificial lenses. Cataracts will lead to blindness if left uncorrected. Another condition called **glaucoma** appears more frequently in people over 50 years of age. Glaucoma is a build-up of pressure from excess fluid inside the eyeball. If left untreated, glaucoma causes blindness. Glaucoma can be detected early during routine eye examinations and can be treated with medication or lasers.

Altogether, the changes to the eye in older adults cause them to see more glare, have less sensitivity under dim lighting conditions, and have difficulty with near vision. Distance vision also shows a steady decline in old age after peaking in the 20s and staying steady in middle age. Research has also shown that older adults perform more poorly on tests of selective attention and visual search compared with younger adults.

Hearing

Changes in hearing with age are caused by changes in the inner ear. The inner ear contains hair cells that are bent when vibrations of the eardrum cause fluid of the inner ear to move in waves. Hair cells degenerate and are lost in increasing numbers with age. The loss of hearing associated with aging is called **presbycusis**. At first there is a loss of sensitivity to high frequency sounds. Later, after the age of 50, low frequency sounds are also more difficult to hear. About 2 percent of adults aged 45 to 54 have disabling hearing loss. In adults aged 55 to 64, the rate increases to 8.5 percent. In adults 65 to 74 years of age, the rate is nearly 25 percent, with a rate of about 50 percent for those who are 75 and older. Understanding speech becomes more difficult for the older adult, particularly when there is background noise in the room. Some hearing loss can be corrected with hearing aids or more sophisticated devices, such as cochlear implants.

Taste and Smell

Older adults may have difficulty discriminating among salty, bitter, and acidic flavors. Sensitivity to sweetness, however, does not change. There is an increased absolute threshold for taste, so food tastes blander to an older person. The same is true for detecting odor. The absolute threshold rises even more for odor than for taste. Among older subjects, females are better at detecting odors than males.

Touch, Temperature, and Pain

Sensitivity to temperature and body temperature regulation both decline in older adults. Absolute thresholds for touch and for pain do not change significantly. Older adults are no more or less sensitive to strong pain stimulation than younger adults.

CHAPTER 6

LEARNING THROUGH BEHAVIORAL CHANGE

Recall (from Chapter 2) that the behaviorist perspective of development is also called "learning theory." This is because behaviorists assert that all behavior is learned, and the learning takes place through a certain set of procedures. (Also recall that other theories have alternate ways to explain learning.) With this in mind, it is important to be aware that although this chapter has "learning" in the title, it is exclusively devoted to only the behaviorist perspective on learning. Other chapters deal with learning as described by other theoretical perspectives.

According to behavioral psychology, learning is defined as a relatively permanent change in behavior as a result of experience, practice, or both. Learning theorists have described three different learning processes, including:

1. **classical conditioning**
2. **operant conditioning**
3. **observational learning**

These mechanisms of learning are viewed as remaining the same throughout development. Learning, therefore, is believed to be a continuous versus discontinuous process. In other words, behaviorists view learning throughout the life span as a series of similar processes, not influenced by differences in life stages or maturation.

CLASSICAL CONDITIONING

Classical conditioning always involves a reflexive or respondent behavior. This means that classical conditioning produces an automatic (involuntary) response to a stimulus. This kind of conditioning occurs when a neutral stimulus that does not trigger a reflexive behavior is conditioned in the person or animal so that it will elicit an automatic response. In other words, conditioning occurs because a neutral stimulus has been associated with a stimulus that has always triggered a certain response.

It appears that both humans and animals may be biologically prepared to learn some associations more readily than others. The associations that are more readily learned may be ones that increased chances for survival in the past.

Ivan Pavlov (1849–1936), a Russian physiologist, classically conditioned dogs using the salivary reflex. Dogs automatically respond to food by salivating, so it is called a reflex. No conditioning is necessary to elicit this response; they do not have to be trained or conditioned to salivate to food. Dogs do not, however, automatically salivate to the sound of a bell ringing. This is what Pavlov conditioned them to do. He would ring the bell, present the food, and the dogs would salivate. He repeated this procedure until the bell alone would cause the dogs to salivate. They had learned to associate the sound of the bell with the presentation of food. (This use of the word "learn" is not describing a conscious or voluntary process.)

The terms used to describe classical conditioning include:

Unconditioned Stimulus (UCS)—The stimulus that automatically produces a reflex. (In Pavlov's study, this was the food.)

Unconditioned Response (UCR)—An automatic response to the UCS; a natural response that does not require conditioning for it to occur. (In Pavlov's study, this was salivation to the food.)

Neutral Stimulus (NS)—A neutral stimulus (object or event) that does not normally elicit an automatic response. (In Pavlov's study, this was the bell.)

Conditioned Stimulus (CS)—A neutral stimulus that is repeatedly paired with a UCS so that it is no longer neutral, but instead elicits a conditioned response. (In Pavlov's study, this was the bell.)

Conditioned Response (CR)—The learned response that occurs when the CS is presented alone, without the UCS. (In Pavlov's study, the CR was salivation that occurred to the bell alone; no food was present.)

The standard classical conditioning paradigm is:

Step 1		**UCS** (food)	⇒	**UCR** (salivation)
Step 2*	**NS ⇒ CS** (bell) NS becomes CS from repetition	+ **UCS** (food)	⇒	**UCR** (salivation)
Step 3		**CS alone** (bell alone)	⇒	**CR** (salivation)

*Step 2 is repeated until the NS becomes a CS that will prompt the CR by itself.

After classical conditioning has taken place, the conditioned stimulus (CS) must be paired with, or reinforced by, the unconditioned stimulus (UCS) at least some of the time or else the conditioned response (CR) will disappear. **Extinction** is the process of eliminating the conditioned response (CR) by no longer pairing the unconditioned stimulus (UCS) with the conditioned stimulus (CS). Extinction will take place if the conditioned stimulus (CS) is presented repeatedly without the unconditioned stimulus (UCS). Extinction is a method that is used intentionally to eliminate conditioned responses (CR). It can also happen naturally if the CS-UCS pairing ceases for some time.

Stimulus generalization occurs when a conditioned response (CR) occurs to a stimulus that only resembles or is similar to the conditioned stimulus (CS) but is not identical to it. For instance, Pavlov's dogs were classically conditioned to salivate to a bell (the CS), but if the first time they heard a buzzer they also salivated, this would be stimulus generalization. They were never conditioned with the buzzer, but they responded because the sound resembled that of the bell.

Stimulus discrimination occurs when the differences between stimuli are noticed and, thus, the new or different stimulus is not responded to in the same way as the original conditioned stimulus. For instance, stimulus discrimination would occur if Pavlov's dogs did not salivate to the sound of a buzzer, even if it sounded similar to the bell. This would indicate that the dogs could discriminate between these two sounds and, as a result, respond differently to each.

Researchers have used humans as well as animals in classical conditioning studies. In humans, emotional reactions occur sometimes as a result of classical conditioning, because emotions are involuntary, automatic responses. For instance, phobias (intense, irrational fears) may develop as a result of classical conditioning. (Phobias will be discussed further in Chapter 14 on Developmental Psychopathology.)

The most famous classical conditioning of emotions using a human subject was one conducted by American researcher **John Watson** (1878–1958). Although this study is considered unethical today and some have suggested that it is more myth or legend than fact, most textbooks mention the **Little Albert study** when discussing classical conditioning. Little Albert was an 11-month-old infant who initially was not afraid of laboratory white rats. Watson classically conditioned Albert to fear these rats by pairing the presentation of the rat with a loud noise that scared the infant. The diagram of this study would be:

Noise (UCS)	→	**Fear response** (UCR)
Rat + Noise (NS) (UCS)	→	**Fear response** (UCR)
NS becomes CS by repetition		
Rat alone (CS)	→	**Fear response** (UCR)

Example of Classical Conditioning

Higher-order conditioning occurs when a new neutral stimulus is associated with a conditioned stimulus (CS) and eventually comes to produce the conditioned response (CR). If, after Albert was classically conditioned, a dog was always paired with the rat, eventually Albert would display the fear response to the dog. A diagram of this higher order conditioning example would be:

Rat alone (CS)	→	**Fear** (CR)
Dog + Rat (new NS) (CS) by repetition	→	**Fear** (CR)
Dog alone (CS)	→	**Fear** (CR)

Example of Higher-Order Conditioning

OPERANT AND INSTRUMENTAL CONDITIONING

In **operant** or **instrumental conditioning**, responses are learned because of their consequences. Unlike classical conditioning, the responses learned in operant/instrumental conditioning are voluntary (but not necessarily consciously voluntary). **B.F. Skinner** is best known for his research in this area and for the principles he laid out. Skinner began with the research findings and theories of **Edward Thorndike**, whose "law of effect" stated that a behavior will be repeated if it gives pleasurable results and not repeated if it gives unpleasant results. (Refer to Chapter 2: Theories of Development, for more background on this.)

Hundreds of experiments have produced these principles of operant conditioning:

Reinforcement

Reinforcers are consequences for behavior and can be anything that increases the likelihood that a behavior will be repeated. Reinforcers can be positive or negative, and both have the potential to increase behaviors. Positive reinforcers are rewards or other pleasant consequences that follow behaviors and increase the likelihood that the behaviors will occur again in the future. Giving your dog a biscuit each time it sits on command is an example of **positive reinforcement**.

Negative reinforcers are anything a subject will work to avoid or terminate. Nagging behaviors are examples of **negative reinforcement** because we often will do whatever it takes to stop the nagging. Escape conditioning occurs when a subject learns that a particular response will terminate an aversive stimulus. Here are two examples of negative reinforcement:

- A parent buys a whining child candy to escape the embarrassing or annoying behavior. The child's whining is a negative reinforcement, and the mother is being conditioned to prevent or end whining by giving candy.
- A child cleans her room to avoid her mother's nagging. The parent is conditioning the child through negative reinforcement. Nagging will stop (or be prevented) by performing cleaning behavior.

Reinforcers can also be classified as primary or secondary. Primary reinforcers are necessary to meet biological needs, such as food, water, air, etc. Secondary reinforcers have acquired value and are not necessary for survival. Grades, money, a pat on the back, and praise are examples of secondary reinforcers.

Extinction occurs in operant conditioning when the reinforcement is removed before the target behavior becomes consistent and automatic. For example, an owner gives his dog a treat every time it sits on command. If the owner stops giving the treat suddenly after only a few trials, the dog will stop sitting on command. **Spontaneous recovery** can also occur in operant conditioning, as when the dog sits on command after treats have stopped. However, the behavior might not be consistent or last very long unless reinforcement is re-initiated.

How easily a new operant response takes hold and becomes automatic depends, in part, on how often that response is reinforced, or its **schedule of reinforcement**. A continuous schedule of reinforcement happens when every response is reinforced (100 percent of the time). Each time the dog sits on command, it receives a treat. Behaviors that are continuously reinforced are easier to extinguish than behaviors that are not reinforced 100 percent of the time. In the case of the dog, the disappearance of treats will cause the dog to stop sitting on command very soon.

Behaviors that are not reinforced each time they occur are said to be on an intermittent, or partial, schedule of reinforcement. There are four possible partial schedules of reinforcement:

- **Fixed ratio schedule:** Reinforcement is given after a fixed number of responses (e.g., every third time your dog sits, it receives a biscuit). Being paid on a piece-rate basis is an example of a fixed ratio schedule. The fixed ratio schedule produces a high rate of responding with a slight pause after each reinforcement is given. Fixed ratio schedules produce the fastest rate of extinction because the subject realizes quickly that reinforcement has stopped at the expected times.
- **Variable ratio schedule:** Reinforcement is given after a variable number of responses. For instance, on one occasion, reinforcement may occur after 2 responses, on the next occasion after 5 responses, and after 3 responses on the following occasion. The rate of reinforcement depends upon the rate of responding: the faster the rate, the more reinforcers received. This schedule produces steady, high rates of responding and is extremely resistant to extinction. Slot machines are based on variable ratio schedules.
- **Fixed interval schedule:** Reinforcement is given after the first response—after a given amount of time has elapsed. This may mean a reinforcer every 5 minutes, for example. Being paid once per month is another example. Fixed interval schedules produce a low rate of responding at the beginning of each interval and a high rate toward the end of each interval.
- **Variable interval schedule:** Reinforcement is given after the first response after a varying amount of time has elapsed. Pop quizzes often

occur on a variable interval schedule. The variable interval schedule produces a steady, slow rate of responding.

In general, ratio schedules produce higher response rates than interval schedules. Variable schedules are usually harder to extinguish than are fixed schedules because variable schedules are less predictable.

Skinner devised a chamber, known as a **Skinner box**, to study the effects of various schedules of reinforcement on the behavior of small animals such as rats and pigeons. During acquisition, or learning, each time a lever in the Skinner box was pressed, a food pellet was dispensed into a food dish. A speaker or light signal was also used to indicate conditions of reinforcement or extinction. In some studies, the grid floor was electrified, and the electric current could be turned off by pressing the lever. The speaker or lights signaled when the current would be turned on and, in avoidance trials, the animal had a certain amount of time to press the lever to avoid the shock.

Shaping involves systematically reinforcing closer and closer approximations of the desired behavior. When a rat is first placed in the Skinner box, it doesn't know that pressing the lever will result in a food reward and may never press the lever on its own. Lever pressing can be conditioned through shaping—each step closer to the lever results in a food reward. Shaping by approximations is used with humans to teach complex tasks. A task is broken down into parts and a person is rewarded during the process of mastering each part. This is particularly effective in training people with low cognitive skills how to master routine tasks.

A **discriminative stimulus** can serve as a cue to indicate a response is likely to be reinforced. The light in the Skinner box would be a discriminative stimulus. When the light is on, lever pressing results in a food reward. When it is off, lever pressing is not reinforced. The animal will eventually learn to discriminate and to press the lever only when the light is on.

Punishment

Just as reinforcement is used to increase a behavior, **punishment** is an operant conditioning technique used to decrease a behavior. Punishment involves the presentation of an aversive stimulus, or undesirable consequence, after an unwanted behavior has occurred. Something unpleasant can be added or something pleasant can be taken away.

- Receiving a ticket for speeding can be an example of positive punishment when it leads to adding unwanted "points" to one's driving record and increasing insurance premiums. Making a teenager do extra and unpleasant chores after breaking curfew is also an example of a punishment that adds something undesirable.

- Receiving a ticket for speeding can also be an example of a negative punishment when it leads to a fine or driving privileges being taken away. Placing a teenager on house restriction ("grounding") after breaking curfew is also an example of a punishment that takes away something positive, namely freedom.

Timing is very important for punishment to be effective—the sooner the punishment is delivered after the undesired behavior occurred, the better or quicker the learning. Even very short delays can reduce the effectiveness of punishment. Punishment must also be severe enough to eliminate the undesirable response.

Punishment can also have undesirable side effects:

- When punishment is accompanied by anger or aggression, the person punished may learn that aggression is a viable method for solving problems.
- Punishment alone does not teach appropriate behavior.
- The person providing the punishment can become a feared agent to be avoided.
- Punishment can get out of hand and become abusive.

Many behaviorists today suggest that punishment should be avoided as a conditioning method. Instead, they recommend the use of extinction to weaken an inappropriate response and reinforcement to increase appropriate behaviors. When punishment needs to be used, behaviorists recommend it be done with a firm but dispassionate attitude. Some also recommend that the punishment "fit the crime," i.e., making the punishment relate to the behavior that needs to be extinguished. Making a child clean up his or her own mess after a tantrum is an example of this. (This topic will be discussed again in Chapter 13: Schooling, Work, and Interventions.)

OBSERVATIONAL LEARNING

Very young infants exhibit habituation, and they can be conditioned with either classical or operant conditioning techniques. However, the third type of behavioral learning, observational learning, does not emerge until later in an infant's life. This is because observational learning requires greater cognitive demands for attention, memory, and deferred imitation.

Observational learning occurs when we learn new behaviors by watching others. This is sometimes called **social learning** or **modeling**. It is guided by four processes:

- **Attention**—Attention must be paid to the salient features of another's actions. Prestige or status of a model can influence whether another's actions are noticed and valued.
- **Retention**—Observed behaviors must be remembered in order to be carried out.
- **Reproduction of action**—The observer must be capable of carrying out the behavior that was observed.
- **Motivation**—There must be some reason for carrying out the behavior. Observing someone being rewarded for a behavior increases the likelihood that the behavior will be imitated.

Vicarious learning occurs when we learn the relationship between a response and its consequences by watching others. Vicarious reinforcement occurs when we observe the model receiving reinforcement for a behavior. Vicarious punishment happens when we observe the model being punished for engaging in a behavior.

The classic research on observational learning was conducted by **Albert Bandura** and his colleagues. This research included children watching and imitating an adult's aggressive behavior toward an inflated Bobo clown doll. Bandura found that children learned the aggressive behavior even when the adult was not reinforced for this behavior. Later research indicated that children who watched an aggressive model being reinforced were much more aggressive in a similar situation than children who saw the model punished for the aggressive actions. Through his research, Bandura demonstrated that both classical and operant conditioning can take place through observational learning—by observing another's conditioning.

Applications of observational or social learning will be discussed in Chapter 10: Social Development throughout the Life Span and Chapter 13: Schooling, Work, and Interventions.

CHAPTER 7

COGNITIVE DEVELOPMENT THROUGHOUT THE LIFE SPAN

Cognition, or thought, is defined as the manipulation of mental representations. Cognition includes the mental activities involved in the acquisition, storage, retrieval, and use of knowledge. The most intense cognitive development takes place during the first few years of life when the brain is developing rapidly. As the following discussion shows, however, cognitive development is best described as a lifelong process.

Before discussing theories of cognitive development, it is important to define the basic elements of cognition.

CONCEPTS

A basic element of thought is the **concept**. A concept is a label that represents a class or group of objects, people, or events that share common characteristics or qualities. We organize our thinking by using concepts, and concepts allow us to think about something new by relating it to a concept we already know.

Some concepts are well-defined, and each member of the concept has all the defining properties, while non-members do not possess all the properties. An example would be registered voters—you either are or are not registered to vote. Other concepts are not so clearly defined but are encountered frequently in our everyday life. These natural concepts do not have a definite set of defining features but instead have characteristic features, so members of this concept must have at least some of these characteristics. "Bird" is a natural concept. **Prototypes** are objects or events that best represent a natural concept. A sparrow or robin would be considered a prototypical bird by many individuals, while ostriches, penguins, or hummingbirds are not prototypical. New concepts are easier to learn if they are organized around a prototype.

Also, there are abstract concepts, such as "freedom" or "happiness," which have different definitions or prototypes for different people depending on their experience or ideals.

Reasoning

Reasoning involves processing information to reach a conclusion or to make sense of something. Reasoning should employ **logic**, which involves using systematic procedures based on valid arguments or suppositions to reach valid conclusions. There are two types of reasoning that we use commonly and in professional settings:

- **Inductive reasoning** involves reasoning from the specific to the general. For example, drawing conclusions about all members of a category or concept based on observing or measuring only some of the members is inductive reasoning. Research that uses random sampling of a population attempts to generalize the results to the whole population through induction.
- **Deductive reasoning** is reasoning from the general to the specific. Making a prediction about a person's behavior, based on a theory, involves deductive reasoning. Using the theory of observational learning, you might deduce that a healthy child with an irregular walking gait learned this behavior from imitating an older family member.

Problem Solving

Problem solving is the mental activity used to reach a certain goal. Problem solving includes understanding the problem, planning a solution, carrying out the solution, and evaluating the results. **Problem representation** is the way we think about a problem. We can represent problems visually, verbally, symbolically (e.g., mathematically), with analogies, or with concrete objects. The representation is supposed to make it easier to solve a problem, but one's choice of representation could make it harder by closing off other possibilities.

THEORIES OF COGNITIVE DEVELOPMENT

Piaget's Stage Theory

Jean Piaget's **cognitive-developmental theory** asserts that humans are born with certain cognitive abilities or predispositions which are developed as individuals mature physiologically and as they gain experience in their environment. Through a process he called **adaptation**, children construct cognitive **schemata** (singular: schema) to organize their experiences. He described the processes of **accommodation** and **assimilation** that occur when an individual is confronted with a stimulus that does not conform to previous experiences.

Imagine the brain as a very sophisticated filing system, mostly empty at birth. As a young child experiences the world, the filing system gets filled with file folders of concepts and **schemata**. (Piaget used the word "schema" rather than "concept." Both words can be defined as "mental category." But a schema can be more complex, including a series of thoughts or actions rather than just a single idea.)

Folders created early in life contain few items, because experience is limited. There might be a folder called "things that are soft," and another called "things that are dangerous," and another called "what makes things get called dogs," and so forth. Imagine that the dog folder has some descriptive items inside, such as "four legs" and "furry" and "black" and "tail"—all based on previous experiences in which someone said "dog" when a black, four-legged, furry, tailed creature was in sight. Suppose a furry four-legged *yellowish* creature appears. The child is told it is a dog, which creates a state of **disequilibrium** (confusion, being off-balance). So now the child must **assimilate** this new information about what colors a dog can be. The dog folder gets a bit bigger.

Now suppose another new and similar creature appears—four-legged, furry, black, with a tail. The child refers to the dog file folder, mentally checks off the descriptive items, and shouts "Dog!" But the grownup nearby says, "No, that's a cat." Again, this puts the child in a state of disequilibrium. The child must **accommodate** this new information by reorganizing the filing system. A new file folder must be created, along with some new information that distinguishes dogs from cats—perhaps based on observing eye shape or behavior or sound. The **adaptation** process is now complete—at least temporarily, until the next moment of disequilibrium.

Imagine this whole process repeating itself every time there is a novel situation or stimulus in the environment. For Piaget, this is how learners learn. His explanation is called **constructivism** because he envisioned that children construct concepts of reality by constructing schemata or organized patterns of thought and action based on experiences in their expanding environment. This part of Piaget's theory—adaptation through assimilation and accommodation—stays constant throughout the life span.

Unlike behavioral learning theory that describes learning as the same process throughout the life span, Piaget asserted that certain behaviors and ways of thinking characterize individuals at different ages. For this reason, his theory is considered a **stage theory**. Stage theories share the common tenet that certain characteristics will occur in predictable sequences and at certain times in the life of all individuals.

Piaget theorized that cognitive development proceeded through four stages:

1. the **sensorimotor** stage, which lasts from birth to approximately 2 years of age
2. the **preoperations** stage, which lasts from 2 to 7 years of age
3. the **concrete operations** stage, which covers the years 7 to about 11 or 12
4. the **formal operations** stage, which extends from about 12 years on

Children's thinking becomes more logical as they progress through the stages, resulting in the ability to think logically and to solve problems using abstract concepts. This chart illustrates the challenges and differences among the stages:

Piaget's Stages of Cognitive Development

Name and ages of stage	Characteristics and challenges to be mastered
Sensorimotor Stage Ages birth–2	• Learning through the senses of touch, sight, hearing, and through manipulation of objects • Gaining of focus and attention • Learning object permanence • Imitation of adults and older children • Little intention, mostly random explorations
Preoperations Stage Ages 2–7	• Centration (ability to filter only 1 attribute out of many—e.g., focusing on height, neglecting depth or width) ◦ Learning to "conserve" quantity if it changes form, such as pouring water from a tall to wide container and understanding that the quantity has not changed

(continued)

Piaget's Stages of Cognitive Development (continued)

Name and ages of stage	Characteristics and challenges to be mastered
Preoperations Stage Ages 2–7 (continued)	o Learning to mentally reverse operations (e.g. imagining "tall" water poured into a wide container and back again and understanding that the quantity of water has not changed) • Egocentric viewpoint o Events can only be seen or imagined from "my" point of view o Animism: I am alive, so this doll or rock must be alive. • Learning through play (first solitary, later social) • Rapid increase in language/vocabulary • Learning and stabilizing concepts of gender identity
Concrete Operations Stage Ages 7–11	• Mastery of previous concepts and challenges • Reduction of egocentrism • Logical reasoning o Ability to classify by attribute (all the "red" squares) o Ability to classify by multiple attributes (all the "large red" squares) o Seriation or sequencing things/events in order
Formal Operations Stage Ages 12 and up	• Abstract reasoning o Understanding of literary symbols o Understanding of ideologies and their implications o Full ability for critical and abstract thinking • Ability to understand abstract quantitative concepts (higher math, geometry) • Hypothetical reasoning o Ability to generate hypotheses o Idealization (imagining ideal solutions)

According to Piaget, the order in which children pass through the stages does not vary, but the rate at which children pass through them can vary from child to child. Piaget argued that each stage of cognitive development represents a qualitatively different way of thinking. That is, children in each stage think differently from children in the other stages. Therefore, it is not just that children acquire more information as they grow older, but *how* they think actually changes as they mature.

The following paragraphs offer more detail about these stages, with some added facts and theories that have emerged since Piaget's original writings.

From Birth to 2 Years—Sensorimotor

In the first 2 years of life, children are in the **sensorimotor stage** of cognitive development. They use senses and motor activity to construct schemata and improve their ability to engage in coordinated action. A child in this stage develops skills in problem solving when the problem involves sensorimotor activities or goals. Examples of such goals might be reaching for and grasping objects, climbing steps, and feeding oneself. To accomplish these goals, according to Piaget's theory, newborns use inborn sensory and motor systems that enable them to interact with the environment. Young infants explore their environment by holding and manipulating or mouthing objects and by visually tracking things that move. Out of all this sensorimotor activity, infants construct sensorimotor schema—e.g., organized patterns of action and thought about how the world is organized and how one can interact with the environment.

One of the first achievements to be mastered in the sensorimotor stage is **object permanence**. Piaget tested for object permanence by taking a toy, letting the child see it, then hiding it under a blanket in full view of the child. He then observed the child's reaction. From these and repeated tests, we know that infants 4 to 8 months of age act as if an object that is no longer in their sight must no longer exist. They do not search for the hidden toy. Between 8 and 12 months of age, a child will search under the blanket for the toy. However, these children have not fully grasped object permanence. If you show the toy, then hide it under a blanket, and then move the toy out from the blanket and place it under the couch, children in this age range will first look under the blanket and then go to the couch. It is as if they retrace their actions because they think their own actions had something to do with making the toy reappear. According to Piaget, object permanence is not fully achieved until the end of this first stage.

The final challenges to be mastered in this sensorimotor stage are **symbolic representation** and **deferred imitation**. Symbolic representation is the ability to use one thing to stand for another, illustrated in the pretend play of children. For instance, children can and will use a broom as a horse. Words (and sign language) are also examples of using symbolic material.

Deferred imitation is modeling someone else's behavior some time after observing the model. This requires the ability to create a mental representation of the behavior and later retrieve and use the representation.

When a child engages in pretend play, shows deferred imitation and an understanding of object permanence, he or she has shifted into the second stage of preoperations.

From 2 to 7 Years—Preoperations

The **preoperations stage** describes the way that children in preschool and kindergarten go about solving problems. Preschoolers and even many children in the primary grades may be at this stage in their cognitive development. Piaget gave this stage the name "preoperations" because even though a child in this stage is capable of using mental schemata (operations), these schemata are not particularly logical. (There is a lot of erroneous and "magical" thinking during these years.)

The preoperational child is challenged by certain logical concepts that must be mastered for truly logical thinking:

- **Conservation** is the understanding that the quantity of liquid, or number, or volume does not change unless you add or take some away. Conservation of liquid, for example, is the understanding that the quantity of liquid held in a tall, thin beaker does not change when it is poured into a short, wide bowl. Preoperational thinkers are fooled by the perceptual change in how the liquid looks and believe the quantity has changed. This is due to the child's tendency toward **centration**—focusing on only one attribute at a time. The child in this stage watches the "tall" water become "short" without taking into account that the width has also changed.
- **Seriation** is the ability to rank-order objects on one attribute or dimension. An example could be arranging objects from smallest to largest or from tallest to shortest.
- **Classification** is the ability to organize items into groups based on shared characteristics or attributes. If toddlers are given some red and blue triangles and red and blue circles, and are asked to put together what goes together, they do not group them in a logical way. Rather than putting all the same shapes together or putting all the same colors together, their grouping is unsystematic.
- **Class inclusion** is the ability to represent exemplars of categories in superordinate and subordinate levels. Toddlers have difficulty keeping multiple levels of a hierarchically organized system in mind at the same time. If you show a toddler a collection of five green beads and three red beads and ask if there are more green beads than beads all together, the preoperational child will say there are more green beads.

As a child progresses through this stage, these four concepts will solidify, and the child will be able to apply them easily.

Preoperational thought also has several other characteristic features. Children in this stage engage in **egocentric thinking**. They are unable to take the perspective of another person. Piaget first demonstrated egocentrism with his Three Mountain Task. A child is seated at Position A at a table. On the table are several mountains made of clay that are different sizes and that partially block the view of each other. The child has the view of the mountains that a person would have from being at Position A, but that view is different from the view someone would get if seated at Position B, which is to the right. The child is shown photographs taken from each of four seating positions, including A and B, and asked to pick the photograph that shows what a person sitting at Position B would see. Children using preoperational thinking pick the photograph that shows the mountains from their own view.

Preoperational children also do not reason logically about cause and effect. Piaget called this **transductive reasoning**. They may infer a causal relationship between events that simply co-occur, or they might mistakenly identify an event as the cause, when in fact it has followed the effect. Preoperational children also engage in **animistic thinking** and project human abilities and traits onto inanimate objects. Examples might include statements such as "My doll is sick" or "That rock bumped its head" or "The tree looks sad."

Preoperational thinking also lacks the concept of **reversibility**. That is, the child cannot easily imagine that a thing that has changed could be put back into its original form. A child might think that when "tall" water is turned into "short" water, it could never be "tall" again—except by magic.

From 7 to 11 Years—Concrete Operations

The next two stages, concrete operations and formal operations, describe cognitive development during the times that most young people are in school. The third stage, **concrete operations**, is the beginning of operational thinking and describes the thinking of children between the ages of about 7 and 11. Learners in this stage begin to decenter, meaning that they are able to take into consideration viewpoints other than their own. They can perform **transformations**, meaning that they can understand reversibility, inversion, reciprocity, and conservation. They can group items into categories, and they are capable of seriation and sequencing. They can make inferences about reality and engage in inductive reasoning. Their quantitative skills increase, and they can manipulate symbols if they are given concrete examples with which to work. All these cognitive skills are necessary for learning to read, for doing math, and for general logic and comprehension.

Adolescence—Formal Operations

Formal operations is the last stage of cognitive development. It opens the door for higher-ordered, critical thinking. This stage describes the way individuals think starting around the age of 12, improving over the next few years. For Piaget, this constitutes the ultimate stage of cognitive development—thus also describing adult thinking. Not all people reach this stage, according to Piaget. Learners at this stage of cognitive development are constantly improving their ability to

- engage in logical, abstract, and hypothetical thought;
- use the scientific method—formulating hypotheses, isolating influences, and identifying cause-and-effect relationships;
- plan and anticipate verbal cues;
- engage in both deductive and inductive reasoning;
- mentally operate on verbal statements that do not have concrete terms or examples.

These cognitive abilities characterize the highest level of thought. The end goal of cognitive development is the ability to engage in **hypothetico-deductive reasoning** about abstract concepts such as "justice" and "equity."

Adulthood

Gisela Labouvie-Vief suggested that there is an additional form of thought after adolescence called post-formal operations. This way of thinking is characterized by the understanding that there is often more than one right answer to a problem. To the relativistic thinker, truth is understood as relative to the knower, and problems are understood to have more than one possible solution. An absolute thinker thinks linearly and expects that there is one truth and that every problem has one correct solution. This theory of adult cognition assumes that post-formal operations is a distinct cognitive stage. It could also be argued that this flexible thinking is not a stage, but rather a type of thinking brought about by social-emotional factors. In other words, these are thinkers who have learned to allow a diversity of possibilities and viewpoints in their use of formal operations.

Vygotsky's Sociocultural Theory

Lev Vygotsky developed an alternative to Piaget's explanation of cognitive development. He argued that children develop cognitively as they interact not only with objects in their environment, but also with people in a **sociocultural** context. He described how the interactions that children have with more sophisticated thinkers will help their own thinking develop.

Guided participation is Vygotsky's term for how adults (or even older children) transmit concepts, skills, values, and beliefs to young children. Through a mutual communication process, learning takes place as the older person demonstrates, explains, and guides while participating in an activity that the child has not yet mastered. As an example, you can think of an adult and child playing "catch" as the adult gives suggestions for improvement. Or you can think of an older sibling helping a child pour milk into a cup, at first with both holding the milk container, then later with just verbal suggestions.

Vygotsky used the term **zone of proximal development** (ZPD) to describe children's problem-solving ability with and without the aid of an older guide. The ZPD pinpoints the gap between what the child knows or can do alone and what the next step of learning will be. Working alone on a skill, the child performs at the lowest level of his or her zone of proximal development. Working with a teacher or parent, a child can perform at the upper level of that range. Vygotsky observed that teachers and parents will **scaffold** the learning experience as they break the learning into manageable steps or provide progressively less help in the task. Scaffolding can be tailored to the individual and to the circumstance as the child shows more sophisticated problem-solving behaviors. In other words, teachers and parents notice what the child needs to learn next in a set of skills and provides clues or help to allow the child to experience that next step. As an example, consider a child who is trying to reach a toy on a shelf—trying strategies such as jumping or standing on tiptoes, but not being successful. An older sibling, rather than getting the toy for the child, pulls over some pillows or a chair for the child to use to climb up higher. Or think of the game of "catch" where the adult moves farther away or increases the speed or height of the throw. The concepts of ZPD and scaffolding also apply to the way adults teach children to read or do progressively harder math problems.

Vygotsky believed that language also plays a role in thinking. **Social speech**, i.e., speech that involves talking with other people, leads to **private speech**, i.e., talking aloud to oneself, which eventually becomes silent **inner speech**. Children from 3–4 years old often talk aloud while engaged in an activity, but older children tend to use inner speech during problem solving. He suggested that preschool children talk aloud to themselves when engaged in a task because the language directs their thinking about the task at hand. Incorporated into the private speech of these children are conversations and solutions they remember from their earlier collaborations with adults. Often, children increase the use of private speech when they get stuck on a problem or with a task. Private speech goes inward to become nonverbal inner speech in the elementary school years.

Play

It has been said that play is the work of childhood. The time from 2 to 5 years has even been called the play years. Play serves a variety of functions in children's development. It both reflects and stimulates cognitive development, and it helps children develop social interaction skills. It is interesting to note that the nature and value of play fit into both Piaget's constructivism and Vygotsky's social learning theory. Children engage in play in a series of stages:

Stages and Types of Play

Name of Stage	Typical Activities
Sensorimotor (functional) **play**	Infants manipulate objects to learn about their qualities and properties and to give tactile or oral pleasure. Toddlers push objects around in random fashion.
Solitary play	Toddlers and young preschoolers prefer to play with toys by themselves.
Parallel play	Young preschoolers play with toys or sand near each other, but do not interact. They do similar actions, yet do not interact with each other in any intentional way.
Associative play	Games such as Musical Chairs fit here. Toys or games might be shared, but with no mutual goal. "Playing house" in its earliest form fits here, where children dress, talk, and act out behaviors, but they are not really listening to or playing with each other in an organized fashion.
Cooperative play	Older preschoolers and elementary-age children play games or with toys and interact with others as they do so. "Playing house" in its more mature form fits here, where children agree on roles and rules and interact continuously. This is also a type of **sociodramatic play** because children are acting out social roles and sharing facts and opinions. This lays the groundwork for interpersonal relationships.

Play that is not just random exploration and not just for the pleasure of motor activity can be classified into two types:

Constructive play involves manipulating or building with objects such as blocks. The objects are just objects to the child, and the purpose of play is to test the limits of the material and the limits of the child's motor skills. The pieces or finished products do not represent anything. A tower of blocks is just a stack of blocks that is made to be as high as possible.

Pretend or **imaginative** or **symbolic play** involves games of make-believe. According to Piaget, this type of play requires the cognitive ability of symbolic representation. The child may imagine that he or she is someone or something else, that the activities he or she engages in are something other than what they really are, or possibly he or she imagines that the objects he or she is playing with are something different from what they appear to be. Now the block tower is constructed not for the challenge of building high, but to represent a castle or a fort or a skyscraper for imaginative play.

Daydreaming is a major form of imaginative play. Daydreaming, however, involves no physical activity as compared to the other types of play. It is pure imaginative thinking.

In addition to teaching the child how to interact socially, play is also an influencing factor in cognition. **Sutton-Smith** (1967) considered play an activity in which the infant can work through new responses and operations and increase his or her range of responses. Sutton-Smith called play a mechanism for the "socialization of novelty." Children whose play is varied can experience situations that increase their ability to respond appropriately to novel situations. Children whose play is restricted are less able to respond in unfamiliar situations. Thus, play enlarges a child's repertoire of responses and thereby allows him or her to adjust quickly to novelty.

Information Processing Theory

A relatively new and popular approach to studying cognition comes from the **information processing approach**. Theorists in this approach use the computer as a metaphor for the human mind, which is viewed as an information processing machine. Studying how the brain processes information has led to new understandings about cognitive processes. In this perspective, cognition involves the processes of **executive function**, which are the processes that occur when sensory data (stimuli) become present:

Executive Function in Brain	Comparable Computer Function
Attention	Input
Short-Term Storage	Temporary Memory (RAM chip)
Encoding	Processing (by CPU)
Long-Term Storage	Permanent Memory (hard drive)
Retrieval	Output; opening stored file

Information processing theorists study cognitive development by examining changes to these and other processes that occur with age. They tend to argue that cognitive development is more continuous, rather than discontinuous. Changes that occur with age frequently are described as changes in capacity or speed, not the emergence of qualitatively new processes during the life span. They do not concern themselves with qualitative changes or differences in thinking.

Note: There is one more executive function that humans employ that does not occur in common computers, and that is **feedback**. For us, retrieval can trigger a new input from our own perceptions or from people or things in the environment. This is sometimes referred to as a feedback loop, and it can contribute to expanding and refining what we learn. For instance, we might realize (or be told) that our initial retrieval from storage was flawed (e.g., biased or inaccurate), based on new information in front of us. This gives us the opportunity to adjust our thinking and store newer, more accurate information. Sophisticated computers can "learn" from feedback when they are programmed with artificial intelligence (AI).

ATTENTION is the first step in the information processing sequence. Sensory stimuli are everywhere and never-ending. One of the first tasks of an infant is learning to focus attention on important stimuli and ignore the rest. **Selective attention** is directing one's attention toward a particular aspect of the sensory field while at the same time ignoring other distracting stimuli. Habituation helps with that, but focus involves more than just filtering out "old stuff" in favor of new stimuli. In fact, often there are times when an individual must attend to something old because it is the most important stimulus in the environment at that moment, even if it is not novel.

SHORT-TERM STORAGE is the part of the system that information moves to when it has been given attention. To clarify, the theory describes more than one kind of storage or memory. In fact, researchers have identified different memory systems and have constructed a flow chart showing the transfer of information from one system to another. The memory systems include:

Sensory Memory	⇒ If further attention is given	**Working Memory** (or **Primary** or **Short-term Memory**)	⇒ If encoding takes place	**Long-term Memory** (or **Secondary Memory**)

Information that comes into a person's sensory perceptual system (has gotten attention) registers automatically in **sensory memory**. The sensory register holds information for a very brief period, up to only a few seconds. Information that is not transferred from sensory memory to working memory is lost. (In other words, the person might briefly notice a stimulus, but does not pay enough attention to it to let that stimulus become a thought for short-term memory to use.)

Short-term or **working memory** is where a sensory memory moves to next. Short-term memory is also called working memory because a great deal of information processing takes place in that system. It is where conscious thinking takes place. Whatever you are thinking about right now is in your short-term memory.

ENCODING is the process of making information in short-term memory meaningful so that it can be stored for future use in long-term memory. Information can be held in working memory for slightly longer time periods compared to sensory memory. It can be retained even longer through the process of **rehearsal**. An example of **maintenance rehearsal** is repeating the telephone number of a pizzeria to yourself while you walk over to get your phone. There is also **elaborative rehearsal**, which involves encoding the information through activity or association or relating the information to previous knowledge. If rehearsal stops too soon, information will be lost after 20 or 30 seconds unless it is further processed for long-term storage.

Working or short-term memory is also limited in how much information it can hold at one time. That will affect one's ability to encode. The average adult can hold from five to nine bits, or chunks, of information in short-term memory. **George Miller** proposed the number seven, plus or minus two, as the capacity of short-term memory. However, the capacity of short-term memory can be increased by grouping pieces of information—what Miller referred to as **chunking**. Chunking involves organizing or grouping separate bits of information into larger units or chunks. For example, 5 8 1 2 7 8 6 3 could be chunked into 58-12-78-63. This transforms eight bits of information into four, thereby freeing up space in short-term memory. (Phone numbers are chunked for us, using a 3-digit area code, then a 3-digit prefix, then a 4-digit number.)

LONG-TERM STORAGE is the system that holds information for an extended period of time. Some information processing theorists suggest long-term memories are permanent, and that what we call forgetting is a failure of retrieval, not loss of memory. However, there is a great deal of disagreement, and several competing theories of forgetting have been offered. Unlike short-term memory, long-term memory appears to have unlimited storage capacity. Long-term memory is also a very organized system. Research has suggested that new memories are fitted into a network of preexisting, organized knowledge. (Does this remind you of the file folder analogy regarding schemata?)

RETRIEVAL is the process of remembering something that has been stored in long-term memory. Retrieval can take the form of either **recognition** or **recall**. Recognition is remembering that occurs when the cue for retrieval contains the information to be remembered. Selecting the correct response to a multiple-choice question is an example of recognition. Recall is a much more difficult retrieval process. It involves remembering after being given a less helpful cue. Answering the question, “What did you eat for breakfast yesterday?” is an example of the recall process.

Long-term memory is divided into three categories, and each seems to be controlled by or stored in its own area of the brain.

- **Semantic memory** stores facts and information.
- **Episodic memory** stores experiences and events.
- **Procedural memory** stores “how-to” knowledge and behaviors.

Consider how these three types of memory might interact in life situations. It could lead to enhanced memory of a fact, person, event, or skill. But it could also contribute to a “false memory” if a memory in one category gets associated incorrectly with a memory in another category. For instance, identifying a smell from the past, you might remember vividly interacting with an old friend from that time. But it is possible that you might falsely remember an event from another time or a place that did not have that smell, yet now you think it did.

Another facet of research in information processing deals with people’s knowledge of their own executive functions of attention, memory, and retrieval. **Metacognition** is the awareness of one’s own cognitive processing. **Metamemory** is one’s knowledge about memory. Some psychologists and educators believe that training in metacognition through “memory tricks” will improve one’s executive function when engaged in a new learning task. This will be discussed further in this chapter and in Chapter 13: Schooling, Work, and Interventions.

Before moving on, let us compare the cognitive developmental theory and information processing theory. Piaget described definite stages of cognitive development, because he was looking at children’s abilities to think and learn different kinds of things at different ages. Information processing theorists are not looking at what kinds of things can be thought, but rather at how learning takes place in the brain. So it is possible to subscribe to both cognitive developmental theory and information processing theory. One describes stages of what is possible for a learner to think about, and the other describes a set of processes for how the brain processes, stores, and retrieves what the learner is thinking about.

EXECUTIVE FUNCTION THROUGHOUT THE LIFE SPAN

Research has focused on the ability to control and use all the executive functions while learning and while solving problems. Here is what we know about executive function through the life span:

In early childhood (ages 2–6), children begin to use **inhibitory control**. That is, they start to block their own impulses so that they can focus on something that needs attention, even if it means focusing on a familiar stimulus rather than a novel one. During this stage, working memory becomes apparent, as children show abilities for short-term processing of information. Also, intentional memory strategies appear, with behaviors such as looking, pointing, and naming. Young children's ideas about their own metacognitive abilities are unrealistic and exaggerated.

In middle childhood (ages 7–12), children are still working on controlling attention. Visual scans and searches are more systematic than in younger years, which makes learning to read possible. Older children exhibit longer attention spans. They also exhibit verbal working memory as they can talk about what they observe and how they are thinking about it. They can use rehearsal as a method of remembering, and they can use organization, chunking, and mnemonics as memory tools (when guided by adults). They can plan and organize, and they can demonstrate some cognitive flexibility as they try problem-solving strategies. With all these abilities, it is not surprising that older children possess realistic and effective metacognition.

In adolescence, all of the above executive functions show strong improvement. Visual scanning is more focused and systematic. Attention spans are longer and there is an ability to switch between two ongoing tasks. Teens' metacognitive abilities are greater than children's. All this is due to greater experience, improved myelination of the nervous system, and the development of the prefrontal cortex of the brain.

In adulthood, complete myelination in the prefrontal cortex allows for maximum cognitive ability. (Recall that this process coats nerve cells with fatty myelin, which speeds up processing across nerve synapses.) Cognitive acuity peaks in people's twenties, when they exhibit the finest abilities of selective attention and divided attention tasks. Later in adulthood, memory declines and distractibility increases. Around age 70, cognitive flexibility starts to decline. Some adults show little decline, due to factors such as activity level, diet, training, and level of cognitive stimulation. As for metacognition, adults are very aware of their abilities and shortcomings, and they can take advantage of their long-term knowledge base, especially in specialized areas on which they have concentrated.

PROBLEM SOLVING AND PLANNING

Recall that the brain and nervous system develop with age. Notably, myelin sheathing around neurons increases speed of thought and the development of the prefrontal cortex increases the depth, quality, and abstraction of thought. The effects of these biological changes have been tracked by researchers of memory and retrieval through experiments in problem solving.

Robert Siegler studied problem solving in children, using what he called a "rule assessment approach." He observed problem solving in participants aged 3 to 20 years to determine what aspects or information about the problem they focused on and what rule they developed from that information to solve the problem. Most 3-year-olds will just guess at a solution, but 4- to 5-year-olds will select information they deem to be important and form a rule using that information. However, they tend to fail to take all important information into account when forming the rule. By age 12, children are sophisticated in determining all the information relevant to the problem and then forming a rule to apply in solving it. (And recall that Piaget placed that same age as the peak of concrete operations and the beginning of the formal operations stage.)

Problem-solving strategies can take on many forms. At first, **brainstorming** might be used to help the individual shake off cognitive biases and rigid thinking. **Rule-making**, as mentioned in the paragraph above, is usually based on previous experience, as the person tries to apply what is already known to a new problem. This involves the creation and use of **heuristics**—that is, algorithms, "mental maps," or practical idioms that might be applied to a novel situation. Examples of heuristics are "Righty-tighty, lefty-loosey," for working with tools, and "Moss grows heaviest on the north side of trees," for dealing with navigation. Another problem-solving strategy is to mentally work backward on a problem—envisioning a solution and thinking about the steps necessary to get to that solution.

ENVIRONMENTAL INFLUENCES ON COGNITIVE DEVELOPMENT

There are cultural and environmental influences on cognitive development. You will find references in several chapters of this book regarding how factors in the prenatal environment and in childhood can disrupt the normal course of cognitive development. There are many environmental factors, for example, that can cause intellectual disability in children. Furthermore, although the domains of development (biological, cognitive, psychosocial) are discussed separately, they actually interact throughout life. Poor nutrition or poor social relationships, for instance, can have a negative impact on cognitive development.

Research has shown that long-term stress can affect cognitive ability. Sources of stress can be socioeconomic (e.g., poverty, malnutrition), environmental (e.g., toxins), or family-related. Because stress affects hormones, it affects growth—even brain growth and development.

Early childhood education programs can positively influence cognitive development. There are many different types of programs and many different approaches used in these programs, but research has shown that many early education programs can have a positive effect on cognitive development. The key factor is having a staff that is qualified to create an appropriate curriculum and to respond to the cognitive (and other) needs of children. Such programs take a holistic approach when designing the curriculum, so different domains are integrated. Activities will include and integrate motor skills, cognitive skills, social skills, pre-academic skills, and the arts, such as music, dance, painting, sculpting, etc. Parent participation is also advantageous to a good early childhood program.

Culture can also affect cognitive development. Cultural expectations can mold cognitive functions beginning at a very young age, from gender preferences to what is possible to think about oneself in the present or future. **Caldwell and Bradley** have developed the **HOME** scale (Home Observation for Measurement of the Environment) to assess the amount of intellectual stimulation in the home environment. HOME measures things such as the amount of appropriate play materials, parental involvement with children, and the amount of intellectual stimulation (such as the number of books in the home). Studies have shown that scores on the HOME scale positively correlate with later measures of intelligence. Adopted children show gains in IQ scores when they move from an impoverished household to a stimulating one. In fact, children who live in households with high HOME scores tend to show gains in IQ scores between 1 and 3 years of age, while the opposite is true of children from households with low HOME scores. These patterns hold for European-American and African-American households, but not for Mexican-American households. More research is needed to explore these cultural differences regarding the home environment.

Developmental psychologists have also investigated whether the pattern of cognitive development described by Piaget is universal—that is, found in all children. **Michael Cole** pioneered the study of cultural influences on cognitive development to test this universality. His study of the development of thinking in children from non-Western cultures showed that children in those cultures took longer to achieve concrete operations and were unable to achieve formal operations. The explanation for this difference is that the achievement of concrete and formal operational thought correlates with formal schooling. Cultures that define intelligence as logical, hypothetico-deductive thought are cultures that design schools to foster the development of this type of reasoning. But not all cultures have formal schooling, nor do they all define intelligence that way. Some cultures equate intelligence with good social skills and still others view slow and deliberate problem solving as more intelligent than being quick. This is the opposite of the typical Western view. Children from other cultures are also better able to show their capacity for logical thinking if the problems and the materials are familiar to them. So it is clear that culture influences cognitive development.

EXPERTISE

Older adults often perform best on problem-solving tasks in domains in which they have a great deal of knowledge and experience. They solve problems more efficiently in their area of expertise than outside it. They also outperform younger subjects on problem-solving tasks that involve everyday problems. As mentioned earlier, it may be that this build-up of domain-specific knowledge and experience in solving everyday problems compensates for the slowing down of cognitive processing that has been found in older adults. This distinction of younger versus older cognitive ability will come up again in Chapter 8: Intelligence throughout the Life Span.

The topic of "specialized knowledge" possessed by older adults brings us to the topic of **expertise** as it relates to cognitive ability. It has been said that a person needs to spend 10,000 hours on a subject to master it or to build expertise. Since humans must rest, eat, play, etc., and not just spend all their time getting good at something, it works out that 10,000 hours applied to a single pursuit would normally require at least 10 years. So it is no wonder that older adults (say, about 35 years of age or more) would be the ones to possess expertise in any area that involves cognitive skills of processing and retrieving large amounts of information. And it would follow that these adults would have plenty of experience, heuristics, and "out-of-the-box" thinking to draw from when confronted with a problem to solve.

WISDOM

Does expertise make one wise? Developmental psychologists do not think so. **Wisdom** seems to be something outside anything that can be described by information processing or learning theory or Piaget's constructivism. Wisdom, as researchers have found, is more of a psychological state than a cognitive stage, although age is partly involved. It consists of not just biological and cognitive maturity, but also elements of self-awareness, emotional stability, empathy, and a sense of appropriate words or action in situations. It also seems to evolve from helping and leading others as one matures oneself, all while having an appreciation and understanding of what those being helped are going through. You might find more clues about the development of wisdom in Chapter 10: Social Development throughout the Life Span and Chapter 12: Personality and Emotions.

CHAPTER 8

INTELLIGENCE THROUGHOUT THE LIFE SPAN

This chapter focuses on the components and measurement of intelligence. There will also be discussion of ways that heredity and environment affect intelligence.

CONCEPTS OF INTELLIGENCE AND CREATIVITY

Intelligence

Because **intelligence** is a hypothetical construct, psychologists have disagreed on how to define it. Different intelligence tests, therefore, ask different questions and may measure different abilities. Some definitions of intelligence include:

- The capacity to acquire and use knowledge
- The total body of acquired knowledge
- The ability to arrive at innovative solutions to problems
- The ability to deal effectively with one's environment
- Knowledge of one's culture
- The ability to do well in school
- The global capacity of the individual to act purposefully, to think rationally, and to deal effectively with the environment
- What intelligence tests measure

A key question about intelligence has been whether it consists of a single core factor or several and perhaps unrelated abilities. Responses to this question have included these constructs and theories by researchers:

Charles Spearman — Concluded that cognitive abilities could be narrowed down to one critical **g-factor**, or general intelligence. (The s-factors represent specific knowledge needed to answer questions on a particular kind of test.) The g-factor seems to stay stable throughout life, while s-factors increase with knowledge and experience.

J.P. Guilford — Proposed that intelligence consists of 150 distinct abilities.

L.L. Thurstone — Used a statistical technique known as factor analysis to find seven independent primary mental abilities: numerical ability, reasoning, verbal fluency, spatial visualization, perceptual ability, memory, and verbal comprehension.

Raymond B. Cattell — Argued that a g-factor does exist, but cognitive ability consists of **fluid intelligence** (reasoning and problem solving) and **crystallized intelligence** (specific knowledge gained from applying fluid intelligence).

Robert Sternberg — Proposed a **triarchic theory of intelligence** that proposed three kinds of intelligence:

- analytical (or processing) intelligence that includes metacomponents, performance components, and knowledge-acquisition components,
- experiential (or creative) intelligence that includes abilities to deal with novelty and to automatize processing, and
- contextual intelligence that includes both practical and social intelligence.

Howard Gardner — Proposed a theory of **multiple intelligences** that include eight distinct types of intelligence:

- Language
- Logical-Mathematical
- Spatial
- Musical
- Bodily-Kinesthetic
- Naturalistic
- Interpersonal (Social)
- Intrapersonal (Self)

Creativity

Psychologists differentiate between intelligence and creativity. **Creativity** is the ability to produce something new and unique or something that combines elements in new ways. Creative problem solving involves coming up with a solution that is both unusual and useful. Creative thinking and problem solving usually involve **divergent thinking**, i.e., thinking that can produce many different solutions to the same problem or question. Creating a variety of sentences with the word "corner" would involve divergent thinking, since there is no one specific correct response and many ways to use that word. A response to the question "What is the capital of Canada?" would require **convergent thinking**, because only one correct answer is possible. Convergent thinking does not appear to be related to creativity.

Tests have been developed to measure creativity, and almost all of them require divergent thinking. The Remote Associates Test (RAT) is one example. In general, these tests of creativity have not been good at predicting who will be creative in real-life problem-solving situations.

There is a modest correlation between creativity and intelligence. Highly creative people tend to have above-average intelligence, but not always. More specifically, research indicates that creativity uses three types of intelligence:

- Ability to analyze
- Ability to synthesize
- Ability to make practical changes and applications

Furthermore, having a high IQ does not necessarily mean that a person will ever exhibit creativity. Children who are creative tend to engage in more pretend or fantasy play and enjoy new experiences. But the factors that generally predict IQ in children do not predict creativity. The development of creativity may be fostered by certain types of parenting, or the home environment, and perhaps somewhat by genetics. However, identical twins do not have more similar creativity scores than fraternal twins or siblings.

Creativity seems to be a capacity that is maintained throughout the life span. Even if creative production declines in older adults, or if they score lower on measures of creativity, the capacity to be creative is retained. Some creative people continue to produce great works until the end of their lives.

GIFTEDNESS

Discussion of intelligence and creativity leads to the concept of giftedness. **Giftedness** is often defined as having an intelligence score of 120 to 130 or higher (or having an IQ in the upper 2 to 3 percent of the population). **Lewis Terman** began a longitudinal study of gifted children in the 1920s. He and others followed the lives of these children as they grew up and became adults. The average intelligence score was 150 for the approximately 1,500 children in this study. The study was to officially conclude when the last subject died. The last report by the research team was in 1996, and in 2006 there were still some surviving subjects in their 90s.

The findings of this study have challenged the commonly held belief that the intellectually gifted are emotionally disturbed and socially maladjusted. In fact, just the opposite was found. As adults, this group was also more academically and professionally successful than their non-gifted peers. Although the study contained flaws, it stands as a defining depiction of the mostly successful lives of gifted individuals.

Schools are often pressed to define giftedness and then select students who qualify for special programs. **Joseph Renzulli** proposed a giftedness model that is often used to define giftedness for such programs. In this model, giftedness is composed of these elements:

- High ability and achievement (high IQ and application of intelligence in academics, leadership, or some other pursuit)
- Persistence in tasks (demonstrated perseverance to complete work)
- Creativity or artistry

Other factors that have been proposed to identify gifted students are high verbal skills and imaginative thought and expression. Some students who have been identified as gifted have emotional and social difficulties, while other gifted students are very popular and socially at ease.

INTELLIGENCE TESTS

History of Intelligence Testing

Early interest in intelligence testing dates back to the eugenics movement of **Sir Frances Galton**. Galton believed that it is possible to improve genetic characteristics (including intelligence) through breeding.

The first effective test of intelligence was devised in the early 1900s by French psychologist **Alfred Binet**. Binet was appointed by the French Ministry of Public Instruction to design an intelligence test that would identify children who needed to be removed from the regular classrooms so that they could receive special instruction.

Binet and his colleague Theodore Simon devised an intelligence test consisting of 30 subtests containing problems of increasing difficulty. The items on the test were designed to measure children's judgment, reasoning, and comprehension. This first test was published in 1905 and then was revised in 1908 and 1911. The 1908 revision of the Binet and Simon scale introduced the notion of mental age. **Mental age** is a measure of a child's intellectual level that is independent of the child's chronological or actual age.

Shortly after Binet's original work, **Terman** and his colleagues helped refine and standardize the test for American children. (This was the same Terman discussed in the giftedness section above.) Their version came to be the **Stanford-Binet Intelligence Scale**, and its latest revision (SB-5) is still being used today. A further discussion of this scale can be found later in this chapter.

Researchers and practitioners have adopted **William Stern's** term **intelligence quotient,** or **IQ**, sometimes referred to as the ratio IQ score. To calculate IQ, a child's mental age (MA) (as determined by how well he or she does on the test) is divided by his or her chronological age (CA) and multiplied by 100.

The major advantage of the IQ score over simple MA is that it gives an index of a child's IQ test performance relative to others of the same chronological age. The major problem with the ratio IQ score is that most people's mental development slows in their late teens. But as MA may remain fairly stable throughout adulthood, CA increases over time. Using CA as the divisor in the IQ formula, therefore, results in an individual's IQ score diminishing over time (even though MA has not changed).

David Wechsler corrected this problem with ratio IQ scores by devising **the deviation IQ score**. This deviation IQ score is calculated by converting the raw scores on each subtest of the test to standard scores "normalized" for each age group—that is, graphed on a bell curve. These standard scores are then translated into deviation IQ scores. Wechsler reasoned that intelligence is normally distributed and follows the bell-shaped curve—that is, the majority of people score at or around the mean, or average, score of 100 and progressively fewer people will achieve scores that spread out in either direction of the mean. A group of IQ scores can be depicted as a normal, bell-shaped curve with an average score of 100 and a standard deviation (deviation from the mean) that is the same for any age level. The figure on the next page shows an example of a bell curve of IQ scores divided into standard deviations.

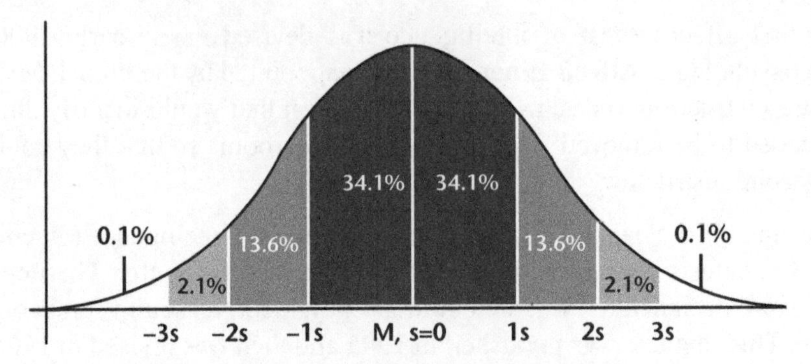

This chart shows a bell curve with standard deviations, derived statistically.
For IQ tests, the center line represents 100.
The 34% of the population to the right of 100 represents scores of 101–115.
The 34% of the population to the left of 100 represents scores of 85–99.
13.6% of people have scores of 116–130.
13.6% of people have scores of 70–84.
About 2% have scores of 131–145.
About 2% have scores of 55–69.
About one-tenth of 1% have scores over 145.
About one-tenth of 1% have scores under 55.
(Source: Wikimedia Commons)

The advantage of the deviation IQ is that the standing of an individual can be compared with the scores of others of the same age, and the intervals from age to age remain the same. Deviation IQ scores, therefore, indicate exactly where a test-taker falls in the normal distribution of intelligence.

Terman adopted the deviation IQ as the scoring standard for the 1960 revision of the Stanford-Binet Intelligence Scale, although he chose a standard deviation of 16 rather than 15. Almost all other intelligence tests today use deviation IQ scores.

Current Intelligence Tests

The most widely used versions of intelligence tests today are described in this section. These tests are meant to be administered individually, which means that they are to be given only by trained psychologists to one test-taker at a time.

The first Stanford-Binet Intelligence Scale was published in 1916 by Lewis Terman and his colleagues. It was revised most recently in 2003 and remains one of the world's most widely used tests of intelligence (although there are criticisms of the scale). It can be used with individuals from age 2 through adulthood.

In the Stanford-Binet Intelligence Scale (Fifth Edition), the term *intelligence* has been replaced by *cognitive development*. Also, the terms IQ and mental age are not used; instead, the term Standard Age Score (SAS) is used. The current edition measures five areas of cognitive development, and the SAS can be calculated for each area as well as an overall composite score. The five areas are fluid reasoning, knowledge, quantitative reasoning, visual-spatial processing, and working memory.

Because the Stanford-Binet initially appeared to be unsatisfactory for use with adults, in 1939, **David Wechsler** published a test designed exclusively for adults. This test has since been revised and is now known as the **WAIS-IV** (Wechsler Adult Intelligence Scale, 4th edition). A fifth edition is scheduled to be released around 2020.

Wechsler also published two scales for children and these are now known as:

WPPSI-IV Wechsler Preschool and Primary Scale of Intelligence, 4th edition (for children 4 to 6 years of age)

WISC-V Wechsler Intelligence Scale for Children, 5th edition (for children 6 to 16 years of age)

The Wechsler scales were known for at least two major innovations when they were first developed. First, they were less dependent on verbal ability than the Stanford-Binet and included many items that required nonverbal reasoning. His tests allow the computation of three scores: a verbal IQ score, a performance IQ score, and an overall full-scale IQ score.

Second, Wechsler developed the deviation IQ score based on the normal distribution of intelligence and abandoned the notion of intelligence quotient. Wechsler's scales of intelligence are still widely used and respected today.

The **Bayley Scales of Infant Intelligence-III** is a test designed to be used with infants aged 2 to 30 months. There are three scales on this test, including the motor scale, the mental scale, and the infant behavior record. The degree to which the infant has achieved developmental milestones, can coordinate goal-directed behavior, and can follow directions, are examples of what is measured on these scales. Infants receive a developmental quotient (DQ). Scores on the Bayley Scales do not predict later IQ very well. However, a low DQ score may be a sign of intellectual disability or neurological problems.

Intelligence tests, as with any other tests, must have **reliability** and **validity** to be of good quality and to be predictive. Most intelligence tests used today (e.g., Stanford-Binet and Wechsler scales) demonstrate good reliability or consistency of scores. In other words, the same individual taking the same or similar form of the test at a later time will score about the same.

The validity of intelligence tests is the degree to which the tests measure what they are intended to measure. Validity is often assessed using criterion validity. This entails correlating test scores with another independent measure of intelligence. The validity of intelligence tests depends on the criterion being used. For example, intelligence tests do a good job of predicting success in school. Although intelligence test scores correlate with occupational attainment, they do not predict performance within a given occupation.

Intelligence tests have been criticized as being biased. Children who have low socioeconomic status tend to score lower than children from middle to upper socioeconomic classes. Some experts suggest that mainstream intelligence tests tap into experiences that people from the middle to upper status groups have, since the tests were developed by white, middle-class psychologists. People from low economic backgrounds and from diverse cultures can have very different background experiences (and language usage) compared to the background of those who created the tests. There is some research evidence to support this claim of bias. This **test bias** has led to several recent attempts to create a **culture-fair intelligence test**. For instance, **Raven's Progressive Matrices test** uses nonverbal items to measure fluid intelligence, thus bypassing language differences in children's culture or experience.

Intelligence test scores can and do change over time. For instance, infant and preschool scores are not good predictors of intelligence in later childhood, adolescence, or adulthood. It is not until late elementary school (after about ages 8–10) that intelligence test scores begin to stabilize. It is also possible, however, to have gains or losses in intelligence during adolescence and adulthood.

HEREDITY AND ENVIRONMENT RELATED TO INTELLIGENCE

The nature-versus-nurture debate finds its way into the topic of intelligence. Does heredity or environment determine one's intellectual abilities? Or is it a combination of the two?

Researchers use the term **heritability** when they attempt to estimate how much of a trait in a population is determined by genetic inheritance. **Twin studies** have become the most popular research tool to examine this issue. Correlational studies with twins suggest that heredity has a great influence on the development of intelligence. For instance, the correlation of intelligence test scores for identical twins (who have identical genetic makeup) is higher than the correlation for fraternal twins. Even identical twins reared apart have more similar IQs than fraternal twins reared together in the same household.

There is research evidence, however, to indicate that environment also exerts a strong influence on intelligence. **Sandra Scarr** and other researchers have shown that underprivileged children placed in homes that provide an enriching intellectual environment have shown moderate but consistent increases in intelligence. Children placed in various enrichment programs have also shown gains in IQ.

It should be noted that racial and cultural differences in IQ are very small when compared to the range of genetic differences within each group. Research has suggested that the differences between mean intelligence test scores for black and white Americans may be due to differences in parental education, nutrition, health care, and schools, as well as differences in motivation for doing well on the test.

REACTION RANGE

The term **reaction range** has been applied to the nature-versus-nurture debate on intelligence. Reaction range of intelligence implies that genetics defines a potential range of IQ, but that environment will influence where along this range an individual's IQ score will fall. This would explain the difference in IQ scores for identical twins who were raised apart. The twin raised in a more enriched environment would tend to score near the top of his or her inborn potential and mutual IQ reaction range, while the twin raised in a sparse or dull environment would tend to score near the bottom of their mutual range.

DEVELOPMENTAL STABILITY AND CHANGE IN INTELLIGENCE

The concept of reaction range in regard to intelligence gives researchers clues about where to investigate to find what influences intelligence differences. Many children show considerable fluctuation in IQ scores through childhood. Children may show both gains and losses. Children who live in poverty or are being raised by parents with low IQs show noticeable declines in IQ. This has been explained by the cumulative deficit hypothesis, which suggests the negative effects of living in a non-stimulating environment build up over time. On the other hand, children who show noticeable gains in IQ tend to be those who are exposed to stimulating environments and have parents who foster their achievement. Some of these children also may have benefited from intervention programs such as Head Start, which have been shown to produce improved IQ scores, although they might not always be lasting.

During adolescence, IQ scores become much more stable and continue to be so through most of adulthood. Research on intelligence in adulthood paints a very complex picture. Early research on intelligence in adulthood was cross-sectional and longitudinal. Recall that both of these research methodologies have flaws. Both types of research reported declines in IQ with some suggesting the decline began as early as the forties and others reporting a decline beginning in the sixties or seventies. There was typical agreement that the steepest decline occurred in the eighties.

Klaus Warner Schaie conducted a groundbreaking sequential study of intelligence in adulthood which he began in 1956 and ended in 1984. Recall that this developmental research method resolves the flaws of both cross-sectional and longitudinal designs. (See Chapter 3: Research Strategies and Methodology.) Furthermore, Schaie measured changes in both **fluid intelligence** (e.g., problem-solving ability) and **crystallized intelligence** (accumulated knowledge). He found that fluid intelligence did show declines in adulthood and that this decline began earlier and was steeper than declines in crystallized intelligence. Crystallized intelligence remained the same or even improved and then started to decline somewhat after the sixties. Not all people showed declines. There were some who maintained the same levels of both fluid and crystallized intelligence into later life. Most importantly, Schaie found large birth cohort differences in the patterns of both fluid and crystallized intelligence in adulthood. Younger birth cohorts retained higher levels of intelligence into late adulthood than members of older birth cohorts.

What has been particularly challenging in the study of intellectual performance in older adults is controlling for the confounding factors of disease or health issues. Diseases such as cardiovascular disease are correlated with steeper intellectual decline. There is also a phenomenon that has been observed called **terminal drop**. This is a rapid decline in intellectual performance shortly before death.

CHAPTER 9

LANGUAGE DEVELOPMENT

Language development is related to cognitive development. However, it is such a unique feature of human development that it requires a separate discussion. This chapter focuses on the components and development of spoken language, as well as cultural and environmental influences.

LANGUAGE AND THOUGHT: THEORIES OF LANGUAGE DEVELOPMENT

An ongoing nature-versus-nurture debate has been whether language is tied to an innate biological process or is a learned phenomenon. Many researchers hold the view of the **nativist theory**, which maintains that humans are somehow biologically programmed to learn language. According to **Noam Chomsky**, a **language acquisition device (LAD)** gives children an innate ability to process speech and to understand both the fundamental relationships among words and the regularities of speech. Actually, "device" is not a very accurate description, since language acquisition would have to take place in some region(s) of the brain. And in evolutionary terms, it would most likely reside in the "new" or mammalian brain. As it turns out, researchers have identified two areas in the dominant (usually left) side of the cerebral cortex that seem to hold major keys to language: Broca's area and Wernicke's area.

Researchers have also proposed a sensitive period for language learning during childhood. If exposed to language during this sensitive period, fluent language learning will take place. After the sensitive period has passed, language learning will be much more difficult.

The **empiricist theory** of language development argues that humans are born with a mind that is a tabula rasa or blank slate and that all aspects of language are learned. B.F. Skinner and other **learning theorists** (behaviorists) argue that language learning takes place similar to other forms of learning. That is, parents selectively reinforce and shape babbling sounds into words. This happens when parents speak to their young children after an utterance, giving their children attention and often affection as well. Children then try to make these reinforcing sounds themselves.

The social cognitive theorists would also side with the empiricist theory, except they would emphasize the child's innate desire to imitate sounds in the social environment—and the adults' desire and efforts to be imitated.

Comparing Theories of Language Development

A sensitive period for language development would support the nativist view. There is some evidence for a sensitive period from studies of abused children, feral children, or children raised by animals, who were not exposed to language until after their discovery. These children can acquire some use of language but do not reach the level of language development found in the normal adult. The sensitive period for language is said to end at or around puberty.

Additional support for the nativist position comes from studies of infants' sound discrimination. Young infants have the capacity to discriminate in their hearing all the phonemes used in all of the world's languages, and they lose this ability over time as they are exposed only to the phonemes of their native language. Infants can also produce all the sounds used in all of the world's languages during the babbling phase, an ability which declines with age. Furthermore, the consistent pattern of errors in children's speech, such as over-regularization, supports the nativist view.

While it seems apparent that there is a good deal of evidence to support the nativist view of language acquisition, learning theory is also helpful in explaining language development. Children's speech clearly undergoes a shaping process as their pronunciation of words improves. The learning mechanisms of imitation and reinforcement likely explain these changes.

Lev Vygotsky, who offered an alternate approach to Piaget's theory of cognition, also fits into this discussion of learning theory in language acquisition. Vygotsky believed that language played a role in the development of thinking. Recall that his sociocultural theory of cognition put great emphasis on the interaction of the learner with older children and adults. This would naturally include the exchange and development of language, much as Skinner might describe the shaping of language skills through rewards and punishments—such as smiles, frowns, and corrections.

There is also ample evidence that the way parents talk to their children affects their language development. This includes socioeconomic status and gender differences in language use. Clearly, both nature and nurture interact in language development.

MAJOR PROPERTIES OF SPOKEN LANGUAGE

Language and abstract thinking are two abilities that make us uniquely human. A spoken language requires the use of vocal symbols (words) within a grammar. Grammar determines how the various symbols can be arranged, since it is the set of rules for combining the word symbols into sentences. Language and grammar allow us to use word symbols to create novel constructions so we can verbalize new thoughts in new situations.

Building blocks of spoken language include:

- **Phonemes**—The smallest unit of sound that affects the meaning of speech. The English language consists of 44 phonemes. By changing the beginning phoneme, the word "hat" becomes "cat."
- **Morphemes**—The smallest unit of language that has meaning. A word can be one morpheme, but morphemes are also roots, stems, prefixes, and suffixes. For instance, when speaking of someone who plays the violin, we add the morpheme "ist."

Language uses those building blocks when creating rules for speaking. The study of language can include these concepts or practices:

- **Phonetics (Phonology)**—The study of how sounds are put together to make words.
- **Grammar**—The set of rules that determines how words are combined to make phrases and sentences.
- **Syntax**—The set of grammar rules for how words should or can be sequenced in sentences.
- **Semantics**—The study of meaning in language.
- **Pragmatics**—The social aspects of language, including politeness, conversational interactions, and conversational rules.
- **Psycholinguistics**—The study of the psychological mechanisms related to the acquisition and use of language.

Chomsky distinguished between a sentence's surface structure (the words spoken) and its deep structure (its underlying meaning). Two sentences, therefore, could have different surface structures but similar deep structures. An example would be, "The dog bit the boy" and "The boy was bitten by the dog." On the other hand, the surface structure of a sentence could also have more than one deep structure or meaning. For instance, "Visiting relatives can be boring" can be interpreted two ways, depending on who is visiting whom. When we hear a spoken sentence, we do not retain the surface structure, but instead transform it into its deep structure. Chomsky referred to this as his transformational grammar theory.

Speech perception is guided by both bottom-up and top-down perception. Bottom-up processing in perception depends on the information from the senses at the most basic level, with sensory information flowing from this low level upward to the higher, more cognitive levels. For instance, the phoneme *t* in the word *cat* is perceived, in part, because our ears gather precise information about the characteristics of this sound. Top-down processing emphasizes the kind of information stored at the highest level of perception and includes concepts, knowledge, and prior knowledge. We are so skilled at top-down processing, for example, that we sometimes believe that we hear a missing phoneme. **Warren and Warren** found that subjects reported they heard the word *heel* in the following sentence in which the * indicates a coughing sound: "It was found that the *eel was on the shoe." Subjects thought they heard the phoneme *h* even though the correct sound vibration never reached their ears. This is an example of top-down processing because prior knowledge and expectations influenced what subjects perceived they had heard.

VOCALIZATION AND SOUND

Infants go through two stages of making sounds. The first stage is cooing—the vocalization of vowel sounds, along with crying. The second stage is babbling—the vocalization of vowels and consonants. Often the babbled sounds are repetitive (e.g., "mamamama"). Both the vowels and consonants include sounds that appear in all languages. In other words, infant babbling sounds are made up of all the possible vocalizations (phonemes) of the human mouth, tongue, lips, and throat.

Cooing
(vowel sounds)
↓
Babbling
(adds consonants at about 4 months)
(all sounds possible)

By 6 months of age, an infant is more likely to babble when an adult is talking to the infant. Babbling appears to be an innate ability because even deaf infants usually babble.

DEVELOPMENT OF SYNTAX

Holophrases
(one-word stage about age 1)
(phonemic discrimination)
↓
Two-Word Stage
(toddler)
↓
Telegraphic Speech
(multi-word, non-grammatical sentences, about age 2)
↓
Verb Tenses, Meaning Modifiers, Pronouns, etc., Added
↓
Syntax Acquired

Infants usually begin to understand several individual words that caregivers are saying by 5 to 8 months of age. A child's first words are ordinarily spoken between 10 and 12 months of age. This is referred to as the one-word stage because they can usually only use one word at a time. The first words that children use tend to be concrete nouns and verbs. By this time, the child has acquired **phonemic discrimination**. This means that the child will only make sounds (phonemes) that occur in the language that he or she has heard.

Children often underextend and overextend the meanings of their first several words. Underextension occurs when a child only uses a word in a specific context (e.g., only says "duck" when in the bathtub with a toy duck, but never refers to this toy as "duck" when outside the bathtub). **Semantic overextension** occurs when a child uses a word to mean more than an adult speaker would. For instance, a child who calls *all* four-legged, furry animals "doggie" is overextending.

Some researchers have referred to children's one-word utterances as **holophrases**—that is, the one word could be interpreted to mean an entire phrase. For instance, a child points at an object and says "cookie." Depending on context, this holophrase could possibly mean, "I want a cookie," or "There is a cookie," or "Is that a cookie?"

Children from 18 to 20 months of age are in the two-word stage of language development because they are now making short, two-word sentences (e.g., "More milk," "Where ball?"). Their vocabulary is also expanding rapidly during this stage. They may learn several new words each day.

Telegraphic speech quickly follows the two-word stage and consists of sentences that do not contain any conjunctions, prepositions, or any other function words. Telegraphic speech only contains the content words necessary to convey meaning, similar to a telegram (e.g., "Mommy kiss Jeff."). Children's first sentences follow the subject-verb-object sequence, and children often rely on this word order to make their meaning clear.

Eventually, children add verb endings, adjectives, and auxiliary verbs to their utterances. Interestingly, children initially tend to use the correct verb tenses, even the exceptions (e.g., "went," "ran"). By age 4 or 5, however, they are often using incorrect forms ("goed," "runned"). These errors, called **overregularizations,** seem to indicate that children are acquiring general rules about their language and, for a period of time, they overgeneralize these rules to include the exceptions. Eventually, children use the exceptions appropriately. By age 5, children have acquired most of the syntax of their native language.

When speaking to infants and toddlers, older children and adults typically use motherese. **Motherese** is speech that contains short sentences that are often repeated. This speech tends to consist of concrete nouns and active verbs. Pronouns, adjectives, conjunctions, and past tenses are usually absent. The sentences are enunciated clearly, often in a high-pitched voice. Many researchers believe that motherese helps children learn language. However, recent research has shown that mothers also use two techniques, **expansions** and **recasts**, which have a positive effect on children's language development. An expansion is when a mother repeats a child's verbalization but makes it more complex. If a child says, "Mommy up," the mother might reply "Oh, you want me to pick you up." A recast is repeating a child's utterance but correcting grammatical mistakes. If a child says "He goed," the mother might reply "Yes, he went away."

SEMANTIC DEVELOPMENT

Susan Carey suggested that vocabulary growth spurts can be explained by a process called **fast mapping**. She argued that children assign a meaning to a word very rapidly after only a brief encounter during this phase of language development. (Think of "fast mapping" as another way of describing a child quickly creating new "file folders" in the brain's organizational system.) Other theorists explain rapid vocabulary growth as a function of children guessing at meanings when they first use them, then refining later.

Another aspect of semantic development is the fact that young children use language literally. This makes their semantics completely concrete as they talk about objects and events and meanings. They cannot understand or use metaphors, figures of speech, or sarcasm. It will be some time before they can grasp or use non-literal speech.

School-age children continue to improve their pronunciation of language and both school-age children and adolescents continue to increase their vocabulary. While there is a tremendous vocabulary spurt during the preschool period, school-age children and adolescents continue to increase their vocabulary by many words a day.

The understanding of word meanings expands in adulthood, and older adults continue to have gains in vocabulary. While older adults may have more difficulty retrieving words, that may be due to a memory processing deficit, not a language deficit. Language skills are remarkably well-maintained through late adulthood.

PRAGMATICS

School-age children exhibit an improved understanding of the rules of language. In fact, they can become quite adept at the **pragmatics** of language. They learn (mostly unconsciously) to use the "right" kind of language for the environment or situation they are in. Children can speak with one set of vocabulary, syntax, and pronunciation rules at school and another set at home or in their neighborhood.

BILINGUALISM

Bilingualism is having some degree of fluency in more than one language. Over 20 percent of children in the United States are bilingual; many other countries of the world have significantly higher rates of bilingual speakers. Some bilingual children, called balanced bilinguals, are equally fluent in both languages, but many others are not.

As noted in a previous discussion, there is a sensitive period in infancy for the learning of language. This applies to bilingualism as well. Being exposed to more than one language in the first years of life can result in fluency in each language the child hears.

Early research on the cognitive development and academic achievement of bilingual children in the United States showed they had learning deficits compared to their monolingual peers. However, the earlier studies confounded socioeconomic conditions and the effects of prejudice with bilingualism. Recent work has shown that although there may be some learning delays in the early years, bilingual children catch up in the early elementary years. In fact, after controlling for socioeconomic disadvantages, bilinguals (particularly balanced bilinguals) have cognitive advantages over monolingual peers. They have better linguistic awareness and greater cognitive flexibility.

ENVIRONMENTAL, CULTURAL, AND GENETIC INFLUENCES

Which comes first, language or thought? Can you think about an idea or object without a word for it? There is evidence on both sides of this argument. But why does it matter? It matters because whichever comes first, it is obvious that language and thought are influenced by each other. This is especially true when languages are compared for vocabulary and usage – and how environment and culture also play into what is thought and how thought is expressed.

Benjamin Whorf created the term **linguistic relativity** from his studies of languages from different geographical environments. He was particularly interested in languages of Native American cultures. From his research, he found that differences in grammar, vocabulary, and syntax often led to difficulties in translation to and from English. He theorized that the differences and difficulties were due to the way each language developed in a unique mix of geography, climate, culture, and way of life. Just as the locale and culture shaped the origin of a language, the language would shape or determine the way its future generations of speakers would think. For instance, speakers of Shawnee see and describe the world differently from speakers of English. Their vocabulary, grammar, and syntax would have shaped the way they perceive reality and the way they think about things, ideas, and events. To those who subscribe to this theory of **linguistic determinism**, one's language guides and limits cognition and expression.

What researchers have learned about language differences sheds some light on all of this. For instance, because of cultural and language differences, American children's first words tend to be nouns—names of things. For Chinese children, first words tend to be verbs—describing actions and relationships.

We can refer to Piaget's constructivist theory or information processing theory to imagine the brain developing categories of thought and action (schemata), and those categories being created out of—or alongside of—the development of language. We can also refer to learning theory and social-cognitive theory to see native speakers shaping their children's words and behaviors, and thus their thought processes. And we can imagine children imitating native speakers in order to fit in and get along—and get what they want.

CHAPTER 10

SOCIAL DEVELOPMENT THROUGHOUT THE LIFE SPAN

Social development refers to the development of thoughts and behaviors that people engage in when they interact with others. The need for **social affiliation**—the desire to be with other people—is strong. Evolutionary psychologists describe social affiliation as an example of a species behavior that evolved because of its survival value. Humans seek out the company of others, especially when afraid. In a classic series of studies, **Stanley Schachter** manipulated the fear level of college women by leading them to believe they would receive electric shocks in a laboratory experiment. He then measured whether the women preferred to wait for the experiment to begin either alone or with others. The majority preferred to wait with others.

The process through which young people learn the values and acceptable behaviors of their society is called **socialization**. This chapter will examine social development topics such as attachment and interpersonal relationships, social cognition, gender role development, and moral development. Key influences on socialization—family, school, and media—will be discussed in the next chapter.

At the root of socialization are three processes that occur very early in life: recognition of self, recognition of others, and a sense of relationship between self and others. We must begin with the last one (in its most rudimentary form), since it is the foundation for the other two.

ATTACHMENT

Attachment, or **bonding**, is the close emotional relationship between infant and caretaker(s). Ethologist **Konrad Lorenz** studied attachment in animals. He found that ducklings attach to their mother after birth, following her in a process he called **imprinting**. Lorenz also found that there was a critical period for imprinting to develop. In fact, ducklings would imprint on any moving object (including Lorenz himself) if they were exposed to that object during a critical period of days after hatching. If the exposure did not occur during this time period, the ducklings never imprinted. Ethologists suggest that infant attachment to a caregiver is analogous to imprinting in ducklings, and that attachment is adaptive for an infant since the infant is dependent on caregivers for survival.

Complete social isolation prevents the development of attachment and socialization in primates. Monkeys raised in complete social isolation display either fear or aggression when suddenly placed with peers.

Harry Harlow conducted a seminal study with monkeys to study the formation of attachment. To test the hypothesis that infants attach to a caregiver for survival, Harlow conducted an experiment to see which of two surrogate mothers the infant monkeys would attach to. One surrogate mother was made of wire mesh. The mesh held a bottle with a nipple for feeding. The other surrogate was made of wire mesh with no feeding bottle but instead was covered with soft cloth. Infants attached to the cloth mother even though they would feed from the wire-mesh mother. Harlow concluded that the warmth and comfort given by the cloth mother was the necessary condition for the attachment relationship.

Human infants exhibit inborn attachment behaviors, that is, behaviors that elicit caregiving. (There is also evidence that the size and facial structure of infants—with large eyes and small chins—naturally elicit the caregiving instinct.) Initially, infants attempt to attract the attention, usually through crying, smiling, etc., of no one in particular. Between 6 and 10 weeks of age, infants begin to smile in the presence of a known caregiver. Prior to this time, an infant's smile is merely a reflexive response.

Mary Ainsworth and her colleagues found they could distinguish categories of attachment based on the quality of the infant-caregiver interactions. They developed a method of measuring the quality of the attachment relationship in the **Ainsworth Strange Situation**. They had mothers and infants come into a lab room and then observed the infants' behaviors when the mothers left the room and upon their return. Although this method has been criticized as measuring the quality of attachment in an artificial setting, it remains the most frequently used technique in studies of attachment. Based on their reactions in the Strange Situation, infants are classified as either having a secure or insecure attachment, as detailed in the table that follows. Insecure attachment is further divided into three categories.

Types of Attachment Responses in Infants

Secure Attachment	Children use parent as secure base from which they explore the new environment. They become upset when their mother leaves the room and are glad to see her and go to her when she returns.
Insecure Attachment	
Anxious-Ambivalent	Children tend not to use the parent as a secure base (and may either cling to or refuse to leave their mother). They become very upset when she leaves and may often appear angry or become more upset when she returns.
Avoidant	Children seek little contact with their mother and are not concerned when she leaves. They usually avoid interaction when the parent returns.
Disorganized-Disoriented	Children alternatively approach and avoid contact with their mother. They appear confused about whether to seek or avoid her. Often appears in abused children.

Parents of securely attached infants are often found to be more sensitive and responsive to their child's needs. Some studies have found a relationship between attachment patterns and children's later adjustment. For instance, one study found that securely attached infants were happier and less frustrated at 2 years-of-age than were their insecurely attached peers. Some researchers have suggested that in addition to **sensitive parenting**, other factors come into play. Inborn temperament of the child, genetic characteristics, and **goodness of fit** of child and adult temperaments may be important for both the quality of bonding and a child's later developmental outcome.

Psychologists studying adult relationships have found a correlation between the quality of infant attachment and later adult relationships. This has led to the assertion that securely attached infants develop the capacity to have secure adult attachments. Adults who had insecure infant attachments tend to have insecure adult relationships. A lack of ability to form relationships can manifest in some very severe personality traits and behaviors, such as dishonesty, lack of empathy, cruelty, and criminal behavior.

SENSE OF SELF

Before being able to interact with people other than the primary caregiver(s), infants must develop a sense of self. That is, they need the understanding that they are separate from other people, beginning with a sense of separation from the primary caregiver. Infants show signs of self-awareness at around 12 months. One way they show this is by their reaction to being with unfamiliar people. At this age, infants may cry or otherwise become distressed when preferred caregivers leave the room. This is referred to as **separation anxiety**. Separation anxiety may begin as early as 6 months of age, but it usually peaks around 18 months and then gradually declines.

As another way to determine whether a child has **self-recognition, Lewis and Brooks-Gunn** borrowed the mirror (or rouge) test of self-recognition from a previous test on non-humans. Children ages 9 to 24 months of age were seated in front of a mirror after the experimenter had placed rouge on their cheek. Infants at least 18 months of age rubbed their own cheek when they saw the reflection. Younger infants rubbed the image in the mirror.

The concept of self contributes to a child's later ability for self-control. Toddlers are capable of compliance, i.e., obeying others' wishes, and some **delay of gratification**. Delay of gratification is the ability to exert self-control and wait for an anticipated reward or goal, or put off a desired activity for a later time.

The sense of self also sets the stage for social emotions in later childhood. These emotions include uncomfortable ones such as guilt and embarrassment, but also empathy and other prosocial feelings.

As children mature, their sense of self takes a progression of forms. Children who are younger than 7 or 8, when asked to describe themselves and other people, will refer to physical attributes before using psychological characteristics such as personality traits. Young children might describe themselves as being a boy or girl, having a certain color hair, and having five dolls or a bicycle. By the age of 8 or so, they describe themselves and others with psychological and social attributes, such as being funny or smart. At age 11 or 12, children begin to make social comparisons of their own characteristics, traits, and abilities with their peers. They may judge themselves to be smarter than others or not as smart as others. Social comparison plays a key role in Erikson's model of psychosocial development, which is discussed in more detail in Chapter 12: Personality and Emotions. Adolescents' descriptions of themselves and others get more complex, as they are able to consider more and deeper dimensions of psychological and personality characteristics.

SOCIAL COGNITION

Social cognition is reasoning about social situations and social relationships, based on schemata constructed since infancy. A child is not born with the capacity to understand self and others. But as children gain cognitive skills and social experience, they come to understand that they and others have personalities, thoughts, and feelings. They begin to relate in social role relationships. Social cognition influences all social interactions and social behavior.

Developmental psychologists have identified one of the key concepts that underlies social cognition. This concept is called **theory of mind**. Theory of mind is the understanding that people have mental states and that the content of these mental states guides their behavior. Actions are guided by beliefs, emotions, and goals. **Baron-Cohen** and his colleagues developed the **false belief task** to assess children's theory of mind. In this task, a child witnesses the researcher's confederate place a marble in a basket and then leave the room. While the confederate is out of the room, the experimenter moves the marble from the basket to a box. When the confederate returns to the room, the researcher asks the child where he or she thinks the confederate will look for the marble. Most 4-year-olds will correctly say that the confederate will look in the basket. Four-year-olds understand that since the confederate thinks the marble is still in the basket, that is where he or she will look. They have demonstrated that they possess theory of mind in regard to another person. Researchers also found that 80 percent of autistic children got the task wrong, leading them to hypothesize that autistic children have what they called **mindblindness.**

Theory of mind begins with **joint attention** seen in children beginning around 9 months of age. Joint attention occurs when a child and caregiver simultaneously direct their attention to the same object. An infant at this age will point to an object then turn to the caregiver to see that he or she is looking at the object. This behavior indicates that the child knows the other person has perceptual experiences too.

More sophisticated understandings of theory of mind appear in the second year. Children's pretend play signifies an understanding that there is a difference between reality and pretend. Pretending is creating false beliefs in a sense. Beginning between 2 and 3 years-of-age, children refer to their mental states in their speech. "I want" and "Do myself" indicate the child understands his words and actions are driven by a personal desire. (And the child must also learn that these desires must be balanced with the desires of others.) Young children are also capable of deception and may try to fool someone by planting a false belief. A child may try to play a joke on Mommy by claiming to have eaten all the cookies, when in fact he or she did not. Or the child might say that Daddy ate the cookies when really the child ate the cookies—a deception that is not meant as a joke, but rather as a deflection of guilt.

The quality of an individual's social cognition affects peer acceptance, popularity, and other social phenomena. A child who is not skilled in social cognition may often misinterpret the motives of other people. This child, for example, might push a child who accidentally bumped into him or her. Aggressive children tend to misinterpret the motives behind other people's behavior.

When the child begins schooling, social cognition must expand to include adults and authority figures outside the family. Also, peer group interactions begin, and the child must adjust and add social skills in order to make friends and get along with others.

Role-taking skills also develop as the child has more social experiences and develops cognitively. These role-taking skills are also critical to the child's ability to interact with others. According to Piaget, children are egocentric between the ages of 2 to 6–7 years, lacking the ability to take the perspective of another. Between the ages of 6 to 8, children understand that people have different viewpoints, but they are not capable of judging how other people view them. Later, around the ages of 8 to 10, children understand that there is a view of the self and a view of the other. They view themselves a certain way and they view other people a certain way. They further understand that the other person's view of them can be different from their view of themselves and vice versa. Around ages 10 to 12, children can take the perspective of a third party. For example, they can understand how a third person views their relationship with a second person.

Adolescents acquire the added ability to take a societal perspective. They can understand that a group of people has certain views and beliefs. In adolescence, social cognition shifts almost entirely to maintaining peer group acceptance. During this time, the individual uses peers to measure and validate oneself.

In young adulthood, social cognition must readjust to maintain an intimate relationship and to work with authority and peers as a subordinate or team member. Tact and discretion may need to be learned.

By middle adulthood, social cognition may include one's sense of authority within family and work contexts. On the other hand, social cognition in late adulthood must include the relinquishing of authority.

SOCIAL LEARNING AND MODELING

Much of what we call **social learning** can be explained by cognitive learning theory. From a very early age, children learn by observation, and this applies greatly to social skills. Children observe behavior in others. They also observe and learn about the consequences of those behaviors. Thus they learn what is and is not appropriate.

In early years, children use **social referencing**. They watch behavior; then they watch authority figures, such as parents and teachers, react to that behavior. That teaches them how they should feel about such behavior and whether they should imitate it. In later years, teens and young adults will emulate a role model or a group norm as social reference points in attitude, speaking, and behavior.

Bandura's research on this subject led to a categorizing of two types of **vicarious learning**:

Direct modeling occurs when children imitate behavior they have observed in their environment. For instance, when Bandura had children watch an adult punch an inflated Bobo clown toy that righted itself, they also punched the clown after the adult left the room. However, they tended not to punch the clown if the adult was criticized by another adult for such behavior.

Symbolic modeling occurs when children or teens imitate a behavior they have seen in media, such as movies, TV programs, or online. The behavior is especially attractive for imitation if it is performed by a celebrity.

On the one hand, vicarious learning can lead to improved social skills, motivation, and an increased sense of self-efficacy. On the other hand, this kind of learning can lead to self-deception or unrealistic self-expectations. Consider, for instance, the thousands of young people who are convinced they are destined to be a sports star because they can imitate the moves of a famous athlete.

GENDER

There are definite social aspects in relation to gender. First, it must be recognized that gender is independent of biological sex determination or an individual's **sexual orientation**. Because of that, gender has a relationship with both one's self-identity and one's social relationships. Various theories come into play when explaining the development of gender concepts in children:

Learning and Social Learning Theory	Proposes that children learn gender roles because they are rewarded for appropriate behavior and punished for inappropriate gender role behaviors. Children also watch and imitate the behaviors of others.
Psychodynamic Theory	Freud's psychoanalytic theory proposes that children establish their gender role identity when they identify with their same sex parent during the Phallic stage, assuming successful completion of previous stages.

Cognitive Theory	Kohlberg argued that children learn about gender the same way that they acquire other cognitive concepts, and it happens in a sequence of stages. (See Piaget's theory for more detail.) • First, preschool children acquire **gender identity** (ages 2–3). The child can label self and others as boy/girl or man/woman. But the internal definitions are fluid, depending on such things as what oneself or another person is doing or how the person is dressed. • **Gender stability** (ages 3–5) occurs when the child recognizes that a person's gender stays the same and will not change as one grows older. • **Gender constancy** (ages 4–7) occurs when the child recognizes that gender is not affected by change in appearance.

Gender roles are our set of expectations about appropriate activities for females and males—all culturally defined. There is a **feminine** gender role, a **masculine** gender role, and **androgyny**. **Gender stereotypes** are restrictive views about which gender role men and women should adopt and what attitudes and behaviors must belong to each gender. In our culture, the traditional and stereotypical view is that females are feminine, with qualities that include being caring, nurturing, and compliant. Traditionally, stereotypical males are masculine, with qualities that include being aggressive, dominant, and competitive. The androgynous gender role combines elements of both gender roles.

Gender typing starts early in life. This is the process of socializing children about what roles are appropriate for males and females in the society. They learn these gender concepts by differences in toys, in clothing, how people treat them, and from media portrayals. Research has shown that even preschoolers believe that males and females have different characteristics. They also believe it is inappropriate to act like a member of the other gender. Young school-age children are very restrictive about gender roles but become more flexible and tolerant of violations of gender stereotypes. Adolescents regress to being more inflexible about gender roles and conform to gender stereotypes. Adults tend to adopt stereotypical roles when they have children.

All this is subject to change as society debates and reconsiders attitudes and laws regarding gender issues. As society shifts, so do expectations placed on children, which in turn causes changes in children's attitudes and expectations about themselves and others.

In adulthood, there is an androgyny shift hypothesis that argues for a midlife change, in which people start to become more androgynous. This is possibly due to changes in hormone levels and possibly due to changes in attitude and self-expectations.

INTERPERSONAL RELATIONSHIPS

PEER RELATIONSHIPS

Infants up to the age of 2 generally spend their time on solo explorations and family interactions. Their play tends to be **unoccupied** or **functional play** such as moving a toy truck back and forth on the floor. During this time, they are observing interpersonal relationships between parents and other family members.

Preschoolers find themselves thrown together outside the home, and they must work out peer relations. Teachers referee young children's self-centered instincts coming into conflict with each other. In time, most learn to share and take turns and use "inside voices."

During the elementary school years, children prefer same-sex friendships. Boys and girls can antagonize each other during these years. These children tend to play in groups but can start to pair off into sets of best friends. Best friends tend to be fluid in early years and become more stable later.

Peer acceptance and rejection in childhood has significant influences on children's development. Four types of peer status have been identified:

- **Popular** children have good social skills, above-average intelligence, an even temperament, a good sense of humor, and positive self-perceptions.
- **Rejected** children are shunned by peers, often because they are aggressive. They are at risk for dropping out of school, developing delinquent or criminal behavior, and needing mental health services.
- **Controversial** children tend to be rebellious and are not well-liked by peers.
- **Neglected** children tend to be those who are withdrawn and are rather invisible to peers. They could also be "weird" to other children due to behavior or appearance.

Experiences in the family, parenting style, attachment quality, and exposure to aggressive or non-aggressive models influence children's social competence. Many of these factors are discussed in Chapter 13: Schooling, Work, and Interventions.

In adolescence, the timing of the adolescent growth spurt (including puberty) has been shown to have psychosocial effects on adolescents. Early maturing boys and late maturing girls tend to have the best psychosocial outcomes, whereas late maturing boys and early maturing girls fair worse. Early maturing boys may benefit from being larger and appearing older than their late maturing counterparts. Early maturing girls, on the other hand, may face challenges from having an early menarche and/or because other people may treat them as if they were more mature and expect them to act as if they were older.

During adolescence, same-sex and opposite-sex friendships occur as well as dating relationships. Friendships are very important in adolescence. The need to be accepted by peers gets stronger as adolescents spend more time with friends than family. The need to be accepted leads to **conformity** and capitulating to peer pressure. There is also a danger of **co-rumination**. This occurs when two or more teens get locked into negative conversations and emotions that can spiral downward into depression or aggression toward others.

David Elkind pointed out that there is a new form of egocentrism that emerges during this time, which he called **adolescent egocentrism**. This egocentrism takes two forms, the imaginary audience and the personal fable. Recall that the egocentrism of early childhood is caused by the young child's inability to take the perspective of another. In adolescence, teens discover a newfound ability to think about their own and other people's thoughts. This appears to cause a heightened concern about what others are thinking. **Imaginary audience** comes from the belief that other people are focused on what you think is important. For example, if a teenager has a pimple, he or she is very aware of it and believes that everyone else will also focus on it. (But in Elkind's construct, all the other teens are too involved with their own imaginary audiences to notice someone else's flaws.) **Personal fable** is believing that what you feel and experience is unique. According to Elkind, the adolescent believes that no one else has ever been as sad, as happy, as in love, or as disappointed as he or she is right now.

Friendship groups vary in size. A **clique** is a small collection of close friends who spend a substantial amount of time together. Membership in a clique tends to be same-sex and very restrictive. The clique strictly defines acceptable behavior, dress, and attitude.

A **crowd** is a large collection of individuals known by a distinct reputation. A crowd is typically mixed-sex. This is exemplified in literature and movies when teens are portrayed segregating themselves into separate areas of the school cafeteria and campus.

Adolescent opposite-sex friendships occur with greater frequency than in childhood and may help heterosexual adolescents prepare for dating relationships.

Adult friendships remain important to the quality of one's life. In fact, adults who are single report a great need for friendship and companionship. Many single adults report feeling lonely. Erikson argued that young adults especially have a need for intimacy and if they do not fulfill this need, they face feelings of isolation. Developmental psychologists have spent a great deal of time studying mate selection and relationship satisfaction to better understand how relationships form. This is covered in the next section.

INTERPERSONAL ATTRACTION

Interpersonal attraction refers to factors that contribute to a relationship being formed. One theory of interpersonal attraction is **social exchange theory**. This theory views human interactions in economic terms. According to this theory, when two people meet, they each calculate the costs and benefits of developing a relationship. If the benefits outweigh the costs, then the two people will be attracted to each other.

Other theories of attraction suggest that there are key dimensions on which we evaluate others in regard to forming relationships. These factors are discussed below.

Friendship

Studies of friendships have found three factors that are important in determining who will become friends.

Similarity	People are generally attracted to those who are similar to themselves in many ways—similar in age, sex, race, economic status, etc. (There is also complementarity, in which two people are attracted to each other at least in part because they "balance" each other. Both similarity and complementarity can appear in a relationship.)
Proximity or Propinquity	It is easier to develop a friendship with people who are close at hand. Proximity also increases the likelihood of repeated contacts, and increased exposure can lead to increased attraction—the **mere exposure effect**. In a classic study at Massachusetts Institute of Technology, **Festinger** found that friends of women who lived in married student housing were most likely to live in the same building. In fact, half of all friends lived on the same floor.
Attractiveness	Physical attractiveness is a major factor in attraction for people of all ages. We tend to like attractive people. Research in social psychology indicates that physical appearance is the most important determinant of first impressions. It also contributes to effectiveness in persuading others to change their beliefs.

Love

Overall, the same factors connected with friendships (similarity and complementarity, proximity, and attractiveness) are also related to love relationships.

Similarity	Dating and married couples tend to be similar in age, race, social class, religion, education, intelligence, attitudes, and interests. (Complementarity can also come into play regarding personality or temperament traits.)
Proximity	We tend to fall in love with people who live nearby. (In these modern times, "nearby" might mean geographically, or it might mean through social media or an online dating site.)
Attractiveness	We tend to fall in love with people whose attractiveness matches our own according to the matching hypothesis.

Researchers believe that love is a qualitatively different state than merely liking someone. Love includes physiological arousal, self-disclosure, all-encompassing interest in another individual, fantasizing about the other, and a relatively rapid swing of emotions. Unlike liking, love also includes passion, closeness, fascination, exclusiveness, sexual desire, and intense caring. Some researchers have distinguished two main types of love.

Passionate or Romantic Love	Predominates in the early part of a romantic relationship. Includes intense physiological arousal, psychological interest, sexual desire, and the type of love we mean when we say we are "in love" with someone.
Companionate or Affectionate Love	The type of love that occurs when we have a deep, caring affection for a person.

Robert Sternberg has proposed a theory of love that consists of three components:

Intimacy	The encompassing feelings of closeness and connectedness in a relationship.
Passion/ Excitement	The physical and sexual attraction in a relationship.
Decision/ Commitment	The initial cognition that one loves someone and the longer-term feelings of commitment to maintain the love.

According to Sternberg's theory, complete love only happens when all three kinds of love are represented in a relationship. Sternberg called this **consummate love**, while fatuous love is based only on passion and commitment and is often short-lived. Research has shown that successful romantic relationships that last for many years are based on the expression of love and admiration, friendship between the partners, a commitment to the relationship, displays of affection, self-disclosure, and offering each other emotional support.

MORAL DEVELOPMENT

From a very young age, children are usually taught and shown that it is important to treat others fairly, whether those "others" are friends or not. Regardless of culture, some form of the Golden Rule exists around the globe, and adults put in great effort to instill that in their children as early as possible. Typically, we call that moral instruction.

Lawrence Kohlberg developed a model of moral development based on an individual's responses to difficult moral questions called **moral dilemmas**. Kohlberg's theory attempts to explain how children develop a sense of right or wrong. He was influenced by Piaget's theory and therefore maintained that moral development was determined by cognitive development as it progressed through a series of stages.

Kohlberg's theory describes how individuals pass through a series of three levels of moral development, each of which can be broken into two sublevels, resulting in a total of six stages.

Kohlberg's Stages of Moral Development

Level I. Preconventional Morality		
Stage 1.	**Punishment orientation**	A child obeys and complies with rules during this stage to avoid punishment.
Stage 2.	**Self-interest orientation**	An action is determined by one's own needs. Compliance if it will be rewarded, i.e., "What's in it for me?"
Level II. Conventional Morality		
Stage 3.	**Good-girl/Good-boy orientation**	Good behavior is that which pleases others and gets their approval.
Stage 4.	**Authority orientation**	Emphasis is on upholding the law, order, and authority and doing one's duty by following rules of society. Law and order must be maintained.

(continued)

Kohlberg's Stages of Moral Development (continued)

Level III. Postconventional Morality		
Stage 5.	**Social contract orientation**	Flexible understanding that people obey rules because they are necessary for the social order, but rules can and should change if there are good reasons and better alternatives.
Stage 6.	**Morality of individual principles orientation**	Behavior is directed by self-chosen ethical principles. High value is placed on justice, dignity, and equity for all.

Although these are called stages of moral development, it should be noted that Level III (especially Stage 6) actually resides in the realm of ethics, not morality. Morals are based on cultural or religious traditions, which can vary across regions or groups, while ethics attempts to take a universal view of laws and social relationships. It should also be noted that not all individuals attain Stage 5, and even fewer attain Stage 6.

Kohlberg found strategies for helping individuals move up to the next level of their moral reasoning. One method is to have children listen to moral issues being discussed by those who are already at the next level. He also experimented with "communities" within high schools, where teens could share their reasoning on issues that mattered to them.

Criticisms of Kohlberg's theory of moral development include the argument that it may be better at describing the development of morality in males than in females. **Carol Gilligan** conducted similar studies of reasoning about moral dilemmas, but in comparing males to females, she found that females tended to apply a **morality of care** when reasoning about moral issues. A morality of care means basing decisions about morality by considering the impact of actions on other people or on social relationships. Kohlberg's model suggested that a **morality of justice** was the most developmentally advanced type of morality.

Kohlberg's model has also been criticized by those who argue that development may not be as orderly and uniform as his theory suggests. For instance, it is not unusual to find individuals who are reasoning at several adjacent levels of moral reasoning at the same time—rigid in regard to some issues, flexible on other issues. Also, Kohlberg's theory describes moral reasoning but does not predict moral behavior.

The development of more advanced moral reasoning in children is assisted by parents and teachers using **induction**. Parents use induction when they explain to a child how his or her behavior can negatively impact others. For example, a parent might explain to a young child that it was bad to take a toy from another child because it made the other child sad. Punishing a child or withdrawing affection for inappropriate behavior are less effective means of teaching morality.

PROSOCIAL BEHAVIOR

Altruism, or **prosocial behavior**, is the selfless concern for the welfare of others that leads to helping behavior. Altruistic behavior is observed in children as young as 13 months of age. For instance, a young child might offer one of his or her toys to a parent. A toddler might try to console a friend or parent in distress.

Research has found that individuals who are high in **empathy**—the subjective grasp of another person's feelings—are more likely to help others in need. According to the empathy-arousal hypothesis, empathy has the power to motivate prosocial behavior. This empathy-action dynamic can be reinforced by parents in early years, and by peers and teachers in later years. Media and role models can also reinforce the idea that altruism is noble and admirable.

AGGRESSION

Researchers have categorized three types of aggression:

- **Instrumental aggression** is using aggressive behavior to achieve a goal, but is not intended to harm. For instance, a preschooler grabs a toy away from another child or pushes another child to keep a toy from being grabbed.
- **Hostile aggression** is defined as intentionally inflicting physical or psychological harm on others. This might take the form of hitting, kicking, biting, or threatening without provocation.
- **Relational aggression** is a form of hostile aggression that is aimed at damaging other people's social relationships. This is often found in adolescents, and it can take one of two forms:
    - **Social exclusion**—"Go away! You can't be our friend anymore!"
    - **Rumor spreading**— "Don't talk to her. She's a weirdo."

  Note: Relational aggression can be committed in person or on social media.

About one-third of studies show that males are more aggressive than females, and the differences are larger with children than adults, and with physical rather than verbal aggression. The consistency in the differences between males and females has led some theorists to suggest that aggression is due to a biological difference between males and females. This is a nature view of aggression. Cross-cultural research on gender differences in aggression has shown that males are more aggressive than females in each of the cultures studied, but the differences between the two groups vary—smaller in some cultures and larger in other cultures. Therefore, while there may be a biological component, culture clearly influences aggressive behavior.

The frustration-aggression hypothesis states that frustration produces aggression and that this aggression may be directed at the one causing frustration or displaced onto another target, as in scapegoating. However, frustration does not always cause aggression.

According to social learning theory, people learn to behave aggressively by observing aggressive models and by having their aggressive responses reinforced. For instance, children of parents who are belligerent with others or who use physical punishment to discipline tend to be more aggressive than peers not exposed to these parental behaviors. Also, exposure to role models in the media can influence aggression. Some research demonstrates that adults and children as young as preschool age show higher levels of aggression after they view media violence.

RISK AND RESILIENCE

Risk is a natural part of life. Some individuals are cautious, while others take great risks. Why? It may depend on inborn factors such as temperament, and it may also depend on experience. When risk arises, certain factors can influence a person's choice:

- Is the risk seen realistically or unrealistically?
- Is the risk based on fear, on bravado, or on an objective assessment?
- Are the consequences of taking the risk clear or unclear?

Parents and other authority figures can influence risk-taking behavior by helping young people learn to assess risk and by helping them build self-esteem that is not influenced by peers.

Risk-taking behavior can be a symptom of a larger issue: that a young person is "at risk" in their social development. **At-risk** children and adolescents are those who are likely to have serious behavioral and performance issues at school and in their communities. They tend to be male, and they are often candidates for dropping out of school, joining gangs, and committing crimes. They can often be pre-identified at a young age by their demographics, even before they exhibit behaviors that would trouble teachers and other authority figures. Factors that tend to lead to being at-risk include:

- Poverty, i.e., low socioeconomic status (low SES)
- Being a member of a minority ethnic group
- Family instability and dysfunction
- Few resources for help or guidance in community and/or school

There is another demographic that can also be identified for at-risk targeting, and that is **affluence**. This may seem counterintuitive, but statistics show that affluent youth often suffer from any number of problems that dim their future: depression, drug addiction, risky behavior, eating disorders, etc.

Whether from poverty or from affluence, at-risk youth constitute a serious societal problem. If these young people cannot foresee a productive future, they will spiral downward and become a burden to their families and to society. They need hope, and that can only come from knowing that there can be a way out of their sense of hopelessness. They also need school and community services starting at a young age to counter the deficits they must live with.

Resilience is the ability to resist a sense of hopelessness and thrive under adversity. The term applies to attitudes, personal traits, and strategies used to overcome or at least not be defeated by difficulties. Research has shown that successfully resilient young people

- tend to have above-average intelligence.
- are sociable.
- have an easy temperament and optimistic outlook.
- have unconditional love from at least one person in their life.
- have grit or perseverance to take on challenges and stick with them.
- feel upset by circumstances but will adapt and change rather than dwell in anger or feel defeated.

Is resilience learnable? Some researchers think so, and they have brought resilience training to young people in school programs, using strategies found in individuals who have successfully conquered difficult situations. Logically, such training can be helpful in low-economic neighborhoods. But the training has also been given to children in affluent communities, just because such children may never have needed resilience, which makes them unprepared for the "storms and stresses"—and temptations—of adolescence.

WELLNESS

Children and adults can be encouraged and trained to increase their moral development, altruism, and risk assessment abilities. The same is true for **wellness**. This term is meant to convey a sense of health and well-being, beyond simply being free from disease or injury or unhappiness. (You might think of this as an outgrowth of humanistic psychology.) Wellness has been researched by several individuals who have been interested in enhancing individual and societal wellness.

Ed Diener described "subjective well-being" as a combination of cognitive and emotional self-assessments of life satisfaction.

Carol Ryff proposed a wellness model with six factors:

- Self-acceptance
- Environmental mastery
- Personal growth
- Autonomy
- Purpose in life
- Positive relations

Martin Seligman proposed the term **positive psychology** to describe his research and theory on happiness. This theory posits that there are three kinds of life happiness that adults can strive for:

- pleasant life, or enjoyment of life
- good life, or a life with engagement and "flow" (correlation of one's abilities with one's task, duties, or career)
- meaningful life, or a life of purpose and affiliation

These tenets of positive psychology will be echoed in Chapter 13: Schooling, Work, and Interventions, specifically in the section "Occupational Development." After all, life happiness often depends on career happiness.

All these definitions and theories of wellness contain common traits, namely that wellness has personal as well as social factors, and that wellness is achievable through conscious focus and effort. That effort need not be strenuous, but it must be consistently positive in outlook to be successful.

CHAPTER 11

FAMILY, HOME, AND SOCIETY THROUGHOUT THE LIFE SPAN

An infant's primary caregivers are usually parents, and the home and family are the primary context for early development. This means that when the brain is in its earliest growth, learning comes from a very small context. This makes home and family powerful influences. But the home and family reside within a culture, and that culture resides within a wider society. At first, the child only experiences culture and the wider society indirectly, but these influences change over time through schooling and media. This chapter will examine the lifelong interaction of individuals with their families, culture, and the wider world.

BRONFENBRENNER'S BIOECOLOGICAL PERSPECTIVE

Urie Bronfenbrenner asserted that development takes place within sociocultural systems or contexts. Bronfenbrenner's bioecological approach suggests there is a **reciprocal determinism** between the child and the environment. For instance, a child's biological makeup determines some of the characteristics of the child, such as potential intelligence. However, if the child is raised in a non-stimulating environment or by parents who are neglectful, the child may not reach his or her full potential intelligence. Following Bronfenbrenner's lead, developmental psychologists have studied the influence of sociocultural contexts on development.

Bronfenbrenner constructed a model depicting the systems of development and their interrelationships as a series of embedded, concentric circles. The innermost circle is the **microsystem**, an environment in which a child directly participates, such as immediate family, extended family, and, later, day care or school. A **mesosystem** is made up of the relationships among microsystems, as the child's experience in one microsystem might affect his or her experience in others. For instance, a child whose parents are arguing or divorcing may start doing poorly in school.

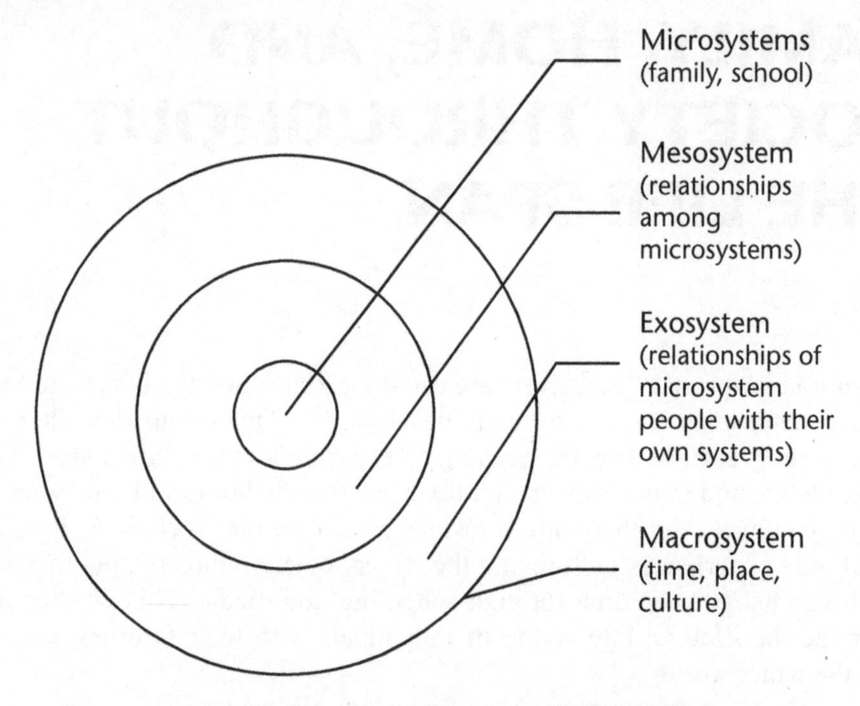

Bronfenbrenner's Bioecological Model

The **exosystem** is where interrelationships between events in contexts in which the child does not directly participate affect the child. For instance, a parent who is experiencing stress at work may interact less with his or her child at home. Finally, the **macrosystem** affects each of the other systems. The macrosystem is the outermost area that encircles all the other systems in the model. This is the sociocultural context and it contains the values and attitudes shared by the members of the culture. For example, social values and parenting customs vary across cultures. These values and customs affect the child's experiences in the microsystem of the family. You can imagine that time and place are also parts of the macrosystem. A child growing up in a time and place of peace experiences very different circumstances from a child growing up in a time and place of war or famine.

Taking this broad perspective as a launching point, the following sections will examine these widening circles of influence, beginning with family.

FAMILY STRUCTURES

There are different family structures that can be found in our society:

- Traditional nuclear family headed by married heterosexual couple
- Family headed by unmarried heterosexual couple
- Family headed by married or unmarried same-sex couple
- Extended family, e.g., grandparent(s) living with children and grandchildren
- Blended or reconstituted family that is the result of remarriage
- Single-parent families
- Any of the above with fostered or adopted children

More households are non-traditional today due to the high rate of divorce and remarriage, and the increasing numbers of same-sex parent households, interracial households and single-parent households.

Many households are headed by dual-working parents, raising concern regarding the degree of supervision children have after school and the amount of time parents spend with their children. **Latchkey children** are children who go home to an empty house after school. This situation became a major issue in the 1980s, when many women were entering the workforce, but the phenomenon has not gone away. Today, it is estimated that about 15 percent of children have no adult supervision when they come home from school. This percentage is higher in low-SES neighborhoods.

Many latchkey children suffer no ill effects, especially those whose parents monitor them through phone calls or online/smartphone apps and establish rules for what the child can and cannot do. Second, research clearly shows that it is the quality of time parents spend with their children that affects their development, not the quantity of time. Working parents who come home and engage in meaningful activities with their children tend to have well-adjusted and competent children. Also, fathers in these households participate more in childcare than those in households with stay-at-home mothers.

There are currently conflicting parenting philosophies regarding the care of children outside of school. On the one hand, some parents have come to schedule their children's afternoons, holidays, and summers with great detail and thoroughness. These **helicopter parents** fill up their children's free time with playdates arranged with other parents and with activities in music, martial arts, dance, gymnastics, and other kinds of private and group instruction. This is seen as giving their children both safe and enriching experiences.

On the other hand, some parents have come to adopt the philosophy of **free-range parenting**. This involves allowing children to be unsupervised and unscheduled outside of school. These parents want their children to be resourceful and imaginative, choosing their own friends and activities in the neighborhood—similar to life as lived in the 20th century—in spite of possible dangers.

PARENTING STYLES

Diana Baumrind conducted a longitudinal study of parenting and developed a system of **classifying parenting styles**. She found that she could classify parents into three styles and that there are predictable developmental outcomes for children raised with each parenting style. A fourth parenting style, neglectful/uninvolved, has subsequently been added to the classification system, which is described below.

Authoritative Parents	Affectionate and loving. Provide control when necessary and set limits. Allow children to express their own point of view—engage in "verbal give and take." Their children tend to be self-reliant, competent, and socially responsible.
Authoritarian Parents	Demand unquestioning obedience. Use punishment to control behavior. Less likely to be affectionate. Their children tend to be unhappy, distrustful, ineffective in social interactions, and often become dependent adults.
Permissive Parents	Make few demands. Allow children to make their own decisions. Use inconsistent discipline. Their children tend to be immature, lack self-control, and are poor in judgment and decision-making.
Neglectful/Uninvolved Parents	Provide little or no attention to the needs of the child. Provide no discipline or guidance. Provide no love or affection. Their children are at risk for antisocial behavior.

Bear in mind that these descriptions apply to the most "pure" or extreme examples. In real life, parents who could be classified in one style will at times employ attitudes and strategies of a different style. For instance, a typically authoritative parent might use a very stern and commanding voice when a child is caught doing something dangerous. Also, a parent might "tone down" their use of a style, compared to the "pure" descriptions in the chart. For instance, an authoritarian parent might always use a very calm and matter-of-fact voice to maintain compliance from a child.

These four parenting styles can be compared on two dimensions: demandingness/control and acceptance/responsiveness.

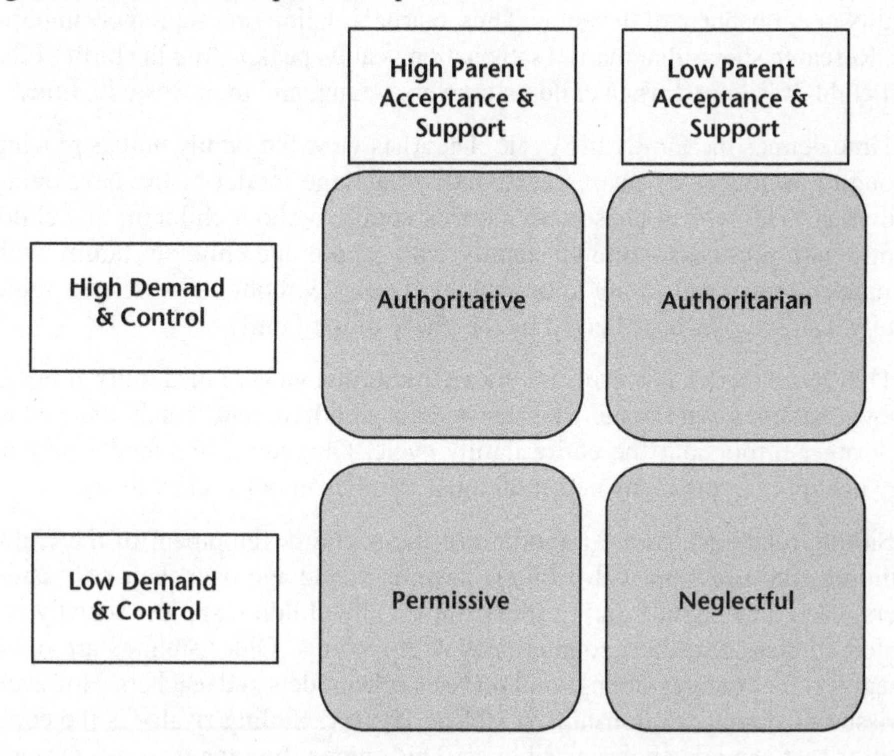

Parenting Styles Compared on Two Dimensions

Longitudinal research has also shown that parenting style changes across the stages of family life. They may adopt one style when children are young, then adjust their style as children age. Also keep in mind that culture influences the parenting style and children's developmental outcomes. This will be discussed later in this chapter.

FAMILY RELATIONS

Family systems theory is the perspective that views the family as an organized, whole unit with integrated parts. Members of the family adopt roles that form reciprocal interrelationships, such as mother-child, father-child, and mother-father. The behavior of each family member affects the whole system, and relationships between two or more members of the family affect the entire system. The father-child or the mother-child relationship can impact the mother-father relationship. In this perspective, the child influences the family system as much as the family influences the child.

The mother-father relationship, being the oldest and most mature, defines the quality or atmosphere of the home. Thus, marital relations are supremely important. Research shows that marital satisfaction is at its peak before the birth of the first child. It is lowest when children are very young, and improves with time.

Time defines the family life cycle. Theorists view the family unit as moving through a sequence of phases analogous to a stage model of the developing individual. The typical phases are married couple without children, first child, family with preschool children, family with school-age children, family with teenagers, family launching young adults, family without children, and aging family. Family roles are affected by the phase of the family.

This entire model, however, assumes a traditional view of the family as headed by a heterosexual couple who marry, have children, and remain married to each other throughout the entire family cycle. Obviously, this model may or may not apply to the many non-traditional families in our society today.

Sibling relationships are important to the social development of the child. Children who grow up with siblings have an advantage over their only-child peers when they begin forming friendships. Only-children are less socially accepted compared to their counterparts with siblings. Older siblings are often caregivers for younger siblings and serve as role models and teachers. However, an issue in sibling relationships is **sibling rivalry**. Sibling rivalry is the competition that can arise between siblings. This competition tends to rise through childhood as school-age children experience more things on which they can compete. It tends to decrease in adolescence as teenagers spend less time in the home and more time with friends. Ambivalence may be the best way to describe sibling relationships. Siblings can be very close, benefit from interactions with each other, yet argue and fight fiercely. All this is greatly influenced by culture and cultural expectations.

ADOLESCENT-PARENT RELATIONSHIPS

The quality of the adolescent-parent relationship depends on the degree to which parents and adolescents successfully renegotiate their previous relationship. A major task of adolescence is achieving autonomy, including the ability to make decisions independently. To accomplish this task, adolescents need to attempt independence even if these attempts sometimes fail. If parents are too restrictive and continue to control their adolescents' lives as much as when they were children, adolescents will not have the opportunity to develop independence. This can result in rebellious behavior, through confrontation and/or sneaking.

Parents tend to give greater autonomy as the adolescent shows more responsibility. Under this system, adolescents must show responsibility if they expect to be given more freedom to make their own decisions, and parents must give adolescents more freedom to be independent. The authoritative parenting style leads to the best outcomes with adolescents, as it did with younger children. Parents who provide rules with consistent consequences for violations, reason with their teenagers, allow their teenagers a voice, and continue to provide warmth and affection have teenagers who will most likely become autonomous and well-adjusted.

ADULT-PARENT RELATIONSHIPS

The **launching phase** (or **empty nest stage**) is when young adult children leave the home. Psychologists once described the empty nest as a period of crisis for parents, particularly for mothers. But recent survey research indicates that most parents enjoy a renewal in their relationship and are very satisfied during the launching phase.

Normally, young adulthood is a time for individuals to leave home, begin their work lives, and experience full independence. During times of economic stress, children may live at home after graduating from high school or even college. Some psychologists refer to this as an extended adolescence, which can range into the late 20s, or longer. The children may have employment, and may even have intimate relationships, but they cannot afford to live on their own. The parent-child relationship is usually renegotiated in these situations, since the child is now of legal age. Good renegotiations result in a relatively adult-adult relationship, although the child is still economically dependent.

Most adult children living outside the home continue strong relationships with their aging parents. These relationships become more mutual, comparable to friendships, rather than parent-child relationships. Adult children continue to have significant contact with their aging parents even if they do not live together or nearby. As parents age they may rely on middle-aged adult children for their care, a change that has been referred to as **role-reversal**.

The **middle generation sandwich** or squeeze occurs when adult children are responsible for the care of aging parents as well as their own children, who are most likely teens or young adults. This is a source of significant stress for middle-aged adults, and the weight of the responsibility tends to fall more heavily on daughters and daughters-in-law of the aging parents. The growth of the assisted care industry in the United States has helped to ease the burden on adult children. Many assisted living facilities are well-designed to provide a high quality of life and a continuous level of care for elderly residents.

GRANDPARENTHOOD

The grandparent role is usually a source of great satisfaction for middle and older adults. While there are differences in styles of grandparenting and degrees of grandparent involvement, grandchildren, their parents, and the grandparents all benefit from the grandparenting role in the family.

There are instances in which grandparents must take on a parenting role due to the custodial parent(s) dying, abandoning their offspring, being incarcerated, or becoming incapacitated by illness or drug addiction. Currently, there are over 2.5 million children being raised by grandparents. There are important issues and concerns for grandparents who take on a parenting role. These concerns can include stress and exhaustion, resentment, and the disruption of routines, plans, and intimacy. Grandparents in this situation can turn to support groups to help ease the stress and to share ideas.

It is also worth noting that during difficult economic times, there is an increase in the number of households that include grandparent(s), parent(s), and child(ren). This can cause stress even while it relieves economic hardship. It is important for the adults to come to terms with issues such as authority over children, household noise, and establishing roles and routines.

INFLUENCES OF DIVORCE AND SINGLE-PARENTHOOD

There have been three major trends facing the developing family over the past several decades: an increase in divorce, an increase in single-parent families, and an increase in working mothers. Because every household is different, it is difficult to generalize the effect of divorce or single-parenting on the family. There are general trends, however, that do appear. Research has shown that certain factors contribute to the stability of all family members involved in divorce or single-parenthood:

- A parent who is secure and rewarded in the workplace deals better with the situation.

- A positive network of friends and family can provide support, lending a more positive aspect to the situation.
- When both parents play a role in raising the child, there is a more positive outcome.
- The quality of the relationship of the custodial parent with the non-custodial parent is a key factor that predicts outcomes of divorce. The quality of the relationship can be predicted by the degree of post-divorce conflict between the two parents. The better the quality of this relationship, the better the children's developmental outcomes.

There are five factors that affect the development of a child dealing with divorce. They are:

- the levels of stress and amount of support at the time of the divorce;
- the sex of the child;
- the age of the child;
- the amount of time since the change; and
- the parents' response to the change.

These factors also influence how parents will talk to the child about the change, as well as what kinds of reactions they might expect from the child. On this last point, it should be noted that sometimes children will blame themselves for the divorce, thinking that some action they committed caused the family disruption. Such erroneous thinking needs to be brought into the open and put to rest.

MULTICULTURAL PERSPECTIVES

Culture influences many aspects of family life and child development. As mentioned above, parenting styles can be heavily influenced by culture. There are fairly consistent differences in parenting style across the two broad types of cultures, **collectivist cultures** and **individualist cultures**. A collectivist culture values the greater good. Members are rewarded and revered for working toward the goals of the group (family, nation, etc.), rather than individualistic or self-improvement goals. Individualistic cultures are the reverse. Members of these cultures value and reward individual achievement, personality individuation, and healthy competition among individuals.

Hispanic, African, and Asian cultures are traditionally more collectivist, while European-descended culture tends to be more individualistic. Parents of Hispanic, African, and Asian descent tend to be more authoritarian in their style of parenting because those collectivist cultures value respect, conformity, and obedience to authority. Parents of European descent (especially middle and upper classes) tend to be more authoritative in their orientation because they value the development of independence and autonomy.

The relationship between parenting style and culture is more complex, though. As described earlier, the authoritarian parenting style has been associated with poor outcomes in studies conducted in the United States. However, the developmental outcomes of the authoritarian parenting style depend on how that style is viewed within the culture. For example, if authoritarian parenting is viewed as an indication that parents love and care about their children, as it is in the Chinese culture, the developmental outcomes are positive. (Remember that strict discipline is not necessarily angry, violent, or loud. It can be carried out with a firm tone and a sense of helpfulness.)

Culture affects more than just parenting style. It also affects how gender roles will be modeled by parents and expected of their children. Culture also influences how and what parents expect regarding a child's obligations toward siblings. And culture influences the kinds of long-range goals parents have in their child-rearing—in other words, the kinds of aspirations and traits they aim for as they nurture their children with love and discipline. You might expect these cultural influences to reflect the individualist versus collectivist viewpoints.

Another aspect of cultural influences is the development of **ethnic identity**. This is not the same as racial identity, since there are many ethnic cultures and nationalities within each race. Ethnic identity is related to a person's self-concept and self-identity. The conscious search for ethnic identity and meaning begins in adolescence, when abstract thought becomes possible. The child has grown up within a culture, but now can hold the culture at arm's length and think about how (and how much) that culture will influence future development.

A teen begins to think about his or her relation to the ethnic group, and how the group relates to other groups. This can lead to close and committed identification with the group, or the beginning of distancing oneself from the group. The process solidifies in adulthood, but it does not necessarily become static. Identification with and participation in one's ethnic group can change throughout the life span.

SOCIAL AND CLASS INFLUENCES

Parents from different social classes tend to adopt different parenting styles and customs, and value different developmental outcomes for their children. Lower- and working-class parents tend to adopt the authoritarian parenting style more than middle- and upper-class parents, because they tend to value obedience. Obedience to authority may be valued because parents assume their children need strict rules within a dangerous neighborhood, or because they assume their children will one day have working-class jobs that require compliance. These parents usually express less affection toward children. Perhaps this is due to the greater number of stressors they have in their lives, including economic hardship and a poor living environment. They also are less educated and therefore may lack knowledge about how to parent more effectively, and how and why to provide enrichment experiences for their children. (Keep in mind that low socioeconomic status [SES] includes less leisure time for parents, as well as less disposable income. So even if enrichment experiences are free, parents may not have the time or energy to take advantage of them.)

With all the stressors that accompany low SES, children in low SES households may be nutritionally deficient. This can cause stunted physical growth, delayed menarche in girls, and poor performance at school—possibly started by having lower vocabulary from an early age compared to middle-class students. Males are most affected by all these factors, and they are especially at risk for social problems and grade retention. Once these negative things happen, they can feed on each other and spiral downward into low motivation, low achievement, and behavior problems in and out of school. (See Chapter 10: Social Development throughout the Life Span.)

ABUSE AND NEGLECT

Child abuse can take one of three forms: physical, emotional, or sexual. All three forms are found in all cultures and across all socioeconomic classes. Child **neglect** is failure to protect children from harm or failure to meet their biological and medical needs. Here are some general facts about these behaviors:

- When young infants are abused or neglected, they often develop a syndrome called **failure to thrive**. This was discussed in Chapter 4: Biological Development throughout the Life Span as a phenomenon that might have no obvious cause. However, abuse or neglect can certainly be a cause.
- Studies of child mistreatment have found a link between abuse and a child's temperament. The difficult temperament is the hardest temperament for caregivers to deal with, which may be why children with this temperament are at greater risk for physical abuse.
- Parents are most often the abuser. Parents who abuse their children tend to be those who have a history of abuse themselves, have little

social support, low self-esteem, and are hypersensitive to their children's bad behavior. Studies have shown that abusers have significantly higher levels of emotional arousal under stressful conditions compared to non-abusers. That is, they get upset more quickly when under stress than other people. Intervention programs that focus on social support for these parents tend to be most successful.

Physical Abuse

Physical abuse is any use of force that can harm an individual's health, survival, development, or dignity. It can include hitting, kicking, shaking, scratching, pinching, scalding, burning, forcing ingestion, or forcing a postural position. It can lead to personality disorders, post-traumatic stress disorder, depression, anxiety, aggression, substance abuse, or eating disorders.

Emotional/Psychological Abuse

Psychological abuse is anything that isolates, terrorizes, humiliates to convey worthlessness, or denies emotional response. It can lead to self-blame, abnormal attachment, internalization, and learned helplessness.

Sexual Abuse

Sexual abuse includes pressure to engage in sexual activities, indecent exposure, creating or displaying pornography, and sexual/genital contact. Sexual offenders tend to target children who are isolated and needy. They will play on these children's vulnerabilities and may gain the trust of children because they are socially isolated and crave attention.

Victims of child sexual abuse frequently develop guilt, eating disorders, and post-traumatic stress disorder. They may develop sexual dysfunction or engage in sexualized behavior, such as behaving promiscuously or in an overly seductive manner. A small number of victims develop more serious psychological disorders, such as dissociative identity disorder. These disorders are also discussed in Chapter 14: Developmental Psychopathology.

Neglect

Neglect includes lack of supervision, care, or nourishment. It manifests itself in school absenteeism, lack of adequate clothing, poor hygiene, and medical and dental needs. It can lead to delays in physical development, poor social skills, and poor executive (cognitive) function.

MEDIA AND TECHNOLOGY

In addition to the family, media such as smartphones, tablets, television, computers, and other digital devices have a significant effect on children's development. Research has shown that preschoolers engage in television viewing more than any other activity other than sleeping. Children between the ages of 2 and 5 watch an average of about 30 hours of media per week, mostly TV, but also DVDs and streaming media. Children between 6 and 11 watch slightly fewer hours of media. There is also a decline in teenagers' viewing; in fact, they watch less than adults—although they are likely online more than other groups.

Educational television programs have been found to have a positive effect on children's cognitive development and prosocial behavior. However, as Bandura and his colleagues showed in a classic experiment, children will imitate an aggressive model that they see on television. Children who watch more violent television than their counterparts show a positive correlation with aggressive behaviors. Younger children are also frightened by the content of some television shows and may not understand the difference between reality and fiction. Television viewing is also negatively correlated with the amount of family interaction and communication, and positively correlated with obesity.

Computer technology is potentially both beneficial and harmful. The World Wide Web provides children access to a great deal of media that is appropriate and educational. (Software or games that are both educational and recreational are sometimes called "edutainment.") However, the Web also has content that is inappropriate and harmful to young people.

Video games can be very violent and, unlike merely observing violence in a television program, violent games reward children's violent behavior. Players earn points by killing or destroying. However, one must make a distinction between aggression, which is angry verbal or physical action, and violence, which is action meant to causes serious physical harm. With that distinction in mind, research tells us that violent video games, much like passive TV watching, do tend to lead to more aggressive attitudes and behavior, but they do not tend to lead to violence.

We do know this: Use of any media, whether passive or interactive, tends to decrease the time family members spend interacting with each other. That can have an impact on development, since so much social and emotional learning comes from family interactions.

There is also a need to distinguish between children and teenagers regarding media use. For children, the main questions for parents are:

- How much "screen time" is appropriate and healthy for the age of the child?
- How much physical playtime is all right to lose because the child is involved in media?
- How much parental supervision and/or regulation is appropriate for the child at this age?

For adolescents, who might spend large amounts of time on social media, these questions need to be addressed:

- Is my teen using screen time for connection purposes, which might include collaborative learning, friendship, or activism? These are positive aspects of media and help develop social skills.
- Is my teen using screen time for alienation purposes, which might include rumor-spreading, cyberbullying, or avoiding direct contact with peers? These would indicate that positive social skills are not being used or developed.

DEATH AND DYING

Elisabeth Kübler-Ross provided the first psychological model of death and dying. She studied this by conducting in-depth interviews with terminally-ill patients. Those interviews led her to propose a stage model of death and dying. Psychologists have attributed the same stages to those who experience the death of a loved one in their **grieving** or **bereavement**. These stages might also describe what transpires in **anticipatory grief** before the loved one's death. Family members often begin the grieving process when they learn that a loved one has a terminal illness.

Stage 1 – Denial. The first stage in this model is denial, in which the person refuses to accept the diagnosis and prognosis of death. A patient in this stage may spend a lot of time and money seeking other medical opinions. Loved ones might try to continue to have a hopeful outlook.

Stage 2 – Anger. When the person has no recourse but to accept the reality, he or she reacts with anger—at God, at the medical profession, and even perhaps at significant others.

Stage 3 – Bargaining. After the anger phase, the person enters the stage of bargaining. He or she tries to find ways to delay the inevitable reality. An example is a person saying, "Let me live to see my daughter's wedding."

Stage 4 – Depression. When the person realizes that anger and bargaining do not change the situation, depression follows.

Stage 5 – Acceptance. Kübler-Ross reported that people do finally come to accept the reality of death. In this final stage, patients may participate in planning for their own funeral and put their affairs in order. Those who grieve finally accept the absence of the loved one and find comfort in memories and memorials.

Critics argue that all people do not progress through these stages in the same order or at all, and that all dying patients do not come to accept their death. How stages are managed, and for how long—or whether stages are skipped—is all affected by the circumstances of the loved one's death. Culture also affects how people deal with death and the dying process. Each culture has unique attitudes about death, expectations for the behavior of those who are bereaved, as well as death and bereavement rituals.

Medical advancements now make it possible to extend a person's life through artificial means. Examples of these measures are resuscitation, oxygen ventilation, and feeding tubes. Medical ethics is a field that has emerged to deal with the ethical and moral dilemmas that have appeared as a result of these life-extending measures. Family members often must make decisions about end-of-life treatments because the patient is incapacitated. Many people believe that it is unethical to keep a person alive who has no quality of life and no hope of recovering. End-of-life choices for individuals or for caretakers include several options:

- Dying at home, with minimal or no medical support, is not typical in our society in modern times.
- Dying in a hospital with medical care often occurs. How much care or intervention will be allowed can be influenced by a patient's **advance care directive** or by electing to have a **DNR** (Do Not Resuscitate) posted.
- A **hospice** is a comprehensive support program for terminally-ill patients and their families. The goal of a hospice is to give **palliative care**, i.e., help the dying person have a pain-free death in a comfortable environment, either in the home or in a non-medical facility, surrounded by their loved ones.

- **Euthanasia**, i.e., actively assisting the death of a terminally-ill person who has a very poor quality of life, is controversial. It has become an issue on state ballots, and it continues to gain support while it is being debated.

In order to help family members make decisions about end-of-life care, it has become common practice for people to have a **living will**. A living will is a legal document that outlines the individual's wishes with regard to end-of-life care. The document might include a DNR directive so that no extreme measures should be used if there is no hope for recovery.

CHAPTER 12

PERSONALITY AND EMOTIONS

Personality is a psychological construct defined as the relatively stable and characteristic set of traits and behaviors of an individual. There is a debate, however, between personality theorists who believe that a person's behavior is greatly influenced by a stable and internal personality and other theorists who believe that behavior is more situationally controlled and that there really is no such thing as personality as a stable or consistent construct.

The first group, the personality theorists, consider personality as a viable construct, although they disagree with each other on whether personality shows more stability than change throughout the life span. Two influential theories of personality development are Freud's psychoanalytic theory and Erikson's psychosocial theory. These two theories will be discussed at length later in this chapter.

The second group of theorists claim that personality theorists and their supporters commit a **fundamental attribution error**. That error, they claim, is assuming that people's personality or beliefs cause their behavior. In other words, these theorists assert that people who think that personality causes behavior tend to underestimate the power of external factors in controlling behavior and overestimate the power of internal factors. (You might think of these theorists as behaviorists, who do not attribute learning to internal processes, but rather to external consequences to behaviors. In that same vein, these theorists do not attribute behavior to a personality, but rather to external factors that shape habits of action.)

Developmental psychologists study two phenomena closely associated with personality: temperament and emotions. **Temperament** is considered a rudimentary form of personality found in newborns. Temperamental differences among newborns suggest that personality is, in part, influenced by nature as well as shaped by experience.

Emotional development is a more complex study. An **emotion** is a conscious experience or feeling that has a stimulus component, a cognitive component, a bodily or physiological component, and a behavioral component. Emotional development includes becoming able to express different emotions, regulate emotional responses, and interpret the emotions of self and others.

Temperament and emotions are discussed below.

TEMPERAMENT

Temperament refers to a person's characteristic mood and activity level. Even young infants are temperamentally different from one another. The New York Longitudinal Study (1956), carried out by **Stella Chess** and **Alexander Thomas,** investigated temperament. The study followed 140 children from birth to adolescence. The researchers interviewed parents when the infants were between two and three months of age and rated the infants based on activity level, rhythmicity, approach/withdrawal, adaptability, intensity of reaction, and quality of mood. They found that infants could be classified into different groups based on temperament.

Easy Infants (40%)	Adaptable to new situations. Predictable in their rhythmicity or schedule. Positive in their mood.
Difficult Infants (10%)	Intense in their reactions. Not very adaptable to new situations. Slightly negative mood. Irregular body rhythms.
Slow-to-Warm-Up Infants (15%)	Initially withdraw when approached, but may later "warm up." Slow to adapt to new situations.
Average Infants (35%)	Do not fit into any one of the above categories.

Chess and Thomas found that temperament was fairly stable over time. For instance, they found that 70 percent of the difficult infants developed behavior problems during childhood, while only 18 percent of the easy infants did so. There were, of course, individual differences in whether specific children showed continuity or dramatic changes in their temperament over time.

Although early temperament appears to be highly biologically determined, environment can also influence it. Researchers have used the term **goodness of fit** to describe the degree to which the environment of people and things matches an infant's temperament in terms of opportunities, expectations, and demands the infant encounters.

DEVELOPMENT OF EMOTIONS

Robert Plutchik proposed that emotions evolved because they help a species to survive. He asserted that emotions are inherited behavioral patterns and are modified by experience. Emotions have four components: external stimuli that are interpreted by the person, feelings, physiological arousal, and behavioral responses. However, there are various theories that attempt to explain the origin and order of our experience of emotions.

William James and **Carl Lange** theorized that people experience physiological changes and interpret these changes as emotions. In other words, emotions follow behavior and not vice versa. Under this theory, the dog does not run because it is scared; it is scared because it runs.

Walter Cannon and colleague **Philip Bard** noted that the physiological changes in many emotional states were identical. For instance, if someone reports sweaty palms, pounding heart, and tension, is that love, jealousy, fear, or hate? Because of this, people cannot determine their emotional state only from their physiological state. The **Cannon-Bard Theory** argues that emotion occurs when the thalamus sends signals simultaneously to the brain cortex and to the autonomic nervous system.

Stanley Schachter and **Jerome Singer** offered a cognitive approach to emotions. It is referred to as the **Schachter-Singer Two-Factor Theory**. This theory proposes that emotion occurs when physiological arousal causes us to search for reasons for this arousal. We examine the environment for an explanation for this arousal. Emotions are determined, therefore, by labeling our arousal based on what is occurring in our environment.

Other researchers have studied the origin of emotions in humans. **Paul Ekman** and his colleagues studied people's ability to judge emotions based on facial expressions in photographs of adults. (They are somewhat successful at recognizing emotional expressions in photographs of infants as well.) The researchers found that there are six facial expressions corresponding to six emotions that people can recognize, and that this interpretation of facial expressions is universal. Out of that, it was proposed that there are **six basic emotions**: happiness, anger, disgust, sadness, fear, and surprise.

Secondary emotions are understood to be shadings and combinations of those basic ones. For instance, hurt is sadness plus anger, worry is sadness plus fear. Curious is a combination of surprise and happiness, while startled is a combination of surprise and fear. There are also **social emotions** that develop, such as embarrassment and empathy.

Newborns do not seem to have a set of emotions. They do, however, exhibit one negative emotion: distress. Other psychologists argue that infants are born with the emotions of interest, distress, and disgust. Joy develops between four and six weeks; anger, surprise, sadness, fear, and shame between three and eight months; and contempt and guilt in the second year. Critics argue that infants may experience all these emotions before they can express them.

Psychologists do agree that there is a biological component to emotion, but that emotions are also affected by experience. Learning theory (behaviorism) suggests that emotional responses are learned through classical conditioning or observational learning. Classical conditioning theory would explain a child's fear of dogs as a conditioned response. For instance, if a child sees a dog and at the same time experiences an unconditioned fear stimulus such as a loud bark, the dog (CS) becomes associated with the loud noise (UCS). Observational learning could also produce fears in children who observe their own parents' fear responses.

EMOTIONAL EXPRESSION AND REGULATION

As humans develop, they feel and express more and more complex emotions. A major challenge is to learn how to regulate those feelings and the behaviors that accompany them. The goal of emotional development is to have a balance between emotional expression and emotional control. Emotional control is associated with social competence and prosocial behavior.

Infants exhibit behaviors that elicit support when distressed—crying being the primary one. Distress is not always alleviated, so around 6 months of age, infants discover self-soothing behaviors, such as sucking on a favorite toy. If such behaviors do not appear, an infant can be trained to self-soothe with some success. Toddlers usually have developed their own self-soothing strategies, which tend to include retreating from unwanted stimuli, since now they are mobile.

Children are typically conscious of their own social emotions (e.g., embarrassment), yet they need help in learning how to control their emotions, especially negative ones such as frustration or anger. When stressed, a child needs strategies that conform to socially accepted norms. Parents and teachers have the biggest role to play in this, so it is imperative that these adults handle a child's outbursts in a way that teaches, not punishes or shames. Other children are also important to emotional regulation. Children develop more emotional control as they engage in more activities with peers. In fact, children control their emotions most when with peers, less when they are with family, and the least when they are alone.

Teens have complex social awareness. They develop coping strategies that can be quite sophisticated and/or devious. Adults can help by keeping their own emotions intact while dealing with teens and by "checking in" with a teen's emotional state regularly.

EMOTIONAL INTELLIGENCE

In the 1960s, **Walter Mischel** devised the marshmallow test at Stanford University. A child was seated at a table and offered a marshmallow (or similar treat) on a plate. The experimenter told the child that he or she could eat the marshmallow, but if the child waited until the experimenter came back into the room in a few minutes, a second marshmallow would be added to the plate. This was a test to observe and measure children's ability to delay gratification. Obviously, some children ate the one treat, while some children waited to get two treats. Follow-up over the next several years revealed that the ones who exhibited **delayed gratification** at a young age had higher SAT scores in high school, better health measures, and other more positive life outcomes than the children who had eaten the one treat. From that study, theorists determined that **impulse control**—the ability to delay gratification—was a predictor of lifelong satisfaction and happiness.

Out of that experiment and the later work of **John Mayer** and **Peter Salovey**, psychologist **Daniel Goleman** proposed a construct of **emotional intelligence** (**EI** or **EQ,** to distinguish it from intellectual IQ). He argued that:

- Children as well as adults vary in their capacity to interpret their own and other people's emotions.
- Competence in correctly identifying one's own or another person's emotional state would lead to a better understanding of motivation.
- People with high EQ tend to be socially competent and successful.
- EQ could predict success in life better than IQ.

Following years of research and interpretation, attributes of high EQ now include:

- High self-awareness of one's own emotional state
- High self-regulation of one's behavior based on emotions

- Adept social skills
- High motivation
- Empathy, i.e., ability to understand and act positively on what another person is feeling

This has led to schools and businesses promoting and training for EQ, hoping to lead young people and adult workers to a higher level of self-awareness and social proficiency.

There are critics of EQ. Some insist that emotional intelligence is just a part of acquired intelligence, not something separate. Some claim that it is more about morals than about emotion or intelligence. There is even some refocusing on the testing that started it. For one thing, Mischel's original delayed gratification test was not performed on a broad spectrum of children. Cultural and economic factors and necessities were not considered when timing a child's ability to wait for gratification. Adding in such factors can reduce the reliability of predicting a child's degree of impulsiveness or predicting future success.

FREUD'S PSYCHODYNAMIC THEORY OF PERSONALITY DEVELOPMENT

Freud's Representation of Personality Development

Freud used his experience with adult patients (mostly female) to build a theory of personality development. His theory emphasized three main points:

1. Childhood experiences—mainly those involving parents' attitudes and actions—determine adult personality.
2. Unconscious mental processes (especially those originating from childhood experiences) influence everyday behavior.
3. Inner conflict (mostly unconscious) causes most human behavior.

This notion of "inner conflict" arises out of what Freud theorized as the three components of personality. These components conflict with each other due to their differing motives or roles. You might recognize that much of this has become accepted in our society, as evidenced by people often speaking of unconscious motives in others. For example: "He must have had a terrible childhood to have that attitude" or "She obviously isn't aware of her own motives for doing that…."

Freud's Personality Components

Personality component	When it develops	How it functions
Id	Present at birth	Pleasure principle; unconscious instincts; irrational; animalistic; seeks instant gratification; contains the libido
Ego	Around 6 months	Reality principle; mediates id and reality; executive branch
Superego	Around 6 years	Morality principle; personal conscience; personal ideals

According to Freud, the **id** is unconscious and has no contact with reality. It works according to the pleasure principle—always seeking pleasure and avoiding pain. The id contains the libido or sexual energy.

The **ego** evolves from the id and deals with the demands of reality. It is called the executive branch of personality because it makes rational decisions. The reality principle describes how the ego tries to reconcile the demands of the id with the norms of society. The ego, however, does not determine whether something is right or wrong, only if it is acceptable.

The **superego** evolves as a mechanism that determines whether something is right or wrong—our conscience. The superego does not consider practical nuances of situations, only rules about moral behavior.

Taking these three components into account, behavior is the outcome of an ongoing series of conflicts among the id, ego, and superego. Conflicts that deal with sexual and aggressive impulses are likely to have far-reaching consequences, because social norms dictate that these impulses should be curbed. When the id takes too much control, behavior will be antisocial and destructive in some way. On the other hand, when the superego takes too much control, the individual will feel and act guilty or ashamed (whether it is warranted or not), and normal functioning will be inhibited.

Freud considered personality to be like an iceberg, in that most of it exists below the level of awareness, just as most of an iceberg is hidden beneath the surface of the water. Freud referred to the hidden part of our personality as the **unconscious**. Through a process of **repression**, unwanted thoughts (originating from impulses in the id) are pushed down into the unconscious. Even though many thoughts, memories, and desires are unconscious, they nonetheless influence our behavior because of the process of repression.

Above the surface of the personality iceberg, the **conscious** part consists of whatever we are aware of at any point in time. The **preconscious**, according to Freud, contains material that is just below the surface of awareness but can be easily retrieved. An example of preconscious awareness would be your mother's birthdate. You were not thinking of your mother's birthdate but can if you need or want to.

Anxiety results from the irrational demands of the id or from the superego causing guilty feelings about a real or imagined transgression. **Defense mechanisms** are unconscious methods used by the ego to distort or reinterpret reality and thereby protect us from anxiety. However, continued and deepening use of defense mechanisms can lead to neuroses, such as anxiety disorders in the form of obsessions, compulsions, and phobias. In extreme cases, defense mechanisms can lead to psychoses which take the individual out of reality altogether. The major defense mechanisms are described in the chart below. Negative results of those mechanisms are discussed in Chapter 14: Developmental Psychopathology.

Name of Defense Mechanism	Definition and Example
Rationalization	Creating false but plausible excuses to justify unacceptable behavior. Example: Reducing guilt for cheating on your taxes by insisting "everyone does it."
Repression	Pushing unacceptable id impulses out of awareness and back into the unconscious. Example: Having no memory of an unpleasant experience.
Reaction Formation	Behaving exactly the opposite of one's true feelings. Example: A mother who feels resentment toward a child may be overly cautious and protective.
Regression	Reversion to immature patterns of behavior. Example: Temper tantrums or emotional outbursts.
Projection	Attributing one's own thoughts, feelings, motives, or shortcomings to others. Example: A wife who constantly suspects her husband of having an affair because she has thought of having an affair.
Displacement	Shifting unacceptable feelings from their original source to a safer, substitute target. Example: You are mad at your boss, but you do not yell at your boss; instead you become angry with a family member when you return home.
Sublimation	A useful, socially acceptable course of behavior replaces a socially unacceptable or distasteful impulse. Example: A person who feels aggression due to a lack of control plays an aggressive game of basketball with friends every other day.

(continued)

Intellectualization	By dealing with a stressful situation in an intellectual and unemotional manner, a person detaches from the stress. Example: A person who has lost a family member due to an illness will speak of the medical terminology of the illness but will not discuss the emotional aspects of the illness.
Denial	Refusing to admit that a very unpleasant thing has happened. Example: A person with constant stomach pains, possibly an ulcer, refuses to see a doctor because he or she insists it is only indigestion.

It is interesting to note that **Carl Jung**, a younger colleague of Freud, did not see personality as an iceberg, but rather as an island partially rising above the surface. Just as with real islands, each personality island is connected to the ocean floor. This metaphor is meant to indicate that all personalities are connected to each other at the deepest level, what he described as the **collective unconscious**. This level of the unconscious would include racial memories from the remote past. Jung analyzed folktales, rather than dreams, to discover elements of the collective unconscious.

Freud's Stages of Psychosexual Development

Freud theorized that the three main components of personality were fully formed during early childhood. However, he theorized that there are other facets of personality that form during and after that time. He described five stages of **psychosexual development**. In each stage, pleasure that satisfies the id comes from a different erogenous zone, or the part of the body where pleasure originates. In each stage there is a **psychosexual crisis** because the ego (and later in development, the superego) must find socially acceptable ways to satisfy the id's focus on each erogenous zone.

According to Freud, children experience conflicts between urges in their erogenous zones and societal rules. **Fixation** can result when these urges are either frustrated or overindulged in any one erogenous zone. Fixation results in one's personality becoming permanently locked in the conflict surrounding that erogenous zone. Freud felt that the first three psychosexual stages were the most important for personality development. Examples of possible personality distortions resulting from fixations in the first three psychosexual stages are presented in the following chart.

Freud's Psychosexual Stages

Stage	Age	Erogenous Zone	Description	Fixation Traits
Oral	0–1 year	Mouth	Stimulation of mouth produces pleasure; infant enjoys sucking, biting, and chewing. Weaning is major task or conflict.	Obsessive eating Smoking Drinking Sarcasm Overly demanding Aggressiveness
Anal	1–3 years	Anus	Retaining and expelling feces produces pleasure. Toilet training is major task or conflict.	Extreme messiness Overly orderly Overly concerned about punctuality Fear of dirt Love of bathroom humor Anxiety about sexual activities Overly giving Rebelliousness
Phallic	3–6 years	Genitals	Self-stimulation of genitals produces pleasure. **Oedipal** (for boys) and **Electra** (for girls) **complexes** occur. Children have unconscious erotic desires for opposite-sex parent as well as feelings of fear and hostility for same-sex parent. Successful resolution of this conflict results in **identification** with same-sex parent.	Excessive masturbation Frequent flirting Excessive modesty Excessive timidity Overly proud Promiscuity
Latency	6–12 years	None	Sexual feelings are repressed. Social contacts beyond immediate family are expanded. Focus shifts to school and same-sex friendships.	
Genital	Puberty onward	Genitals	Establishing intimate, sexual relations with others is main focus.	

ERIKSON'S PSYCHOSOCIAL THEORY OF PERSONALITY DEVELOPMENT

Erik Erikson was trained in Freudian psychoanalytic theory and practice. Erikson's theory, however, is very different from Freud's. For instance, Erikson believed that personality continues to develop over the entire life span (not just through childhood). Also, Erikson did not stress unconscious psychosexual urges, but rather emotional and social challenges at each stage of life. However, like Freud, Erikson did feel that events that occur early in development can leave a permanent mark on one's later social-emotional development.

Erikson contended that each person is faced with a progression of social-emotional tasks, challenges, or crises that will determine his or her ability to function in the social world. At each stage in development, the person can master the challenge and gain ego strength or fail the challenge and develop an ego weakness that makes social adaptation more difficult.

For each of the eight life stages, he described the developmental task in terms of two polarities. The polarities are pairs of potential positive and negative resolutions to the psychosocial crisis at each stage. The reason a psychosocial crisis arises at each stage is partly due to physical and cognitive maturation, and partly because the individual's social environment is expanding and must be accommodated. Thus, the goal for each of the eight stages of development is to resolve the current crisis in a positive way and hence add to one's ego strength.

Erikson's Stages of Psychosocial Development

Infant	Toddler	Young Child	Older Child	Adolescent	Young Adult	Middle Adult	Older Adult
Trust vs. Mistrust	Autonomy vs. Shame & Doubt	Initiative vs. Guilt	Industry vs. Inferiority	Identity vs. Role Confusion	Intimacy vs. Isolation	Generativity vs. Stagnation	Ego Integrity vs. Despair

The significance of Erikson's theory should not be underestimated. Many human development textbooks are organized in accordance with the stages outlined in this theory.

A more complete description of Erikson's eight stages of psychosocial development follows. Each stage represents a specific task or challenge called a **psychosocial crisis** that must be resolved with some degree of success for further development. Related and supporting research from other psychologists will also be discussed where appropriate.

Erikson's Eight Stages of Psychosocial Development

Stage 1: Trust versus Mistrust (Birth–1 year)

The infant's needs must be met by responsive, sensitive caretakers. If this occurs, a basic sense of trust and optimism develops. If not, mistrust and fear of the world and the future will result.

Research: This crisis is related to the topic of attachment discussed in Chapter 10 of this book. Recall Harlow's experiment with wire and cloth mothers for infant monkeys and research on eastern European orphans.

Stage 2: Autonomy versus Shame and Doubt (1–3 years)

Young children begin to express self-control by walking, climbing, exploring, and toilet training. Parents can foster a sense of autonomy by encouraging the child to try new things and giving the child a safe space to explore. If the child is restrained from exploration, or is shamed or punished when mistakes are made, self-doubt can develop.

Stage 3: Initiative versus Guilt (3–6 years)

Children are asked to assume more responsibility. Through play, children learn to plan, undertake, and carry out a task. Parents can encourage initiative by giving children little chores and the freedom to play, to use their imagination, etc. Children who are criticized for or discouraged from taking initiative learn to feel guilty.

Research: During this time, children have a primitive **self-concept**. Their sense of self is typically described in terms of physical attributes only.

Stage 4: Industry versus Inferiority (6–11 years)

In elementary school, children learn social skills, work habits, and academic skills that are valued by society. Success or failure while learning these skills can affect a child's feelings of adequacy. Success can engender a lifelong attitude that effort will result in reaching one's goals. Failure to meet the challenge of this stage can engender a sense of inadequacy in meeting expectations and goals.

Research: Related research tells us that children in this stage have a more sophisticated self-concept. Now they describe themselves in both physical and psychological terms, and they have a realistic view about how their abilities compare with others (**social comparison**). Therefore, success at this stage means a heightened sense of **self-efficacy** (perception or confidence level of ability) and **self-esteem** (pride and feelings of self-worth).

Research: Researchers have found that adults can help build these feelings if they encourage children to try new things, especially tasks that are challenging but with a high probability of success.

Of course, culture can influence self-concept and self-esteem. This happens in two ways:

- Children of minority cultures can develop low self-esteem due to bias and prejudice toward their culture.
- Children of cultures that value collectivism rather than individualism are not expected or trained to have high self-esteem.

Stage 5: Identity versus Role Confusion (Adolescence)

The development of identity involves finding out who one is, what one values, and where one is headed in life. In their search for identity, teens experiment with different roles or lifestyle choices. If they establish an integrated image of themselves as a unique person, then a sense of identity is established. If not, role confusion results. This can be expressed through anger and resentment or through tension and confusion regarding one's personal or sexual identity.

Research: Another theory fills in details about Erikson's concept of the adolescent identity crisis. **James Marcia** proposed that adolescents going through their identity crisis will find themselves in one of four categories of **identity status**. This is not a stage theory, but a set of "landing places" that teens experience for certain amounts of time as they explore or "try on" identities.

- **Foreclosure** = makes early decision about one's identity, career, etc. without exploring options; commitment that avoids identity crisis
- **Moratorium** = continues to experiment and explore options, so there is no decision yet; uncommitted, still in crisis
- **Diffusion** = confused, not sure what to do; does not explore; no crisis, no commitment
- **Achievement** = has explored and is now comfortable with chosen identity; identity crisis now resolved with commitment

On another topic, research tells us that male adolescents tend to have higher levels of self-esteem than females. This may be because males have more positive body images than females.

Stage 6: Intimacy versus Isolation (Young Adulthood)

Erikson asserted that young adults are concerned with, or in crisis of, establishing intimate, long-term relationships. If this is successfully resolved, then they can be warm and open with others, which eventually would lead to committing to a significant and permanent relationship. If they are unable to master emotions and engage with others sincerely, then they might avoid others or keep them at an emotional distance, creating social and emotional isolation.

Stage 7: Generativity versus Stagnation (Middle Adulthood)

The full-grown adult wants to use accumulated skills and resources to create, contribute, and nurture. Success at this stage is demonstrated by adults sharing their life-acquired wisdom and caring for the growth of the family and community. Complacency or negativity in this stage leads to stagnation and potentially to depression and loneliness.

Stage 8: Ego Integrity versus Despair (Late Adulthood)

If a person looking back on his or her life can believe that it has been meaningful and relatively successful, then a sense of integrity develops. There is also a measure of self-wisdom about one's circumstances and abilities. If the individual only sees a life of wasted opportunities and meaninglessness, then the person will be disgusted. Despair will follow disgust if the person feels it is too late to change.

Research: Related to Erikson's model, psychologists have studied differences in late-adult lifestyles and attitudes. **Activity theory** suggests that adults who remained active and connected with other people are more satisfied. **Disengagement theory** suggests that satisfied older adults follow a natural tendency to become less engaged and to focus inward.

Research has found four personality or lifestyle types in late adulthood as it relates to activity and engagement:

- The **integrated** type has chosen to be very active and is satisfied, has chosen to engage in a few activities and is satisfied, or has disengaged voluntarily and is satisfied.

- The **armored-defended** type remains active in the hope of maintaining abilities and is satisfied or disengages after experiencing losses and is satisfied.
- The **passive-dependent** type is emotionally needy and satisfied only if he or she has others to lean on, or disengaged rocking-chair adults who have low satisfaction.
- The **unintegrated/disorganized** type has lost or never had normal psychological functioning.

In conclusion, Erikson believed that the way each psychosocial crisis is resolved affects the person's ability to successfully resolve the next crisis. As a positive example, basic trust from infancy allows the toddler to explore his or her world to gain a sense of autonomy. As a negative example, the toddler who leaves the second stage with a sense of shame or self-doubt, rather than autonomy, will hesitate to plan activities and hence will not develop initiative to do well in school or in cooperation with peers. And so it goes through the stages, where solid self-identity in adolescence is necessary to manage an intimate relationship in early adulthood, and where the ability to be intimate in early adulthood can allow the older adult to be generative rather than isolated or failure-prone.

STABILITY AND CHANGE

Does personality remain stable throughout the life span, or does it change in significant ways? There is evidence to support both sides of this argument. Here are examples:

A Case for Stability

John Holland developed a test that attempted to match personality types to employment. He found six distinct personality types:

- Realistic: works well with animals and tools
- Investigative: good at cognitive tasks and problem solving
- Artistic: good at creating
- Social: good at helping others
- Enterprising: good at leading, selling, persuading
- Conventional: good at methodical planning and creating order

He found that personality types tended to stay stable regardless of age. In other words, an artistic person would stay creative; a conventional person would stay orderly. A change in employment would mean finding work in a new career, but one that required the same personality traits as the previous employment.

A Case for Change

Laura Carstensen offered a socio-emotional theory of personality. It was found that as people age, they tend to invest in more emotionally meaningful goals and activities. In other words, as people mature, their perspectives—and personalities—seem to change toward more altruistic or personally satisfying pursuits. This includes shifts in motivation, shifts in cognitive processing, and even a shift toward a more positive outlook.

A Case for Both

Psychology has long had a **Big Five model of personality traits**, each with its spectrum or range of expression in each person:

- Agreeableness
- Extraversion
- Neuroticism
- Openness
- Conscientiousness

Research has revealed that across the life span, the first four remain stable. In other words, the degree of agreeableness or extraversion a person has at age 20 will be the same at age 50. But the fifth trait, conscientiousness, does change across the life span. It tends to increase over time.

Longitudinal research on self-concept and self-esteem shows a mixture of patterns that "prove" both stability and change. Some report a dip in self-esteem from age 12; others show stability in self-esteem from grade five through adolescence. It may be the case that self-esteem, once formed, tends to be stable but can be affected by positive or negative experiences. Getting involved in drug use is an example of a negative influence.

ATTRIBUTION STYLES

Attribution style is the term for the characteristic way an individual interprets the causes of his or her behaviors, successes, and failures, as well as the behaviors, successes, and failures of other people. We tend to take credit for our successes and good behavior, and we blame others or situational variables for our mistakes and failures. However, we don't always extend that consideration to others. When other people make mistakes, we tend to hold them completely responsible and discount any situational variables that may have influenced them. (This is the **false attribution error** discussed earlier.)

Bernard Weiner proposed an attribution theory of motivation which relates attribution style to the achievement motivation model originated by **Richard DeCharms**. He distinguished four causes to which people attribute success and failure: effort, ability, task difficulty, and luck.

- People with an **internal locus of control** will consistently attribute success and failure to effort and ability. Examples: "I succeeded because I tried hard." "I failed because I didn't have the ability."
- People with an **external locus of control** will consistently attribute success and failure to luck and task difficulty. Examples: "I succeeded only because I was just lucky." "I failed because it was just too hard."

Children with an internal locus of control have higher academic achievement than those with an external locus of control. It is particularly problematic when children have a very stable external locus of control. These children have developed the perception that no matter how much effort they put into a task, they are helpless to control the outcome. Studying for a test and working harder in school are behaviors that such children perceive as useless. It is equally problematic when children have a stable internal locus of control, but perceive themselves as lacking in ability.

The development of one's orientation toward achievement motivation is influenced by childrearing practices and values in the home. If parents give their children responsibilities, stress independence, and praise them for genuine accomplishments, their children are more likely to have an **internal locus of control** and **high achievement motivation**. Children's achievement motivation is positively affected by experiences that bring a feeling of mastery. Children with a mastery orientation thrive on challenges and tend to stick with difficult tasks. They have feelings of pride and competence.

The opposite orientation is the **external locus of control** or **learned helplessness** orientation. Children of parents who set very high standards for their achievement, but at the same time communicate to them that they are not capable of achieving those standards, show signs of learned helplessness. Learned helplessness is a syndrome first noted by **Martin Seligman**. Seligman placed animals in an experimental chamber from which they could not escape. Animals who received electric shocks through the floor of the chamber first tried to escape but they eventually stopped trying. Even when an escape route became available to them, they could not learn to escape. Parents who communicate high standards but have little confidence in the children's abilities produce children who avoid challenges and do not try to succeed.

There are also cultural factors in this regard. People raised in a collectivist culture tend to have an external locus of control—seeing little that is, or even should be, within their personal control. People raised in an individualistic culture tend to have an internal locus of control—seeing that personal opportunity is available everywhere and at all times.

CHAPTER 13

SCHOOLING, WORK, AND INTERVENTIONS

This chapter covers the settings, institutions, and programs that most individuals experience throughout their life span. These include care facilities for young and old, formal schooling, and work environments. Special programs to help those who are disadvantaged will also be discussed.

Professionals in these settings have established a variety of practices to maximize the success of those they serve and employ. Those practices are grounded in theories that were discussed in previous chapters. You can consider this chapter as an overview of how developmental theories are applied every day in our society.

DAY CARE

There are day care facilities for both infants and toddlers. For most, it will be their first extended exposure to adults and peers outside their families. Day care is considered "high quality" if

- there is a good ratio of children to supervising adults (as determined by state law).
- there are plenty of interaction times of children with children, and children with adults.
- there are age-appropriate activities that stimulate body and mind.

Research shows that day care can boost children's social skills in areas of cooperation, confidence, and perspective-taking. These children have a boost in vocabulary. They may score higher on tests of intelligence than children who do not attend day care, but the non-day-care children usually catch up once they enter kindergarten and elementary school.

Conversely, day care can also boost children's aggressive tendencies. They may be more noncompliant, i.e., less likely to carry out an adult's request. Some have suggested that this is because day-care children have learned to think for themselves, not that it is a symptom of maladjustment. There is a slight tendency for day-care children to be classified as insecurely attached.

PRESCHOOL

Preschool attendance is usually limited to those children who have been toilet trained. A preschool is expected to have a learning curriculum, which sets it apart from day care. Curricular areas include:

- social and emotional skills
- language and pre-literacy skills
- quantitative and pre-math skills
- motor skills and physical dexterity skills
- self-help skills

Preschools that overemphasize academics do not always have the expected results. Children from these programs may experience a temporary advantage in achievement when they start kindergarten, but they do not maintain these gains over children who did not attend preschool. They can actually have lower **achievement motivation** and have more negative feelings about school. The best preschool programs balance play and academics. Preschool programs are particularly beneficial to children from impoverished backgrounds.

APPLICATIONS OF COGNITIVE DEVELOPMENTAL PRINCIPLES IN SCHOOL

Applications of Piaget and Vygotsky

Most modern schools of education train teachers in Piagetian principles of learning. This means providing a full understanding of cognitive stages and constructivism. Teachers in training also learn about applying the other theories of cognitive development, such as Vygotsky's learning principles and information processing. (See Chapter 7: Cognitive Development throughout the Life Span.) With knowledge of these theories and how they can be applied, teachers can teach in ways that relate to how learners learn.

Recall that Piagetian theory describes cognitive development in discrete and predictable stages that move from simple to complex, from concrete to abstract. Piaget believed that cognitive development could not be speeded up, but subsequent research has shown that given familiar materials to interact with, children can reason at higher levels than what Piaget predicted.

Also recall that Piaget advocated constructivist learning. He observed children being in a constant process of creating and refining schemata to better understand how the world works. In other words, children are in a continuous process of constructing their personal understanding. Thus, constructivism should be "discovery learning" —active, hands-on exploration and experimentation. This works exceedingly well with preschoolers and young elementary students, who are in the preoperations stage and learn best by manipulating concrete objects. But constructivism works well with older elementary students and teens, with the concrete slowly being replaced by abstract principles in math, science, literature, and social studies.

Teachers also incorporate Vygotskian principles in their practice. By analyzing students' struggles and errors, teachers can determine their zone of proximal development during a series of lessons on a skill or concept. They can then scaffold learning tasks to help students, using examples and opportunities to engage learners in extended dialogue. Recall that Vygotsky advocated conversational interactions with adults as a key component in cognitive development. Teachers encourage children's cognitive development when they reveal their own complex ways of thinking and solving problems to students. Vygotsky also would predict more effective learning takes place when tasks are presented in a natural context.

Achievement Motivation

In middle childhood, many essential skills and concepts are taught in the classroom. So the study of achievement motivation has become important to educators, because if children are motivated to learn, their confidence about learning is boosted. And when children feel competent and confident, they have high self-efficacy, which means they will be willing to take on new challenges. (See Chapter 11: Family, Home, and Society throughout the Life Span.)

Two achievement orientations have been identified from research in child development by **Martin Seligman** and **Carol Dweck**. These are **mastery orientation** and the **learned helplessness orientation**. (See Chapter 12: Personality and Emotion.) Mastery orientation is attributing successes to one's own ability and effort—an internal locus of control attribution style. On the other hand, a learned helplessness orientation (an external locus of control attribution style) causes children to avoid challenges because of the perception that no matter what they do, they likely will not succeed.

In the previous chapter, there was discussion of how parents can foster their children's mastery orientation. In school settings, children need to have experiences with success and the associated feeling of mastery to develop a mastery orientation. Teachers help develop mastery orientation in children in these ways:

- They provide opportunities for children to succeed in moderately challenging tasks.
- They communicate confidence in each child's competence and ability by appealing to their intrinsic motivation, rather than using praise or rewards. For instance, a teacher might say, "Keep up your efforts and you'll succeed."
- They help children correctly interpret the results of their attempts so that they can have a realistic view of their growing abilities. This also helps children see how effort relates to having control over success.
- They lessen anxiety when necessary while children are learning or being tested. Achievement is not possible when anxiety levels are high, although moderate amounts of anxiety will not hamper achievement.

Information Processing

Recall that information-processing theory attempts to describe how learners learn, based on a computer metaphor of input, processing, storage, and retrieval. Information processing begins by determining the processing demands of a cognitive challenge or problem to solve. The study of information processing includes detailed task-analysis of how the brain changes external stimuli or events into retrievable knowledge, and how strategies can make the process efficient and effective. This is similar to the way a computer programmer writes code so a computer will perform a function or the way a computer user creates files and documents. Thus, information-processing theory focuses on finding the best ways to arrive at a solution or to remember information.

Information-processing theory is of interest to educators because it holds promise that effective performance can be facilitated through direct instruction and training. In other words, efficient thinking procedures can be taught. **Sternberg** urged teachers to identify the mental processes that academic tasks require and to teach learners those processes. He challenged teachers to teach learners what processes to use, when and how to use them, and how to combine them into strategies for solving problems and accomplishing assignments.

Here are some examples of learning strategies that teachers might train their students to use to maximize encoding, storage, and retrieval of information:

- effective note-taking
- memory devices, such as mnemonics (e.g., HOMES to remember the names of each of the Great Lakes)
- visual mapping (mind-mapping) of related concepts and vocabulary terms
- chunking of long strings of items
- setting and using criteria for analyzing and evaluating an event or argument

A teacher who wishes to follow Sternberg's advice might also use backward planning prior to teaching. She would begin by identifying instructional objectives, that is, what students should be able to know or do at the end of instruction. Second, she would create an assessment that would measure the degree of achievement of those objectives at the end of instruction. Third, she would create tasks or activities that would prepare students for the objective-based assessment. Those activities would need to include necessary information as well as information-processing strategies for collecting, analyzing, and storing the information for later retrieval.

After following these three steps of identifying instructional objectives, preparing an assessment on the objectives, and preparing activities based on objectives, the teacher might conduct a pre-assessment (or pretest) to determine what students already know about the topic. Instruction would then be based on the results of the pre-assessment, with the teacher focusing on teaching the information students do not yet know, as well as the cognitive skills needed in order for students to process the new information. Following instruction, the teacher would administer the final assessment (or post-test) to evaluate the results of instruction. Further instruction would be based on the results of the post-assessment, based on whether students had achieved the expected outcomes on the instructional objectives.

Regardless of whether teachers follow all these steps for every lesson, it is helpful for them to consider if they are structuring their classrooms to satisfy learners' needs. Furthermore, if teachers' goals are to increase learners' knowledge and skill acquisition, then they will engage continuously in a process of self-examination and self-evaluation of their strategies.

Bear in mind that constructivism and discovery learning seem to be in opposition to information-processing principles of direct instruction. Often constructivism is associated with early childhood education, while direct instruction is associated with late childhood and adolescent education. This is an oversimplification, since there are times when each age group can benefit from both of those methods. Sometimes young children need direct instruction, and sometimes older learners gain valuable skills from open research and experimentation.

APPLICATION OF OPERANT CONDITIONING IN SCHOOLS

Skinner's operant conditioning principles have many applications to life in the classroom, especially in the area of behavior management. An intervention strategy called **behavior modification** was derived from Skinner's theory. Behavior modification is the use of reinforcement to shape behavior. Some effective classroom management strategies flow from this approach:

- Teachers are more effective at controlling classroom behavior if they consistently reinforce students for good behavior.
- In early school years, when a teacher praises or rewards a student's behavior, it causes a "ripple effect" as other students quickly imitate what that praised student was doing. (This could also be considered an example of observational learning.)
- Setting up a "token economy" can help establish good motivation regarding behavior and school work. This can take the form of rewarding students individually or as a group to earn tangible prizes or privileges for appropriate behavior.
- Initially, unwanted behavior should be ignored, because it takes away attention (reinforcement) from the child who is exhibiting that behavior. If the behavior is repeated and disruptive, other strategies must be used.
- Punishment for unwanted behavior should include removing the child from the setting to prevent peers from reinforcing or imitating the behavior. **Time out** is an effective strategy for this, as well as taking away a privilege that others have.
- Punishment in the form of physical or verbal abuse is not effective and creates a negative classroom atmosphere.

- Punishment is most effective when it is done without anger and "teaches" something about the unwanted behavior, such as making a child apologize and clean up after a tantrum. This is the idea behind **restorative justice** rather than traditional punishment.

LEARNING STYLES

Psychologists have observed that people have different, preferred ways of processing new information. Their theory is that if information is processed through these preferred channels, learning is more successful. Three **learning styles** have been identified:

- Visual—learns through pictures, graphs, shapes, text
- Auditory—learns through listening, rhythm, singing
- Tactile/Kinesthetic—learns through manipulating objects, body movement, rhythm

Teachers have been encouraged to assess students' learning styles and then develop instructional strategies to match their styles. However, it is difficult to tailor instruction to each student's learning style in a classroom with 20 or more students. An alternative and more reasonable approach is for teachers to present material in different ways (multimodal) to accommodate all learning styles during instruction. In practice, this means that a teacher would employ visual, auditory, and tactile/kinesthetic activities when teaching each topic or skill.

Learning styles theory is still controversial. There is evidence that a child's learning style may change over time or depend on the task being learned. For instance, a child might be a visual learner when reading comprehension is needed, but a tactile learner when math concepts are being learned. Also, there is logic in forcing students to use non-preferred styles at times, since they need to learn how to be adaptable. Still, teachers do well to make learning experiences multimodal so that all students have equal and varied chances to gain mastery of concepts and skills.

INTERVENTION PROGRAMS AND SERVICES

Childhood intervention programs have been developed by the federal government and by private educational agencies and foundations. They were set up on the supposition that intelligence is strongly influenced by environment, so people in economic stress are at an academic disadvantage. The best known of these intervention programs is **Project Head Start**. In accordance with the theory of environmental influence, underprivileged children who were getting ready to enter first grade—about 5 years old—were given experience with toys, books, and games that most middle-class children were familiar with. It began as a summer program and lasted 8 weeks. It was not completely successful.

The new philosophy of Head Start makes the program an ongoing preschool experience. Notably, it involves the mothers, who are taught how to be effective teachers and nutritionists at home. This has been successful in getting low-income children ready for elementary grade learning. Children's IQ scores rise, thus lessening the disparity in group IQs when compared to affluent students in elementary grades. Moreover, there is a secondary benefit to this kind of intervention. When a mother is involved as the teacher, her self-esteem is raised, her cooperation increases, she becomes closer to her child, and she can spread her learning to other mothers in the area.

Other early childhood interventions are now available in most cities and neighborhoods. Parents can have their child screened for disabilities, autism, attention deficit disorder (ADD), and overall school readiness as preparation for kindergarten or first grade. Once a child is in school, various federally mandated programs are often available. Title I is the best known of these. Children and schools that qualify for Title I funds receive academic and nutritional support. There are also programs for children to receive academic support for learning disabilities, regardless of economic status.

Later in the school career, or during early adulthood, job training programs are available for students with cognitive or physical disabilities. These are usually conducted by non-profit organizations that are subsidized by federal and charitable funds.

OCCUPATIONAL DEVELOPMENT

Eli Ginzberg suggested that career choice develops over a three-stage process. The first phase is the **fantasy phase** in which young children talk of career goals like becoming a firefighter or a doctor. During elementary grades, children are exposed to "career awareness" in one form or another. Guest speakers often come to schools to talk about their professions and careers.

In adolescence, one aspect of identity formation centers on a career identity. It is often difficult and stressful for an adolescent or young adult to decide on a career. Teens will consider a career but start to calculate their perceived aptitude as well as the likelihood of getting a job in that career. This is Ginzberg's **tentative phase**. Adolescents can explore the match between their personalities and abilities and different careers using the model developed by **John Holland.** His research found a relationship between personality traits and characteristics of different occupations. Based on this research, he developed a system to match personality types with occupational types. This sort of testing is administered by high school guidance counselors, although teens can probably find similar resources online. (For details on Holland's system, see Chapter 12: Personality and Emotions.)

In middle and high schools, **tracking** is used to place students in different levels of academic rigor. Higher-tracked students are encouraged to take college preparatory classes, while lower-tracked students are given less rigorous academics with more emphasis on basic academic and life skills. This practice has raised some controversy, especially when students are tracked at a relatively early age or by a single aptitude test score. It also can prevent some college-bound students from learning practical skills that are taught to lower tracks. But the practice has benefits, such as when some high school students can earn credits for classes in trade-related careers, such as automobile repair or electrical wiring, or when others can take advanced placement or even college credit exams or courses.

The final phase in Ginzberg's theory on career choice is the **realistic phase**. Between the ages of 18 and 22, adolescents/young adults select the career or a few career options that they want to pursue. Young adults often enter careers as interns or in entry-level positions. This gives them opportunity to learn necessary work skills under experienced supervisors. It also gives them opportunity to learn necessary social skills for the workplace.

It should be noted that many men and women are still making decisions about their careers or changing careers in their mid-30s or even later. Career counselors understand career development as a life-long process. Research shows that most people will change jobs numerous times and/or pursue different careers in adulthood. They emphasize the need for extensive career exploration in adolescence and young adulthood and encourage individuals to intentionally plan the entire course of their careers. This might not be possible in all cases, since new technologies create new careers that could not have been anticipated.

Middle adults can advance to become supervisors and mentors of entry-level workers. They have experience and expertise to share as they move up their own career ladder. On the other hand, middle adults sometimes feel the need to use their expertise to become entrepreneurs—in other words, become their own boss.

The Japanese concept of *ikigai* or "life value" fits here. According to the World Economic Forum, this concept defines the ideal working life as lying at the intersection of these four questions:

- What do you love?
- What are you good at?
- What does the world need from you?
- What can you get paid for?

This concept of working with purpose and passion can be an important source of motivation for young workers and a source of career reassessment later in a person's working life.

As working adults age, they find themselves at the peak of their careers. But they are also nearer the end of their working lives. They might use some of their time training ("grooming") younger workers to take their place. This happens in business and trades, and it also happens in education when experienced teachers mentor student teachers or first-year teachers.

FACILITATION OF ROLE TRANSITIONS

There are numerous small and large transitions in a person's life. At each juncture, it helps to have guidance from those who know the issues and challenges of the upcoming stage.

It is important to note that there is a difference between a person who guides people through a transition and a person who officiates at a ceremony for a transition. An officiate is a person authorized by a government and/or religion to hold a traditional ceremony, such as a wedding or funeral. In some places, a layperson who is authorized to do this is known as a celebrant.

A guide is someone who has experience and knowledge regarding a transition and can help another person make the transition through discussion, advice, or training. Examples are older friends and colleagues, service volunteers (e.g., retired executives), or paid experts (e.g., financial advisors). In some situations, an officiate can also act as a guide, such as when a member of the clergy holds counseling sessions with a couple before presiding over their wedding ceremony.

The following paragraphs examine some of the transitions that are common in our society, but which may not have any traditional associated ceremony.

Transition into Schooling

Parents and early grade teachers can help children make the transition from home or day care to formal schooling. Children need encouragement in social skills and impulse control, and they need to get used to concepts and practices such as routines and time management.

Transition into the Workforce

Young adults may not come into their first full-time job with all the skills they need. Human resource (HR) departments in businesses are somewhat responsible for getting new hires oriented, and experienced workers often train new workers in a trade. Besides the skills of the job itself, there is a need to develop and use skills in scheduling, in workplace ethics and interactions, and in personal finance. They might also need help finding a balance between work and social life or family.

Transition into Parenting Roles

Studies show that behaviors, positive and negative, are passed down through generations. Often, parents react to situations in the way their own parents responded. This is particularly threatening in the case of abusive or neglectful parenting behavior.

Today, it is commonly believed that the best way to end a cycle of poor parenting is through **parent training**. Parents are taught, through discussion and role play, how to deal successfully with routines and with stressful situations arising in the family. These situations vary from dealing with a crying baby to dealing with a rebellious teenager. Because parents' habitual response might have been learned vicariously through watching their own parents, adults need to be (re)trained in more appropriate methods of parenting. Parenting classes have proven effective for both male and female parents.

Transition into Retirement

As individuals come to the end of their working lives, they may face questions and challenges they had not considered or planned for. They might need to go to multiple sources for answers and guidance, since there is no formal training for the retirement years. Some of the common questions and challenges will be discussed in the next section.

RETIREMENT

Retirement, the final phase in career development, also should be a planned process. Planning for retirement, financially and otherwise, can increase the likelihood that a retired person will be satisfied during this phase of life. Retirement satisfaction is also related to having opportunities to engage in meaningful activities. Research shows that:

- If retirement is chosen rather than forced, individuals tend to be more prepared.
- Retirees need to make decisions about how to spend their retirement based on factors such as health, finances, and outside interests.
- Retirees can benefit from participating in hobbies and avocations, in educational opportunities, in volunteering, or in activism.
- Retirees can benefit from downsizing—moving from a large home to a smaller one. This can free the retiree from financial burdens and contribute to health and safety. For instance, leaving a two-story home for a one-story home can help with possible future mobility issues.

ELDER CARE

Elder care has become a large issue (and industry) in our society. Life spans are longer than in previous generations, so this creates a larger cohort of elderly people. Older adults, possibly in consultation with their children, can consider various options regarding lifestyle:

- **Age in place**—Elderly people live in their own home, with occasional support from family and/or professionals.
- **Assisted living**—Elders live in a facility with a range of support services. Some will live in small apartments, while others will live in rooms with full meal service in a dining hall. There will be opportunities for exercise and recreation, depending on physical and cognitive ability.
- **Nursing home**—Elders live in custodial conditions, such as simple private rooms, with medical services available around the clock.

Elder abuse is a major concern during these years. Caretakers have been known to forge signatures, steal or trick people out of money, and commit physical and verbal abuse of the elderly. There are local and state agencies that are supposed to monitor elder care facilities, but it is usually up to families to monitor the situation of their elderly loved ones. It is also important for family members to monitor each other, since some elder abuse is committed by relatives.

CHAPTER 14

DEVELOPMENTAL PSYCHOPATHOLOGY

This chapter outlines the many ways that normal development can be thwarted. This can include physical illnesses and impairments, cognitive dysfunctions, and personality distortions caused by trauma or other factors. Some of these disorders can be treated or cured, while others are lifelong or life-threatening. But all are debilitating and harmful to natural growth and development.

CHRONIC ILLNESSES AND PHYSICAL DISABILITIES

Chronic illnesses can show up very early in life, while others appear later. Most have some genetic component, but other factors often come into play, such as lifestyle choices and socioeconomic status (SES). Once they appear, development is affected for long periods, or for the rest of the life span. Medical and/or physical interventions then become necessary, unless cures are found.

- **Asthma** is a condition in which bronchial airways become congested and inflamed. Breathing becomes difficult, thus limiting the ability to exert or participate in strenuous activity.
- **Arthritis** is a condition in which joints become stiff and painful, and sometimes swollen. Depending on which joints are affected, large and/or fine motor activities may be curtailed.
- **Diabetes** is a condition in which blood sugar remains high unless treated. Type I diabetes, known as childhood diabetes, is congenital. Type II diabetes, or adult-onset diabetes, is caused mostly by poor lifestyle choices in diet and exercise. Symptoms include frequent urination, increased thirst, and increased hunger. Left untreated, it can lead to complications that damage sight, kidney function, and cardiovascular function. Individuals with diabetes must constantly monitor their blood

sugar level and keep it balanced by dietary adjustments, with oral medications, or with injections of insulin.

- **Cardiovascular disease (CVD)** is a class of conditions in which there is damage to the heart and/or blood vessels. This can include angina (chest pains), heart arrhythmia, blood clots or aneurysms in arteries and veins, heart attack, or heart failure. CVD can be congenital, or it can be caused by smoking, obesity, diabetes, or a number of other conditions. Individuals with CVD must limit and monitor activity, exertion, and stress levels. Medical intervention can range from prescription drugs to surgeries.
- **Cancers** can develop in several body parts and organs. They have multiple causes, including smoking, obesity, lack of exercise, excessive alcohol use, infections, and pollutants (teratogens). Since malignant tumors are life-threatening and can spread to other areas of the body, cancer patients must devote much of their time and life energy to battling the disease. Treatments include chemotherapy and radiation therapy. Some patients turn to a variety of alternative treatments outside of the medical profession.

Physical disabilities can have various causes, depending on when or how the disability occurs. Disabilities require interventions such as surgeries, prosthetics, physical therapy, or just accommodations to function in the world.

- Prenatal causes: abnormal fetal development, teratogens (see Chapter 4: Biological Development throughout the Life Span)
- Perinatal causes: complications at birth, premature delivery
- Postnatal causes: accident, infection, disease

Types of Impairments

Visual impairment ranges from low vision to blindness. Children with visual impairments may appear to be unresponsive to caregivers as infants and have fewer facial expressions than other infants. They usually are developmentally delayed in their physical development in terms of both fine motor skills and gross motor skills.

Auditory impairment ranges from low hearing to deafness. Hearing impairments are caused by prenatal anoxia, exposure to Rubella, or hereditary conditions. Hearing impairments are often not diagnosed until the second year of life. Treatments for hearing impairments include hearing aids that amplify sound, or cochlear implants that activate the auditory nerve. Teaching children American Sign Language (ASL) is the best accommodation, and it should begin as early as possible. Like learning other languages, there is a sensitive period for learning ASL. The optimal treatment plan for children with hearing impairment may be to enable them to communicate with the hearing community through lip-reading or hearing devices and with the non-hearing community through ASL.

Speech impairment can be caused by a hearing impairment. It can also be caused by malformations such as a cleft palate or neurological damage. Speech therapy is recommended in childhood.

Motor impairment includes physical defects and organ or structural abnormalities. Motor disabilities can be caused by injury, congenital disease, or inherited diseases such as muscular dystrophy.

Children with impairments are often rejected or isolated by peers. They may be teased or avoided. However, many can overcome these hardships and develop normal social relationships. Families of children with disabilities have added stress. How families cope with this stress influences the child's adjustment as well as the family's well-being. Families who use problem-focused coping fare much better than those who resort to emotion-focused coping. Problem-focused coping means working to define the source of the stress, and then generating solutions to those problems. Emotion-focused coping means focusing on feelings and emotions, avoiding the actual problem or source of stress, and does not involve any active steps in finding a solution to the problem.

Federal law requires that children with impairments be mainstreamed into public schools as much as possible. The **Americans with Disabilities Act (ADA)** is intended to prevent discrimination against children with disabilities and to provide them with an educational experience comparable to their non-impaired peers. However, depending on the degree of impairment, some children benefit from specialized resource rooms staffed with teachers who have specialized training. Others benefit from "mainstreaming" in regular classrooms, although many require one-on-one aides to accommodate their learning needs. Special schools for disabled children provide an alternative to public schools.

Note: The following disabilities and disorders are part of the compendium known as the **Diagnostic and Statistical Manual of Mental Disorders (DSM)** published and periodically updated by the American Psychiatric Association (APA). DSM-5 was published in 2013.

INTELLECTUAL DISABILITY

Two extremes of intellectual performance are exhibited on the far left and far right of the normal distribution (bell curve) for intelligence. Extremes of the far right are discussed in Chapter 8, on Intelligence, particularly in the topic of **giftedness**. In this chapter, attention will be paid to extremes on the left, or lower, side of the distribution curve for intelligence.

To be classified as having an **intellectual disability** (formerly called mental retardation), an individual must meet all three of the essential features described below:

1. Intellectual functioning must be significantly below average. Intelligence test scores below 70—or two standard deviations below the mean—are considered significantly below average.
2. Significant deficits in adaptive functioning must be evident. Adaptive functioning refers to social competence or independent behavior that is expected based on chronological age.
3. Onset must be prior to age 18—demonstrating delays in motor skills, delays in speech, and/or self-help difficulties.

Four general categories or ways of classifying intellectual disability include the following:

Severity Levels of Intellectual Disability

Category	Percentage	IQ range	Characteristics
Mild	80 percent	50 – 70	May complete sixth grade academic work; may learn vocational skills and hold a job; may live independently as an adult.
Moderate	12 percent	35 – 49	May complete second grade academic work; can learn social and occupational skills; may hold a job in a sheltered workshop.
Severe	7 percent	20 – 34	May learn to talk or communicate; through repetition, may learn basic health habits; often needs help for simple tasks.
Profound	1 percent	less than 20	Little or no speech; may learn limited self-help skills; requires constant help and supervision.

There are hundreds of known causes of intellectual disability. Many of them are biological, genetic, chromosomal, prenatal, perinatal, or postnatal in origin. Intellectual disability can also result from environmental influences, such as sensory or maternal deprivation. In some cases (especially in the case of mild intellectual disability), the cause of an individual child's intellectual disability is unknown. **Behavior modification** techniques have been used successfully to teach simple tasks to severely or profoundly impaired children.

COGNITIVE DISORDERS INCLUDING DEMENTIA

Cognitive disorders (re-labeled neurocognitive disorders in DSM-5) can be caused by factors or events in the womb or after birth by brain injury. These disorders can affect any number of cognitive functions, such as perception, memory processing, language, and problem solving. Perceptual disability (especially dyslexia) will be discussed in another section of this chapter. The most common cognitive disorders will be discussed here.

There are cognitive disorders that appear in older adults that have common characteristics. These are collectively referred to as **dementia**. Dementia is a progressive loss of cognitive functioning, including declining intelligence, impaired memory, poor judgment, disorientation, and personality changes. The disease eventually causes death or leads to death from health complications. Dementia symptoms can be temporary if they are caused by agents such as drug interactions. It is important not to misdiagnose reversible dementia as Alzheimer's or multi-infarct dementia. Furthermore, dementia is not an inevitable part of growing old, as many mistakenly believe. These are diseases, not the product of aging. Approximately only 5 percent of people who are 65 or older have dementia. This rate does increase to 16 percent in those people 85 and older.

The two irreversible dementia disorders are Alzheimer's disease and multi-infarct dementia. **Multi-infarct dementia** is caused by a series of strokes that reduce blood flow and hence oxygen to the brain. Its progression involves sudden noticeable declines in functioning rather than the slow and steady progression of Alzheimer's disease.

Alzheimer's disease is the most prevalent of the dementias. The DSM-5 re-labels this as a major neurocognitive disorder, while other forms of dementia are labeled either mild or major neurocognitive disorders, depending on how severely a person's functioning is affected. Alzheimer's can begin as early as middle adulthood, and some people can live 10 or more years after their diagnosis. The rate of diagnosis increases with age. As the disease progresses, individuals lose not just memory of time and events, but also suffer the loss of self-identity and recognition of relationships. They will lose the ability to name objects and their functions. They may have bouts of anger, and they might wander off away from their home or care facility if not monitored carefully.

The brains of patients with Alzheimer's disease have distinctive **neurofibrillary tangles**, which are twisted neural fibers, and senile **plaques,** which are deposits of amyloid protein. Since Alzheimer's disease has different ages of onset and the progression of symptoms varies somewhat, it may be that this is not one disease, but a collection of related diseases.

It is difficult to point to a single cause of Alzheimer's disease. Some research suggests a link to Down's syndrome, as people with Down's syndrome reliably develop Alzheimer's in adulthood. Geneticists have found a gene on the 21st chromosome that is common in members of families who have high rates of Alzheimer's disease. Other theories suggest that a virus that lies dormant for most of one's life causes the disease, or that it is caused by an immune system response that attacks the brain. Finally, since the distinctive symptom is cognitive impairment, researchers suggest that the disease is caused by a deficit in a necessary neurotransmitter, the chemical that causes neural impulses to travel across synapses through brain circuits. New drug and physical activity interventions have been shown to slow the disease's progression and even improve patients' cognitive functioning.

TRAUMA-BASED SYNDROMES

Psychological trauma can be triggered by personal or environmental events. Victims of natural disasters can develop trauma, as well as victims of abuse, hate, and violence.

Post-traumatic stress disorder (PTSD) is characterized by a variety of symptoms in four areas:

- re-experiencing a traumatic event in nightmares or waking flashbacks
- avoiding social situations or thoughts that remind a person of a trauma
- reactivity, e.g., being easily startled or "on edge" or having difficulty sleeping
- cognitive and mood symptoms, e.g., depression, helplessness, or survivor's guilt.

PTSD is seen in people who have experienced violence or war as a combatant or as a civilian, and those who have experienced sexual abuse. About one-third of victims of child sexual abuse develop PTSD.

Dissociative disorders are extreme reactions to trauma and stress. These disorders are characterized by a loss of contact with portions of consciousness or memory, resulting in disruptions in one's sense of self. They appear to be an attempt to overcome anxiety and stress by dissociating oneself from the core of one's personality, resulting in a loss of memory, identity, or consciousness.

The major dissociative disorders are **associative identity disorder** (formerly termed multiple personality disorder) and **dissociative amnesia** with or without fugue (wandering away).

Somatic symptom and related disorders can also fit in this discussion. These disorders are characterized by complaints of physical symptoms in the absence of any diagnosed physical illness. They are slightly more common in women than in men. **Conversion disorder** can be produced by trauma or high anxiety. Its symptoms can include blindness, numbness, or paralysis, with no physiological explanation. **Hypochondriasis** (although no longer labeled as such in the DSM-5) has traditionally been considered another somatic symptom disorder, with patients complaining of pains or dysfunctions of the heart or gastrointestinal tract. Unfortunately, this diagnosis has often been given just because physicians could not find a cause, rather than because there was no cause. Therefore, it is difficult to tell how pervasive this condition is, and it might explain why it has lost its distinctive DSM label.

AUTISM SPECTRUM DISORDERS

Autism spectrum disorders are developmental disorders that are characterized by aberrant social development and language development, as well as repetitive nonproductive behaviors. Autistic individuals vary in the severity of their symptoms along a continuum. An autistic person does not seek social interactions and will not respond very much to people. This individual will likely not make eye contact and will not recognize social cues or body language in others. Some either do not speak, or use disordered language. Their speech may be highly repetitive.

Autistic children need consistency and may be very upset by change. They show an obsessive attachment to chosen objects or an obsessive interest in a single topic. They seem to be calmed by repetitive behavior such as rocking. Behavior modification programs that use conditioning techniques have been successful in teaching language and social skills to autistic children. Intervention programs begun early have been found to have very good outcomes, particularly when parents are involved in the training program. As autistic children enter adolescence and young adulthood, they can have a better self-awareness of their condition, their symptoms, and their need to follow procedures they have learned for social interactions.

Researchers hypothesize that autism is caused by a disturbance in executive function in the prefrontal cortex that integrates information. Another hypothesis is that autistic individuals have damaged brain stems. The brain stem controls the ability to direct attention. Recent research suggests a genetic cause for autism spectrum disorders. Many, but not all, autistic individuals have been found to have a specific gene called HOXA1. Identical twins' concordance rates for autism are around 92 percent, meaning that, most often, if one twin has autism, so does the other. The concordance rate for fraternal twins is only about 10 percent.

ATTENTION DEFICIT/HYPERACTIVITY DISORDER

Children diagnosed with **attention deficit/hyperactivity disorder (ADHD)** have one or a combination of three characteristic symptoms:

- inattention or distractibility
- impulsive and often undesired behavior
- inability to remain still without fidgeting or moving (hyperactivity)

Boys are diagnosed with ADHD three times more often than girls consistently throughout the world. Girls tend to have the symptom of inattention, but not hyperactivity or impulsivity. Males with ADHD are sometimes also diagnosed with a conduct disorder, since their symptoms tend to be disruptive to family and classroom life. Most children with ADHD have social and academic difficulties and may continue to have attention difficulties throughout their life.

In our society, many children diagnosed with ADHD take stimulant medication to control their symptoms. (Stimulants act as mood/behavior suppressors in childhood, then become mood/behavior activators starting in adolescence.) Studies have found that a combination of medication and behavioral therapy to teach children and parents how to control the symptoms yields the best treatment outcomes.

The causes of ADHD appear to involve both nature and nurture. Identical twins have a high concordance rate: If one twin has ADHD, the other twin also tends to have it, suggesting a genetic factor. However, low birth weight, prenatal exposure to nicotine, and several family risk factors have also been identified as potential causes of ADHD.

LEARNING DISABILITIES

Learning disabilities are diagnosed in children whose performance in school is significantly different from their assessed level of competence. Learning disabilities occur in the areas of reading and language, math, and writing. Learning disabilities are believed to be caused by brain processing deficits.

Dyslexia is one of these disorders. Some dyslexics have trouble discriminating speech sounds. Phonics-based intervention programs that provide practice in sound discriminations produce improvements in this ability. Other dyslexics have a visual discrimination problem and have difficulty distinguishing letters that are similar in appearance, or they read words backwards. Still others perceive numbers and letters backward or "swimming around" such that they have difficulty distinguishing the correct order of letters in a word or numbers in a sequence. With all these symptoms and difficulties, it is understandable that emotional, social, and behavioral difficulties can develop in those with learning disabilities.

Because these all seem to be brain "wiring" problems, there is no cure for learning disabilities. Instead, individuals must learn or figure out coping and compensating strategies for their particular difficulties. One strategy that has been tested is the use of special text fonts that make it easier for dyslexics to distinguish letters, words, and numbers on a page or screen.

ASOCIAL BEHAVIOR, PHOBIAS, AND OBSESSIONS

Individuals who exhibit **asocial behavior** can be placed on a range or spectrum of not being willing or able to relate to others. Mild asocial behavior takes the form of **introversion**, which reveals itself in a person's enjoyment of solitude. This person does not feel lonely, but rather prefers his or her own mental activity over the company of others. An extreme type of asocial behavior is found in **schizophrenia**, a psychosis in which the individual is completely caught up in delusional thinking. There will likely be auditory and/or visual hallucinations as well. This person is not able to relate to others consistently (if at all) in real-world conversation or activity.

In between mild and extreme asocial behavior, there are **personality disorders** that make it difficult for a person to relate to others in conventional ways.

- Some individuals might avoid social contact and feel uncomfortable when they are in social settings. To others, they may appear "cold" or aloof.
- Some have odd behaviors and "act weird" and either shun social contact or are avoided by others.
- Some have wild mood swings and self-image problems that others have trouble dealing with.
- Some might constantly seek attention or approval or admiration (narcissism).

Phobias are irrational fears that overwhelm an individual, causing dysfunction in normal living. Phobias can cause panic attacks, as with agoraphobia (fear of public spaces). Some phobias can cause fainting, as with blood phobia. Phobias usually begin in middle childhood or adolescence. They are more prevalent in females.

Obsessions are often accompanied by **compulsions**—giving rise to the term **obsessive-compulsive disorder (OCD)**. Think of it this way: Obsessive thoughts lead to compulsive behaviors. For example, a person thinks "I am germ-ridden!" which leads to excessive hand-washing. Or a person thinks "I am being watched!" and this leads to constantly checking doors and windows throughout the day and night.

ANTISOCIAL BEHAVIOR

Aggression, vandalism, racism, sexism, and criminal behavior or delinquency are examples of **antisocial behavior**. According to **Kenneth Dodge**'s social-information processing model, aggressive children and adolescents show deficits in how they process information. They tend to misinterpret other people's motives and actions, and thus they respond inappropriately. Very aggressive youth tend to assume hostile intent from others even when there is little information to support that conclusion. They set a goal of "getting even" with another person rather than resolving conflict, and they have a bias toward selecting aggressive responses rather than non-aggressive alternatives.

Oppositional defiant disorder (ODD) is a particularly difficult set of problems. Individuals with this condition are often angry and resentful, argumentative, and defiant of rules and authority. They will blame other people or outside forces for their difficulties with others, which justifies their behavior in their own eyes.

Intermittent explosive disorder is the label for those who have occasional and sudden eruptions of anger and aggression. They may be irritable a great deal of the time, with their angry outbursts coming on suddenly.

Antisocial personality disorder (sociopathy) is the label given for those who consistently disregard the rights and feelings of others. They do not show guilt or remorse when confronted with their actions. They may be impulsive, arrogant, or callous. They can be very charming with the intent of manipulating others.

Highly aggressive children tend to be rejected by their peers and have difficulties in school. This in turn tends to cause them to drop out of school, which puts them at risk for further antisocial behavior. Research has shown that delinquent and violent youth tend to come from home environments where parents use coercive means to get obedience and compliance. In these situations, parents and children are often locked in a power struggle.

ANXIETY AND MOOD DISORDERS

Anxiety Disorders

Anxiety disorders are characterized by intense feelings of worry, dread, and expectations of bad things happening. Nearly 20 percent of adults in this country are affected by anxiety disorders. (That percentage is higher for women, lower for men.) Different types of anxieties have been identified:

- existential/crisis anxiety
- performance/test anxiety
- social/stranger anxiety
- choice/decision anxiety

Along with the emotional component, anxiety also has physical symptoms. Individuals might feel muscle tightness and/or fatigue.

Eating disorders will be discussed here, although they are not put in the anxiety disorders category in the DSM-5. **Anorexia nervosa** and **bulimia nervosa** are two eating disorders that are most prevalently found in adolescent females. Anorexia nervosa is characterized by refusal to maintain at least 85 percent of one's expected body weight, a fear of gaining weight, and a distorted body image. About 1 percent of adolescent females have anorexia. This eating disorder is very serious and can be fatal.

Bulimia nervosa is characterized by binge/purge cycles. Bulimics consume a large amount of food and then purge with laxatives or by vomiting. This is also a serious and life-threatening disorder and is found in about 5 percent of female college students. Bulimics also have an extreme fear of being fat and a strong drive for thinness.

The causal mechanism for eating disorders is complicated. There is some evidence for a genetic factor but it may not be expressed unless there are environmental triggers. These triggers may include difficulty dealing with the stresses and physical changes of adolescence, living in a culture that values thinness, emotional or sexual abuse, perfectionism, low self-esteem, self-directed anger, and having overprotective parents.

The DSM has added a new disorder that affects older children and teens. This is **non-suicidal self-injury** (NSSI), commonly known as **cutting**. Individuals with this condition will cut, stab, or bruise themselves, but without intent of serious harm. It is associated with feelings of depression, anxiety, tension, anger, generalized distress, and self-criticism. Little research has been done on this condition, since previously it was considered to be related to attempted suicide. Professionals now consider it a distinct disorder, where individuals feel temporary relief from anxieties by inflicting wounds on themselves. Many young people grow out of this, but others get so deeply entrenched in the behavior that therapy is necessary.

Mood Disorders

Mood disorders (or **affective disorders**) involve moods or emotions that are extreme, unwarranted, and long-lasting. These emotional disturbances are strong enough to intrude on everyday living. The most serious types of mood disorders are major depression and bipolar disorders.

Major depression is characterized by feelings of sadness and/or rejection, excessive or disruptive sleep, comfort eating, and feelings of worthlessness, failure, or hopelessness. This is not the same as having occasional or periodic "blue" moods. This diagnosis is given when symptoms are long-lasting and extreme. Thoughts of suicide might arise, so the individual needs medical and psychological interventions.

Bipolar disorder is characterized by a recurring cycle of high energy and elevated mood followed by low energy and depressed mood. This condition can be a sign of brain chemistry dysfunction, or it might be caused by taking substances that elevate, then depress, a person's mood.

PRACTICE TEST 1

CLEP Human Growth and Development

This practice test is also offered online at the REA Study Center (*www.rea.com/studycenter*). Since all CLEP exams are administered on computer, we recommend that you take the online version of the test to simulate test-day conditions and receive these added benefits:

- **Timed testing conditions** — Gauge how much time you can spend on each question.
- **Automatic scoring** — Find out how you did on the test, instantly.
- **On-screen detailed explanations of answers** — Learn not just the correct answers, but also why the other answer choices are incorrect.
- **Diagnostic score reports** — Pinpoint where you're strongest and where you need to focus your study.

PRACTICE TEST 1

CLEP Human Growth and Development

(Answer sheet is on page 265.)

TIME: 90 Minutes
90 Questions

Directions: Each of the questions or incomplete statements below is followed by five possible answers or completions. Select the lettered choice that best answers each question and fill in the corresponding oval on the answer sheet.

1. Which theoretical perspective emphasizes nature in the "nature-versus-nurture" controversy?

   (A) Behavioral theory

   (B) Social learning theory

   (C) Social-cognitive theory

   (D) Psychodynamic theory

   (E) Sociocultural

2. Which theorist would be most likely to expect cultural differences in development?

   (A) Vygotsky

   (B) Piaget

   (C) Freud

   (D) Skinner

   (E) Bowlby

3. To determine whether boys and girls play differently, a researcher videotaped children at play during school recess. This is an example of a

   (A) field experiment

   (B) naturalistic observation

   (C) cross-sectional study

   (D) survey

   (E) clinical interview

4. The average child begins to walk between

   (A) 4 and 5 months

   (B) 7 and 8 months

   (C) 11 and 12 months

   (D) 13 and 14 months

   (E) 16 and 17 months

5. According to Piaget, adaptation is made up of the two processes called

   (A) equilibration and accommodation

   (B) accommodation and fixation

   (C) equilibration and assimilation

   (D) operation and conservation

   (E) accommodation and assimilation

6. The fact that parents will provide less direction to a child who begins to show competence on a task, supports the theory of

   (A) Bronfenbrenner

   (B) Freud

   (C) Piaget

   (D) Vygotsky

   (E) Bandura

7. According to the information-processing approach, children's memories improve with age mainly because

   (A) they get better at organizing information

   (B) they develop additional memory storage systems

   (C) their perceptual abilities improve

   (D) they are more interested in remembering information

   (E) parents expect older children to remember information better

8. Jane digs a hole in the sandbox while Jim, who is sitting next to her, fills his bucket with sand. They share the shovels in the sandbox and talk about school. They are engaged in

   (A) cooperative play

   (B) parallel play

   (C) mature play

   (D) nonsocial play

   (E) associative play

9. Which of the following research methods is most often used to study rare or unique situations or behavior?

   (A) Survey

   (B) Case study

   (C) Cross-sequential

   (D) Correlational

   (E) Psychosocial

10. Which of the following theories describes stages of development?

    (A) Collectivist

    (B) Continuity

    (C) Discontinuity

    (D) Nature

    (E) Nurture

11. Which of the following is an example of instrumental aggression?

 (A) Sara pushes Joy out of the way so she can get a toy she wants to play with first.

 (B) Sara tells Emma not to play with Joy because she bites.

 (C) Sara is mad at her brother. She hits her doll rather than him.

 (D) Sara yells at Emma because she knocked down her block tower.

 (E) Sara can't get the wrapper off a candy bar, so she throws it across the room.

12. According to statistics, which group commits most of the child abuse in our country?

 (A) Siblings

 (B) Day care workers

 (C) Foster parents

 (D) Parents

 (E) Stepparents

13. Which theoretical perspective assumes there is a bidirectional relationship between the person and the environment?

 (A) Behavioral

 (B) Learning

 (C) Biological

 (D) Sociocultural

 (E) Humanistic

14. A problem with longitudinal research is

 (A) confounding age difference with birth cohort differences

 (B) a lack of control over extraneous variables

 (C) subject dropout

 (D) subject bias

 (E) researcher bias

15. Students who have developed a mastery orientation would attribute a good grade on a test to their ability, and a bad grade on a test to

    (A) the teacher
    (B) their ability
    (C) bad luck
    (D) lack of effort
    (E) test bias

16. According to research, which of the following has shown a correlation with age, but is occasionally found in younger adults?

    (A) Insight
    (B) Metacognition
    (C) The executive process
    (D) Collectivism
    (E) Wisdom

17. Adolescent cliques and crowds differ in what ways?

    (A) Cliques are known by reputation; crowds are known by size.
    (B) Crowds are large and usually same-sex; cliques are small and co-ed.
    (C) Cliques are small and usually same-sex, while crowds are larger and co-ed.
    (D) Cliques are loosely organized; crowds enforce rigid rules.
    (E) Crowds are often rule-breakers, while cliques tend to be compliant with authority.

18. Which of the following indicates the presence of empathy?

    (A) Mollie starts to cry whenever she sees someone else cry.
    (B) Mollie sees Jake crying and gives him a toy to help him stop crying.
    (C) Mollie laughs when she sees something funny on television.
    (D) Mollie tells her Daddy when she doesn't feel well.
    (E) Mollie goes to her room to cry so no one sees her crying.

19. Among the parenting styles that have been studied by Baumrind, which of the following is associated with the most negative impact on development?

    (A) Authoritative

    (B) Authoritarian

    (C) Permissive

    (D) Strict

    (E) Uninvolved

20. Which of the following statements about physical growth is true?

    (A) Physical growth is rapid during infancy, slows during early and middle childhood, and then is rapid again during adolescence.

    (B) Physical growth is rapid from infancy to its completion in middle childhood.

    (C) Physical growth is rapid during infancy, and then is slow from early childhood through adolescence.

    (D) Physical growth is a steady process from infancy through childhood.

    (E) Physical growth mostly comes in "growth spurts" at unpredictable times.

21. Research on the growth hormone (GH) has shown that

    (A) children with normal thyroid function will grow to be taller than their genotype with injections of GH

    (B) children who do not have GH are likely to be intellectually disabled

    (C) children given early treatments of GH develop normally

    (D) children given GH treatments later can still catch up to their peers

    (E) vitamin C can simulate GH production in the body

22. Researchers have studied the impact of late versus early maturation on adolescents' adjustment. Which of the pairs below have been shown to have the best adjustment outcomes?

    (A) Early maturing boys and early maturing girls

    (B) Early maturing boys and late maturing girls

    (C) Late maturing boys and early maturing girls

    (D) Late maturing boys and late maturing girls

    (E) Adolescent adjustment is in fact NOT related to the timing of maturation.

23. One theory of biological aging suggests aging is inevitable and is caused by
    (A) carcinogens
    (B) teratogens
    (C) wear and tear from normal use
    (D) arteriosclerosis
    (E) genetic mutations

24. An effective treatment for the side effects of menopause is
    (A) antipsychotic medication
    (B) psychotropic medication
    (C) estrogen replacement therapy
    (D) testosterone replacement therapy
    (E) hysterectomy

25. Compared to women, the male climacteric is
    (A) a faster decline
    (B) a slower decline
    (C) unaffected by sex hormone levels in the body
    (D) associated with increased risk of heart disease
    (E) more uncommon

26. Osteoporosis is
    (A) a disease of the pancreas
    (B) a circulatory disease
    (C) a bone disease
    (D) a normal product of biological aging
    (E) an arterial disease caused by plaque buildup in the arteries

27. Janet's mother is terminally ill and the doctors have said her death is imminent. A hospital social worker has suggested to Janet that she contact the hospice program. The social worker most likely will tell Janet that hospice

    (A) would immediately stop her mother's pain medication

    (B) would persuade the doctors to keep her mother in the hospital where she can get the best medical care

    (C) would do everything possible to give her mother a pain-free death

    (D) would help Janet make the difficult euthanasia decision

    (E) would be at the hospital to establish brain death

28. Gibson's visual cliff experiment showed that

    (A) depth perception is innate

    (B) depth perception is learned

    (C) six-month-olds crawled across the visual cliff

    (D) six-month-olds did not crawl across the visual cliff

    (E) six-month-olds have an inborn fear response

29. Visual scanning experiments with infants suggest which pattern of looking?

    (A) Newborns actively scan a stimulus if it is black and white but not colored, but the opposite is true in older infants.

    (B) Newborns will actively scan a stimulus if it is colored but not black and white, but the opposite is true of older infants.

    (C) Newborns scan the edges of a stimulus, and older infants scan the center or inside of a stimulus.

    (D) Newborns do not have preferences for what they look at, but older infants do.

    (E) Newborns scan a stimulus quickly, older infants scan a stimulus more slowly.

30. When you see a German shepherd 100 yards away from you in a park, you don't think it is a miniature dog because of

    (A) Gestalt perception

    (B) shape constancy

    (C) lightness constancy

    (D) color constancy

    (E) size constancy

31. Which of the following is the LEAST developed in newborns?

    (A) Taste

    (B) Touch

    (C) Vision

    (D) Audition

    (E) Smell

32. When young infants look away from a familiar object and turn to a novel one, what cognitive process is being exhibited?

    (A) Executive function

    (B) Short-term memory

    (C) Metacognition

    (D) Habituation

    (E) Rehearsal

33. The type of hearing loss associated with aging is loss of sensitivity for

    (A) the human voice

    (B) low-frequency sounds

    (C) high-frequency sounds

    (D) rhythmic sounds

    (E) tympanic sounds

34. One reason older adults experience declining eyesight is
    (A) decreased flexibility of the lens
    (B) a decrease in the size of the retina
    (C) a decrease in the fibers of the optic nerve
    (D) increased pupil diameter
    (E) decreased fluid in the eyeball

35. Which of the following statements represents the learning approach to language development?
    (A) Children learn language through imitating the speech of others, who in turn reinforce and correct children's attempts.
    (B) Children learn language through a gradual imprinting of the grammatical rules of the language.
    (C) Children learn language by formulating and testing hypotheses about the meaning of words and the rules of their combination.
    (D) Children learn language to fulfill their unconscious desire to communicate with others.
    (E) Children learn language to increase their chances of survival.

36. Which of the following is an example of overregularization in language development?
    (A) "I and Mommy went to the store."
    (B) "Mommy went to the store with me."
    (C) "Mommy went to the store with I."
    (D) "We, Mommy and I went to the store."
    (E) "Mommy and I goed to the store."

37. Billy sees a beach ball and says "ball." He sees a basketball and says "ball." He sees a soccer ball and says "ball." Finally he sees a globe on a desk and says "ball." Calling the globe a ball is referred to as
    (A) categorization
    (B) classification
    (C) accommodation
    (D) overregularization
    (E) overextension

38. Noam Chomsky argued that the ability to learn language
    (A) is innate
    (B) shows wide individual variation
    (C) is positively correlated with intelligence
    (D) is positively correlated with creativity
    (E) differs between males and females

39. The first stage of language development is
    (A) cooing
    (B) babbling
    (C) first words
    (D) expressive speech
    (E) receptive speech

40. An indication that we are born prepared to acquire a language is the fact that
    (A) infants can discriminate among all of the speech sounds used in all of the world's languages even better than adults
    (B) children can produce complex sentences by the age of 2 years
    (C) newborns do not habituate to speech sounds
    (D) mothers all talk in a special way called "motherese"
    (E) we can easily acquire a new language at any age

41. Studies of intelligence in adulthood have shown
    (A) while there is some decline in information processing, there is some stability in fluid and crystallized intelligence
    (B) no intellectual decline, even in the very old
    (C) no relationship between health and intelligence test performance
    (D) no relationship between speed of information processing and age
    (E) a steady increase in both crystallized and fluid intelligence into late adulthood

42. Sibling rivalry tends to be worse during
    (A) toddlerhood
    (B) early childhood
    (C) middle childhood
    (D) early adolescence
    (E) late adolescence

43. Compared with children who have siblings, only-children
    (A) have lower self-esteem
    (B) are less well-accepted by their peers
    (C) are less dependent on parents
    (D) do better academically
    (E) experience more parent-child conflict

44. Although the rate of divorce is high, the rate of remarriage is also high. This leads to a large number of reconstituted families referred to as
    (A) hypercomplex families
    (B) blended families
    (C) cohabitating families
    (D) custodial families
    (E) extended families

45. A sexual offender is more likely to target
    (A) an early maturing child
    (B) a late maturing child
    (C) a child who is emotionally needy and socially isolated
    (D) an outgoing, extroverted child
    (E) a popular child

46. One way to help children adjust to divorce is to

    (A) minimize the conflict between parents after the divorce

    (B) lengthen the time of separation before divorce

    (C) minimize their contact with the non-custodial parent

    (D) have each parent decide how to discipline the child his and her own way

    (E) be sure the amount of contact with each parent is equal

47. Researchers examining cultural influences on self-esteem have found that Chinese and Japanese children score lower in self-esteem than American children, most likely because

    (A) self-esteem is not encouraged in those two cultures.

    (B) Chinese and Japanese languages and syntax are very different from English.

    (C) Chinese and Japanese parents tend to use permissive methods.

    (D) The United States includes several cultures, while China and Japan have little diversity.

    (E) American parents tend to use authoritarian methods.

48. Children display learned helplessness if their parents

    (A) use physical punishment

    (B) always encourage them to do their best

    (C) set high standards of achievement for them, but also communicate the belief that the child is not very capable

    (D) compare them unfavorably to their peers

    (E) never let them quit even when a task becomes very difficult

49. The use of a parenting technique called "induction" can help promote the development of a conscience. Which of the following is an example of induction?

    (A) "If you don't put your toys away, I will throw them out."

    (B) "If you put your toys away, you can have dessert."

    (C) "Putting your toys away is a sign that you are growing up."

    (D) "If you put your toys away, I will talk to you."

    (E) "If you don't put your toys away, someone may trip on them, fall, and get hurt."

50. A child who laughs when Daddy dresses up as a woman for Halloween, but knows Daddy is still a boy, shows

    (A) a gender schema

    (B) gender infallibility

    (C) gender holism

    (D) gender constancy

    (E) gender flexibility

51. The most important personality achievement of adolescence, according to Erikson, is

    (A) identity

    (B) generativity

    (C) integrity

    (D) personal space

    (E) intimacy

52. In Freud's theory, resolution of a young boy's Oedipal conflict is achieved through

    (A) identifying with mother

    (B) identifying with father

    (C) repressing aggressive tendencies

    (D) rejection of father as the love object

    (E) embracing one's feminine tendencies

53. The psychosocial crisis of young adulthood in Erikson's model is

    (A) generativity versus stagnation

    (B) intimacy versus isolation

    (C) integrity versus despair

    (D) autonomy versus doubt

    (E) initiative versus guilt

54. Males have a higher risk of sex-linked genetic diseases like hemophilia than females do because

    (A) they have more genes than females

    (B) they have fewer genes than females

    (C) the male sex hormone provides less immunity to disorders than the female sex hormone

    (D) their Y chromosome cannot mask the effect of a trait for the disease on their X chromosome

    (E) they have only one sex chromosome

55. Which of the following is a genetic disorder that can be controlled with diet?

    (A) Encephaly

    (B) Hemophilia

    (C) Turner's syndrome

    (D) PKU

    (E) Phenotype

56. The best way to help profoundly deaf children communicate with the world is to

    (A) homeschool them

    (B) give them speech therapy

    (C) teach them sign language

    (D) teach them to lip read

    (E) teach them sign language and how to lip read

57. Johnny (age 8) is disobedient, loud, and aggressive in the classroom and at home. He recently threatened to hit his teacher. Johnny would most likely be diagnosed with

    (A) conduct disorder

    (B) delinquent disorder

    (C) hyperactivity-impulsivity disorder

    (D) hyperactivity-inattentive disorder

    (E) bipolar depression

58. A key indicator that a child has a learning disability is

    (A) hyperactivity

    (B) impulsivity

    (C) a discrepancy between ability and performance

    (D) a low score on an intelligence test

    (E) eidetic memory

59. When asked what career he wanted to pursue, Julio said: "I am going to be a doctor just like my mother and father. I have always wanted to be a doctor. I can remember pretending to be a doctor when I was just a little kid." Julio's answer illustrates

    (A) moratorium

    (B) identity diffusion

    (C) identity confusion

    (D) identity foreclosure

    (E) identity achievement

60. Recent survey research has shown the period after launching the last child from the home to be a time of

    (A) depression and sadness for parents

    (B) renewal and growth for parents

    (C) depression and sadness for mothers but not fathers

    (D) decreased activity

    (E) lowered marital satisfaction

61. The social smile first appears in infants

    (A) between 10 and 12 hours after birth

    (B) between 1 and 4 weeks of age

    (C) between 6 and 10 weeks of age

    (D) between 6 and 8 months of age

    (E) between 10 and 12 months of age

62. Research suggests it is important to plan for one's retirement because
    (A) it goes by so quickly
    (B) it will reduce the financial costs
    (C) engaging in meaningful activities during retirement is associated with happiness
    (D) you might decide to keep working instead of retiring
    (E) keeping active prevents normal aging declines from occurring

63. The ego, in contrast to the id,
    (A) mediates between wish-fulfilling desires and the outer reality
    (B) is composed of only wish-fulfilling desires
    (C) mediates between reality and internal rules
    (D) cannot mediate with the superego
    (E) is innate, not learned

64. Freud believed that the primary driving force in an individual's life was
    (A) the superego
    (B) psychosexual development
    (C) libido
    (D) bodily functions
    (E) domination

65. Which approach to psychology stresses the importance of the person's environment on development?
    (A) Psychodynamic
    (B) Humanistic
    (C) Behaviorist
    (D) Cognitive
    (E) Biological

66. Suppose you believe that people are capable of developing personally throughout life and that, given the opportunity, they will achieve their full potential. Which approach to personality does this describe?

    (A) Humanistic

    (B) Cognitive

    (C) Psychodynamic

    (D) Behavioristic

    (E) Social learning

67. Ivan P. Pavlov is famous for his research on

    (A) teaching machines

    (B) perceptual learning

    (C) forward conditioning

    (D) classical conditioning

    (E) backward conditioning

68. The role of imitation in social learning was first systematically observed by

    (A) I. Pavlov

    (B) A. Bandura

    (C) S. Milgram

    (D) B.F. Skinner

    (E) J.B. Watson

69. Correlational studies

    (A) indicate causality

    (B) are more valid than laboratory studies

    (C) involve manipulations of independent variables

    (D) indicate a relationship between two variables

    (E) have no predictive validity

70. Which of the following effects does adrenaline have on the human body?
    (A) Constriction of the pupils
    (B) Increased rate of digestion
    (C) Accelerated heartbeat
    (D) Increased hormone production
    (E) Decreased hormone production

71. According to Piaget, a person who cannot consistently use abstract logic has NOT reached the stage of
    (A) concrete operations
    (B) preoperational development
    (C) formal operations
    (D) initiative vs. guilt
    (E) extrovert vs. introvert

Questions 72 and 73 refer to the following passage:

Suppose you are playing "Monopoly" with a group of children. These children understand the basic instructions and will play by the rules. They are not capable of hypothetical transactions dealing with mortgages, loans, and special pacts with other players.

72. According to Piaget, these children are in which stage of cognitive development?
    (A) Sensorimotor stage
    (B) Formal operations stage
    (C) Preoperational stage
    (D) Concrete operational stage
    (E) Intuitive preoperational stage

73. What are the probable ages of these children?

    (A) 10–14 years

    (B) 4–7 years

    (C) 2–4 years

    (D) 7–12 years

    (E) 5–10 years

74. Suppose you teach preschool and you break José's candy bar into three pieces and Mike's candy bar into two pieces. Mike complains that he received less than José. What does Mike lack?

    (A) Conservation

    (B) Constancy

    (C) Object permanence

    (D) Egocentrism

    (E) Accommodation

75. The short-term memory can hold how many items at one time?

    (A) Seven items, plus or minus two

    (B) Ten items, plus or minus two

    (C) Ten items, plus or minus five

    (D) Five items

    (E) It has unlimited capacity.

76. Which of the following problems would require divergent thinking?

    (A) Adding a column of numbers

    (B) Deciding whether to turn left or right at an intersection while driving a car

    (C) Choosing the best move in a card game

    (D) Restoring an old typewriter

    (E) Both (A) and (D)

77. The Language Acquisition Device was proposed by

(A) Piaget

(B) Bruner

(C) Kohler

(D) Chomsky

(E) Mednick

78. In linguistic terminology, the term "boy" is

(A) a morpheme

(B) a phoneme

(C) a stereotype

(D) a prosody

(E) an example of syntax

79. A "normal" average IQ score is

(A) 85

(B) 100

(C) 115

(D) 110

(E) 140

80. Which of the following does NOT describe a true relationship between environmental factors and IQ?

(A) Level of parent education predicts IQ.

(B) Socioeconomic status predicts IQ.

(C) Score on the HOME scale predicts IQ.

(D) Parents' occupational status predicts IQ.

(E) Intensity of separation anxiety predicts IQ.

81. Shortly after birth a duck will follow the first object that walks by it. This illustrates
    (A) conditioned responses
    (B) conditioned stimulus
    (C) sign stimuli
    (D) imprinting
    (E) shaping

82. Which of the following is NOT a factor that influences the degree to which two people like each other?
    (A) Familiarity
    (B) Physical attractiveness
    (C) Similarity
    (D) Conformity
    (E) Proximity

83. Which of the following increases as a person's fear increases?
    (A) Cognitive processing
    (B) Need for social affiliation
    (C) Resilience
    (D) Depression
    (E) Need for validation

84. According to social learning theory, one of the primary means of socializing our children is
    (A) taming their instincts
    (B) developing their superegos
    (C) helping them self-actualize
    (D) observational learning
    (E) providing minimum discipline

85. According to Freud, a developmental halt due to frustration and anxiety is referred to as

    (A) depression

    (B) fixation

    (C) regression

    (D) neurosis

    (E) learned helplessness

86. A stimulus that elicits a response before any experimental manipulation is

    (A) a response stimulus (RS)

    (B) an unconditioned stimulus (UCS)

    (C) a generalized stimulus (GS)

    (D) a conditioned stimulus (CS)

    (E) a specific stimulus (SS)

87. In our society, money is an example of a

    (A) primary reinforcer

    (B) secondary (conditioned) reinforcer

    (C) socio-reinforcer

    (D) negative reinforcer

    (E) simple operant

88. The reinforcement schedule that produces the highest rates of performance is a

    (A) fixed-interval schedule

    (B) variable-punishment schedule

    (C) fixed-ratio schedule

    (D) variable-ratio schedule

    (E) constant reinforcement

89. Mary is a bright student, but she is constantly disrupting the class by trying to draw the teacher into a power struggle for control. The school psychologist might advise the teacher to do all of the following EXCEPT

    (A) not show Mary the anxiety she is causing

    (B) ignore Mary's disruptive behavior

    (C) verbally embarrass Mary until she is more cooperative

    (D) suggest she talk to Mary's parents

    (E) reinforce Mary when she engages in more productive behavior

90. The major affective disorders are characterized by

    (A) extreme and inappropriate emotional responses

    (B) severe behavior problems

    (C) disturbed speech

    (D) hyperactivity

    (E) delusions

PRACTICE TEST 1

Answer Key

1.	(D)	31.	(C)	61.	(C)
2.	(A)	32.	(D)	62.	(C)
3.	(B)	33.	(C)	63.	(A)
4.	(C)	34.	(A)	64.	(C)
5.	(E)	35.	(A)	65.	(C)
6.	(D)	36.	(E)	66.	(A)
7.	(A)	37.	(E)	67.	(D)
8.	(E)	38.	(A)	68.	(B)
9.	(B)	39.	(A)	69.	(D)
10.	(C)	40.	(A)	70.	(C)
11.	(A)	41.	(A)	71.	(C)
12.	(D)	42.	(C)	72.	(D)
13.	(D)	43.	(B)	73.	(D)
14.	(C)	44.	(B)	74.	(A)
15.	(D)	45.	(C)	75.	(A)
16.	(E)	46.	(A)	76.	(C)
17.	(C)	47.	(A)	77.	(D)
18.	(B)	48.	(C)	78.	(A)
19.	(E)	49.	(E)	79.	(B)
20.	(A)	50.	(D)	80.	(E)
21.	(C)	51.	(A)	81.	(D)
22.	(B)	52.	(B)	82.	(D)
23.	(C)	53.	(B)	83.	(B)
24.	(C)	54.	(D)	84.	(D)
25.	(B)	55.	(D)	85.	(B)
26.	(C)	56.	(E)	86.	(B)
27.	(C)	57.	(A)	87.	(B)
28.	(D)	58.	(C)	88.	(D)
29.	(C)	59.	(D)	89.	(C)
30.	(E)	60.	(B)	90.	(A)

PRACTICE TEST 1

Detailed Explanations of Answers

1. **(D)** The psychodynamic theory emphasizes nature in the nature-versus-nurture debate more than the other perspectives listed because of the emphasis on inborn, biological drives within this perspective.

2. **(A)** Vygotsky is the one theorist of the five who argued that culture influences cognitive development. He argued that a child's cognitive abilities develop as a result of engaging in tasks with older, more competent adults. He also argued that language affects thought.

3. **(B)** Since the researcher is recording behavior in a natural setting, and is not controlling or manipulating any variables, it is a naturalistic observation.

4. **(C)** Research on physical development shows that on average, children begin to walk on their own between 11 and 12 months of age.

5. **(E)** Piaget used the term "adaptation" for the process of a child adjusting to the environment. The two complementary processes involved in adaptation are accommodation, when a child constructs a new schema that organizes a new experience, and assimilation, when a child applies an already existing scheme to understand a new experience. Piaget argued that accommodation occurs when an attempt to assimilate new information fails.

6. **(D)** Vygotsky used the term "guided participation" or "scaffolding" to describe the cognitive support that older adults, like teachers or parents, provide to children when they engage in a task. Adults will adjust the amount of direction and support they provide as the child shows greater mastery over the task at hand.

7. **(A)** The information-processing approach argues children's memory improves because children get better at organizing to-be-learned information. The better a child can organize new information, the better that information is encoded for storage in memory and later retrieval.

8. **(E)** The children are engaged in associative play because even though they are talking to each other while playing and sharing tools, they are not sharing the same purpose or goal.

9. **(B)** The case study method of research is designed to collect a great deal of information about a single person or event. By its nature, then, a case study yields conclusions that are difficult to generalize beyond that person or event. There is typically something unique or special about the case that motivates a researcher to study it in such depth.

10. **(C)** The terms "discontinuity theory" and "stage theory" are used interchangeably in this field. Theories of this type describe development as qualitative shifts in ability or behavior that take place through a series of distinct stages. Almost all stage theories argue that the stages are universal and occur in a fixed sequence.

11. **(A)** Instrumental aggression is aggression that is used in order to achieve an end. The child in this question uses aggression as a means toward the end of getting a toy. Instrumental aggression is usually used in battles over toys and is not personal.

12. **(D)** Statistics on child mistreatment indicate that more often, among the types of offenders listed in this question, the abuser is the child's parent.

13. **(D)** The sociocultural view of development argues there is a bidirectional relationship between the child and the environment. A child influences the people and the environments he or she interacts with, as much as those people and environments influence the child's development. For example, an infant's temperament influences the caregiver's responses to the child, and those caregiving responses in turn shape the child's behavior.

14. **(C)** One problem that threatens the validity of the findings of a longitudinal study is subject dropout. Longitudinal research involves collecting data from the same group of participants at several points in their lives. If participants drop out of the study, not only is the research sample size reduced, but the sample may become biased. For example, participants who drop out of a longitudinal study on memory may have poorer memory ability to begin with compared to those who complete the study. The findings of this longitudinal study of memory then would be biased, that is, only apply to people with good memory ability.

15. **(D)** Those with a mastery-oriented attribution style typically attribute successes and failures to internal traits or abilities and effort. This type of person believes that he or she can be successful at tasks that are attempted and will tend to persevere through challenging or difficult tasks.

16. **(E)** Researchers have begun to systematically study wisdom. Wisdom is defined as exceptional insight into the problems of life. Research has shown that, while the majority of people believe wisdom comes with age, wisdom is not a normal product of aging. The key elements that influence the development of wisdom have to do with the quality and amount of life experience, not just chronological age.

17. **(C)** Cliques are small, tight-knit peer groups, usually same-sex, while crowds are larger groupings known by their reputation and common interests.

18. **(B)** A key element of empathy is being able to feel what another person is feeling. Crying because someone else is crying does not necessarily indicate the child feels what the other person is experiencing. However, a child offering a toy to a crying child shows he or she feels the underlying unhappiness causing the child's crying, and he or she believes a toy will make the child feel happy.

19. **(E)** The uninvolved parenting style is characterized by the parent being low on both the acceptance/responsiveness and the control/demandingness parenting dimensions. Children raised with this style of parenting tend to engage in antisocial behavior.

20. **(A)** Physical growth is not a steady process. There are growth spurts that occur in infancy and in adolescence.

21. **(C)** Research on the growth hormone (GH) has shown that as long as children who lack GH are given injections of the hormone early on, they will grow to their full height potential. If GH is given later, children do not catch up.

22. **(B)** Early maturing boys and late maturing girls have been shown to experience better adjustment compared to their counterparts—late maturing boys and early maturing girls. Early maturing boys may benefit from having larger physical stature than their late maturing peers, and early maturing girls may have difficulty adjusting to puberty and the concomitant physical changes in their bodies. Other people may treat early maturing girls as if they were older than their age. Because of this, they may be faced with higher expectations for their behavior than they are capable of meeting.

23. **(C)** The wear-and-tear theory of biological aging suggests that aging of the body is inevitable because of wear and tear on it from normal use. This theory suggests that, like a machine, over time the body will wear out.

24. **(C)** Estrogen replacement therapy (ERT) has been used successfully to treat symptoms of menopause in women. The therapy works to replace the female hormone, estrogen, which decreases substantially in a woman's body during menopause. ERT seems to treat symptoms like hot flashes quite well. Controversy exists, however, over the side effects of ERT. Some research suggests there is an increased risk of uterine cancer in women given long-term ERT (or breast cancer if the estrogen is given along with another hormone called progestin in therapy, called hormone replacement therapy, or HRT).

25. **(B)** The male climacteric is a less noticeable physiological process than the female climacteric. Changes that occur are caused by a decline in testosterone level and are very gradual. These changes include reduced sperm production, reduction in the size of the testes, and enlargement of the prostate gland. These changes do not prevent a male from fathering a child.

26. **(C)** Osteoporosis is a bone disease caused by a decline in bone density. Bones become very brittle and may spontaneously fracture. Osteoporosis is the result of a calcium deficiency and is found in greater frequency among postmenopausal women.

27. **(C)** Hospice is a program that supports terminally ill patients and their families through the dying process. The goal of hospice is to provide a pain-free death for the dying patient in as comfortable a setting as possible.

28. **(D)** Eleanor Gibson's classic visual cliff experiment showed that 6-month-old infants would not crawl across a "visual cliff." The visual cliff was created by placing a Plexiglas cover, half clear and half checkerboard, across the top of a checkerboard box. For a person with depth perception, there appeared to be a drop-off or "visual cliff" halfway across the top. The experiment did not show conclusively that depth perception was innate, because 6-month-old infants have already had experience exploring their environment and may have learned to see depth from this prior experience.

29. **(C)** Visual scanning experiments with infants have shown that newborns will scan the edges of a stimulus while older infants will scan the interior of a stimulus. This might suggest that newborns are born prepared to scan edges to organize the perceptual field into objects. Older infants may be able to do that more rapidly and hence spend their time looking for details found within the edges.

30. **(E)** Size constancy is the perceptual ability to perceive size accurately by adjusting for changing distance. Perception theorists would argue that, by using binocular and monocular cues to distance, we make an unconscious inference that the German shepherd is 100 yards away. Although the size of the retinal image produced by looking at a dog that far away would be quite small, the size of the retinal image of the dog multiplied by the dog's distance yields the perception of a normal-sized German shepherd. Size constancy is achieved by multiplying retinal image size times distance.

31. **(C)** Vision is the least developed sense in newborns. Visual acuity is normally between 20/200 and 20/400 at birth, due to lack of muscle tone in the lenses.

32. **(D)** Habituation is a form of learning that has shown to be present in newborns and is measured by length of looking at a stimulus. Habituation is seen when an infant looks away or stops looking at a stimulus. When a previously seen stimulus is shown along with a novel stimulus, newborns will look longer at the novel stimulus.

33. **(C)** The hearing loss most associated with aging is a decrease in sensitivity to high frequency sounds.

34. **(A)** A decreased flexibility in the lens of the eye due to normal biological aging is one reason for declining eyesight among the aged. The lens of the eye must be able to change shape from concave to convex in order to properly refract light waves to the retina on the back of the eye. When the lens cannot make these accommodations, light waves are either refracted short of the retina or beyond the retina.

35. **(A)** The learning approach to language development argues that we learn a language through imitation. We imitate the speech of those around us and, in turn, these speech utterances are positively reinforced by caregivers. Therefore, language is described as verbal behavior acquired through the general laws of learning within this theoretical approach.

36. **(E)** Overregularization is when a child who is learning a language produces speech errors that are due to exceptions to grammatical rules. The child's speech error indicates she or he assumes grammatical rules are regular and without exception. For example, one grammatical rule of the English language is to add an *-ed* to form the past tense of a verb. To overregularize English grammar rules, a young child would say "goed" instead of the irregular "went."

37. **(E)** Overextension is when a child learning a language applies a category label, e.g., "ball," to an object that does not belong to the category but may share some similar features of category members. A globe is not a member of the "ball" category although it does share some characteristics of balls.

38. **(A)** Noam Chomsky argued that humans are born prepared to acquire a language. He suggested that the human brain is pre-wired for language acquisition. He used the term language acquisition device (LAD) metaphorically to describe this pre-wiring. Evidence for this theory includes the fact that language learning is universal in humans; language learning proceeds through stages that are universal; there appears to be a sensitive period for learning language; infants can discriminate among all the speech sounds used in all of the world's languages; and children show an understanding of syntax in their speech production that does not appear to be directly taught to them. An example of the latter is speech errors of overregularization.

39. **(A)** Cooing is the first stage of language development. Cooing appears about the same age in babies across cultures.

40. **(A)** An indication that we are born prepared to learn a language is the fact that infants can discriminate among all the speech sounds of all of the world's languages and do so even better than adults. Being able to discriminate speech sounds means infants can perceive differences between sounds such as *pa* and *ba*.

41. **(A)** Studies of intelligence in adulthood have shown that fluid and crystallized intelligence show stability until very late adulthood. Fluid intelligence is closely related to reasoning and thinking, while crystallized intelligence is general knowledge that has been acquired. While research does show a steady decline in the speed of processing of information, these two types of intelligence appear to be stable through most of adulthood in adults who are disease-free.

42. **(C)** Sibling rivalry tends to be worse during middle childhood, as opportunities for competition and comparison increase during these years.

43. **(B)** Only-children are less well-accepted by their peers compared to their counterparts who have siblings. A possible reason for this is that children may develop social skills from interacting with their siblings before the school years. Only-children may not have as much opportunity to interact with other children in such an intensive way as children who have siblings.

44. **(B)** The term "blended family" refers to complex familial structures that are the result of remarriages.

45. **(C)** Sexual offenders tend to target children who are isolated and needy. Offenders prey on these children's vulnerabilities and may gain the trust of children because they are socially isolated and crave attention.

46. **(A)** Minimizing conflict after a divorce has been shown to help children's adjustment, because conflict after a divorce tends to interfere with the non-custodial parent's involvement with the children. Good non-custodial parenting is one of the factors associated with children's positive adjustment after divorce.

47. **(A)** Chinese and Japanese children have been shown to have lower self-esteem than American children, most likely because self-esteem is not encouraged in those collectivist cultures.

48. **(C)** Children of parents who set very high standards for their achievement, but also communicate to them that they are not capable of achieving those standards, show signs of learned helplessness. Learned helplessness is a syndrome first observed by Seligman. Seligman placed animals in an experimental chamber from which they could not escape. Animals who received an electric shock through the floor of the chamber first tried to escape, but they eventually stopped trying. Even when an escape route became available to them, they could not learn to escape. Children of parents who communicate high standards but little confidence in the children's abilities, produce children who do not try to succeed.

49. **(E)** Induction is a parenting technique used to teach children morality. A parent is using induction when she explains to the child how the child's actions may negatively affect other people. Providing an explanation for a behavior rule that encourages the child to think of others may induce independent moral reasoning in the child.

50. **(D)** Gender constancy is the understanding that a person cannot change his maleness or her femaleness by simply changing how he or she looks. Prior to the development of this understanding, young children believe that a male who dresses as a female is now a female, and vice versa. Gender constancy is similar to the cognitive structure of conservation described by Piaget in his theory of cognitive development. A child who says that a tall, thin beaker does not contain the same amount of liquid as a short, wide beaker when the beakers in fact have the same amount of liquid is being fooled by the perceptual

characteristics of the containers (i.e., inability to conserve). A lack of gender constancy is explained the same way. Young children think Daddy has changed into a female when he dresses up as a female because the child is focusing on the perceptual characteristics of the father's appearance.

51. **(A)** Erikson suggested that identity development was the most important task of adolescence. The psychosocial crisis of this stage is identity versus role confusion. An identity is the idea of who you are and what you will be like as an adult member of society. Erikson believed a healthy identity is the result of exploration, and that it is normal for adolescents to experience stress about finding their identity.

52. **(B)** According to Freud, boys in the phallic stage of personality development experience an unconscious conflict because they have an unconscious sexual desire for their mother and at the same time, unconsciously fear reprisal and punishment from their father-rival. Freud argued that this Oedipal conflict is resolved through a process of identification. He believed boys unconsciously resolve the conflict by replacing the sexual desire for mother with identification with father. Boys show this process of identification through modeling the father's behavior and by a preference for father over mother.

53. **(B)** Erikson argued that the psychosocial crisis of young adulthood was intimacy versus isolation. Young adults are highly motivated to be with a romantic partner. Erikson suggested a need to be with a significant other occurs at this time because the young adult has achieved a sense of identity and is now prepared to share his or her self intimately with another person. True intimacy is achieved when two people share a deep commitment, and love and trust each other. This strong emotional bond cannot be achieved if one or both partners cannot trust and/or do not have a strong sense of self. Isolation is experienced when a young adult has not found a romantic partner. Erikson argued the social norm for adults was to be in an intimate relationship, so those who are not will feel lonely and isolated.

54. **(D)** Males are at greater risk of inheriting sex-linked genetic diseases because they have only one X chromosome. Females who have two X chromosomes have a greater chance of having a dominant gene to protect them from a genetic disease that is carried on a recessive gene on X chromosomes. Males who inherit a recessive gene on the X chromosome for a genetic disease have no chance of having a dominant gene to protect them. So while a female may be a carrier but not have the genetic disease, males who have the recessive gene will have the disease.

55. **(D)** Phenylketonuria (PKU) is a genetic disease caused by the body's inability to break down phenylalanine. The disease is controlled by a diet kept free of phenylalanine.

56. **(E)** The best approach to teaching deaf children language is to teach them sign language and how to lip-read. This approach has the benefit of helping the deaf child communicate among hearing people as well as communicate within the sign language community.

57. **(A)** Johnny is showing behaviors that meet the diagnostic criteria for conduct disorder. Conduct disorder is diagnosed when a child acts out and is aggressive in many situations and settings. A child with a conduct disorder is disobedient and aggressive.

58. **(C)** To screen for learning disabilities, children are given assessments to determine level of ability and level of performance. If the child's test results indicate a discrepancy between ability and performance, that child will likely be diagnosed with a learning disability.

59. **(D)** Marcia's model of identity development in adolescence classifies adolescents into four identity status groups based on whether or not they have experienced an identity crisis and whether or not they have made an identity commitment. The four statuses are: 1) identity moratorium (identity crisis and no commitment), 2) identity diffusion (no identity crisis and no commitment), 3) identity foreclosure (no identity crisis and a commitment), and 4) identity achievement (identity crisis and a commitment). Julio is an example of an adolescent who has adopted an identity too soon and never experienced an identity crisis. He is therefore showing identity foreclosure.

60. **(B)** The stage of parenthood when parents are launching children from the home is reportedly a time of growth and renewal for parents. Recent surveys of parents in this phase of parenthood break the myth that the "empty nest" phase usually brings on a period of depression and sadness.

61. **(C)** Between 6 and 10 weeks of age, an infant begins to smile in the presence of a caregiver. Prior to this time, an infant's smile is merely a reflexive response.

62. **(C)** Planning for retirement can help make retirement more satisfying if the planning includes finding opportunities for meaningful activities for the retired person.

63. **(A)** The ego is the intermediary between the id and reality. It develops between the ages of 8 months and 18 months, as the child acquires an understanding of what is possible in the outer world. The ego also distinguishes between long-range and short-range goals and decides which activities will be most profitable to the individual. The id and ego work together to determine the individual's goals.

64. **(C)** Freud believed that the primary driving force in an individual's life is the sexual urge (the libido). His theory of motivational development was particularly concerned with sexual gratification, as it changed in relation to the child's body. His theory of the personality structure (the id, ego, and superego) also deals with the sexual urge. The ego has to channel the libido into behaviors that are acceptable to the superego and fit within the constraints of the outer world.

65. **(C)** The behaviorist approach to psychology stresses the control that the environment has on development. In this view, behavior is shaped by reinforcement and punishment. It is argued that environmental stimuli control behavior.

66. **(A)** The humanistic approach, as exemplified by the work of Maslow and Rogers, stresses the process of self-actualization. The cognitive approach stresses the construction of meaning, interpretations, and beliefs. The Freudian psychodynamic approach stresses unconscious conflicts. The behaviorist approach, as seen in Skinner's writings, stresses environmental stimulus control of behavior. Lastly, Bandura's social learning theory stresses the importance of modeling and vicarious reinforcement.

67. **(D)** Ivan P. Pavlov (1849–1936) discovered the phenomenon of classical conditioning and was the first to investigate it systematically. In Pavlov's experiments with the salivating response of his dogs, he established the basic methodology and terminology still used today in classical conditioning experiments. Pavlov referred to food as the unconditional stimulus (UCS) because it naturally and consistently elicited salivation, which he called the unconditioned response (UCR). Pavlov later taught dogs to salivate to a bell. This was accomplished by presenting the bell just prior to presenting the food. After a series of such pairings, the dogs would salivate in response to the bell. In this case, the bell was a conditioned stimulus (CS) and the salivation in response to the bell was a conditioned response (CR). Hence, Pavlov's research elucidated the process of classical conditioning.

68. **(B)** Bandura and Walters conducted a classic experiment in which children shown videotapes of adults hitting and kicking a doll, later imitated the adults' aggressive behavior. The children also hit and kicked the doll.

69. **(D)** In a correlational study, a researcher measures two variables in a group of participants in order to determine if a relationship exists between the two variables. If a consistent pattern appears in the pairs of scores, for example, pairs of scores are very similar, or paired scores go in predictable, opposite directions, a correlation is established.

70. **(C)** Adrenaline is a hormone that stimulates the sympathetic nervous system. One of the many resulting effects of adrenaline on the body is the stimulation of the heart. When stimulated, the sympathetic branch to the muscles of the heart causes the heart to beat more rapidly and vigorously. Thus, adrenaline has the effect of accelerating and strengthening the heartbeat.

71. **(C)** The stage of formal operations is noted for the ability of the individual to deal with abstract problems and concepts. It usually begins around puberty, but research shows that some people never develop these skills and continue to function at the level of concrete operations for life.

72. **(D)** Based on the description of the way these children understood the game rules, one could determine that they are in the concrete operational stage of development. This stage emphasizes concrete understanding of rules and logical thinking as it relates to real concrete objects. Abstract and hypothetical thinking are largely undeveloped.

73. **(D)** The concrete operational stage lasts from ages 7 to 12 years. This is the usual age span, but it may be shorter or longer in an individual child.

74. **(A)** Conservation is a Piagetian concept of recognizing the identity of number, mass, and volume despite transformations that alter their perceptual properties. Mike lacks conservation of mass in not realizing that his candy bar is equal to José's despite the perceptual difference of two versus three pieces. Learning conservation is a key indicator of progression from the preoperational to the concrete operations stage of development. However, learning conservation in one domain, such as mass, does not imply that other domains, such as volume, are understood.

75. **(A)** Short-term memory (STM) is very limited in its capacity. It can only hold about seven items (plus or minus two items) of information at a time. This brief memory span requires deliberate rehearsal to prevent a specific memory from decaying over time.

76. **(C)** In choosing the best move in a card game, one must be able to generate a number of possible solutions; therefore, divergent thinking is the process being utilized. Divergent thinking requires flexibility, fluency of ideas, and originality.

77. **(D)** Noam Chomsky believes that children are born with a certain "something," a certain genetic predisposition that enables them to learn grammar. Chomsky called this predisposition the Language Acquisition Device (LAD). It is believed to exist at birth. Chomsky used this concept to explain the relative ease with which normal children learn grammar.

78. **(A)** A morpheme is the smallest unit of meaning in a given language. In English, morphemes can be whole words such as "boy," prefixes such as "anti-," or suffixes such as "-ing." There are more than 100,000 morphemes in English.

79. **(B)** A "normal" IQ score is considered to be about 100, while 98 percent of the people who take IQ tests fall in the range between 60 and 140. Someone who scores above 140 is considered a genius.

80. **(E)** There are many early childhood environmental factors that have been shown to correlate with later IQ. The IQ is more malleable than many people believe. All of the factors in this question influence IQ except for the intensity of separation anxiety.

81. **(D)** Konrad Lorenz observed that newborn ducks would follow him if they saw him before encountering their mother. He termed this phenomenon "imprinting" and argued that it illustrated the importance of instinctual behavior. This concept, along with sign stimuli that release fixed patterns, comprised some of the central ideas of ethology.

82. **(D)** Research on social attraction indicates that proximity is important for the obvious reason that social interaction is more likely when two people live nearby. Physical attraction and similarity are critical factors. All else being equal, the greater the familiarity, the greater the social attraction. Conformity is not a factor that has been researched as related to attraction.

83. **(B)** The need for social affiliation or a desire to be with other people is great when we are afraid. In a classic series of studies, Stanley Schachter manipulated the fear level of college women by leading them to believe they would receive electric shocks in a laboratory experiment. He then measured whether the women preferred to wait for the experiment to begin either alone or with others. Most chose to wait with others.

84. **(D)** According to social learning theory, we learn new behaviors by observing other people who serve as models for us. This is called observational learning. Choices (A) and (B) represent the Freudian approach, while choice (C) comes from the humanistic approach.

85. **(B)** According to Freud, fixation results from abnormal personality development. Freud stated that a person feels a certain amount of frustration and anxiety as he passes from one stage of development to the next. If that frustration and anxiety become too great, development may halt and the person becomes fixated at the stage he is trying to grow out of. For example, an overly dependent child is thought to be fixated. Development ceased at an early stage, preventing the child from growing up and becoming independent.

86. **(B)** In classical conditioning, the stimulus that elicits a response before any conditioning begins is called the unconditioned stimulus (UCS). It reliably elicits the unconditioned response (UCR) before the experiment. During the experimental manipulation, the unconditioned stimulus (UCS) is paired with a conditioned stimulus (CS) that originally does not elicit a response. After several such pairings, the subject will emit a conditioned response (CR) to the conditioned stimulus (CS) that is very similar to the unconditioned response (UCR). After this conditioned response (CR) is learned, the unconditioned stimulus (UCS) may be removed, but the subject will keep responding to the conditioned stimulus (CS).

87. **(B)** Money is an example of a secondary (conditioned) reinforcer. Conditioned, or secondary reinforcement, occurs when the reinforcing stimulus is not inherently pleasing or reinforcing, but becomes so through association with other pleasant or reinforcing stimuli. Coins and paper currency are not in themselves pleasing, but the things they buy are pleasing. Therefore, an association is made between money and inherently pleasing primary reinforcers, such as food and drink. Hence, the term "conditioned reinforcer" is used.

88. **(D)** The variable-ratio schedule elicits consistently high rates of performance even after prolonged discontinuance of the reinforcement. In fact, once an operant learning response has been established with a variable-ratio reinforcement schedule, it is difficult to extinguish the response.

89. **(C)** Power struggles with authority figures occur for a variety of reasons. Relying on verbally abrasive responses to punish usually results in alienation of the student and deterioration of class atmosphere. All of the other responses are positive ways of dealing with Mary.

90. **(A)** Affective disorders are characterized by a disturbance of mood accompanied by related symptoms. Mood is defined as a prolonged emotional state that colors the whole psychic life and generally involves either depression or elation. In affective disorders, mood tends to be at one extreme or the other. The patient may be depressed, may be manic, or may exhibit bipolar symptoms, an alternation between depression and mania.

PRACTICE TEST 2

CLEP Human Growth and Development

This practice test is also offered online at the REA Study Center *(www.rea.com/studycenter)*. Since all CLEP exams are administered on computer, we recommend that you take the online version of the test to simulate test-day conditions and receive these added benefits:

- **Timed testing conditions** — Gauge how much time you can spend on each question.
- **Automatic scoring** — Find out how you did on the test, instantly.
- **On-screen detailed explanations of answers** — Learn not just the correct answers, but also why the other answer choices are incorrect.
- **Diagnostic score reports** — Pinpoint where you're strongest and where you need to focus your study.

PRACTICE TEST 2

CLEP Human Growth and Development

(Answer sheet is on page 266.)

TIME: 90 Minutes
90 Questions

Directions: Each of the questions or incomplete statements below is followed by five possible answers or completions. Select the lettered choice that best answers each question and fill in the corresponding oval on the answer sheet.

1. Which of the following questions would be best answered using a correlational research design?

    (A) Is there a relationship between depression and age?

    (B) Are people more depressed before or after retirement?

    (C) Does exercise cause a decrease in depression?

    (D) How depressed are 14-year-olds?

    (E) Does drug addiction cause depression?

2. One of the main contributions of Freud's theory is its emphasis on

    (A) the unconscious

    (B) genetics

    (C) the environment shaping behavior

    (D) reinforcement

    (E) adult development

3. If you want to increase the number of times your child does the dishes, Skinner would say you need to

   (A) yell at your child when he or she does not do the dishes

   (B) give your child a cookie when he or she does the dishes

   (C) leave your sink full of dishes until your child does them

   (D) ask him or her to do the dishes

   (E) simultaneously present a reward and dirty dishes several times

4. Who is the person who identified personality types associated with occupational choice?

   (A) Bowlby

   (B) Ainsworth

   (C) Bronfenbrenner

   (D) Marcia

   (E) Holland

5. Which hormone has been shown to have a negative effect on the body's immune system?

   (A) Estrogen

   (B) Androgen

   (C) Testosterone

   (D) Adrenalin

   (E) Progesterone

6. Which of the following is a condition caused by a reduced supply of oxygen to the baby during delivery?

   (A) Anoxia

   (B) Presbyopia

   (C) Apraxia

   (D) Dysphoria

   (E) Mitosis

7. According to Kübler-Ross, the final stage of adjustment to death and dying is

   (A) mourning

   (B) renewal

   (C) acceptance

   (D) depression

   (E) relief

8. According to Daniel Goleman, which of the following may be a better predictor of success than IQ?

   (A) Drive

   (B) Creativity

   (C) Emotional intelligence

   (D) Practical intelligence

   (E) Sociability

9. Preschoolers spend their waking hours engaging in which one of the following activities more than any other?

   (A) Eating

   (B) Playing with adults

   (C) Talking with other preschoolers

   (D) Watching television/media

   (E) Gross motor play

10. Which of the following terms is used to describe a household that has children from the parents' multiple marriages?

    (A) Blended

    (B) Mixed

    (C) Complex

    (D) Beanpole

    (E) Stratified

11. A person with an internal locus of control tends to attribute
    (A) success to luck
    (B) success to ability and effort
    (C) failure to bad luck
    (D) failure to a lack of effort
    (E) both (B) and (D)

12. All of the following are potential teratogens during pregnancy EXCEPT
    (A) recreational drugs taken by a pregnant woman
    (B) radiation procedures carried out on the mother
    (C) the mother's stress hormones
    (D) the father's stress hormones
    (E) environmental pollutants

13. Object permanence in the beginning of the sensorimotor stage is
    (A) not apparent
    (B) present in rudimentary form
    (C) characterized by active searches for missing objects
    (D) fully developed
    (E) characterized by a visual search rather than a motoric search for missing objects

14. Which of the following is a sign of habituation?
    (A) Looking time decreasing
    (B) Looking time increasing
    (C) Smiling decreasing
    (D) Respiration rate increasing
    (E) Yawning

15. Which of the following measures would be found on the Bayley Scales of Infant Intelligence?

    (A) Cognition, such as auditory and visual attention to objects

    (B) Reflexive response to touch

    (C) A measure of verbal ability

    (D) Temperament

    (E) Puzzle completion

16. The stage of adolescence might be best characterized as

    (A) a biologically determined period

    (B) a cultural creation

    (C) a legal fiction

    (D) an outdated historical concept

    (E) both biologically and culturally determined

17. According to Piaget, when a child is confronted with a new experience or idea that does not fit his or her present level of understanding, the child experiences

    (A) accommodation

    (B) disequilibrium

    (C) preoperation

    (D) disorganization

    (E) fixation

18. One of the most powerful attachment behaviors of infants is

    (A) the perceptual preference for looking at colorful objects versus black and white objects

    (B) the social smile

    (C) reciprocal interweaving

    (D) the tonic neck reflex

    (E) the Babinski reflex

19. Given the thought processes of elementary-aged children, cognitive theory would recommend teaching them geography by

    (A) giving them map or globe pieces that they can manipulate and put together

    (B) showing them slides of various places around the world

    (C) having them memorize the names of the countries on each continent

    (D) having them listen to lectures from people from different countries

    (E) frequent drill and practice with country names

20. An example of the achievement of object permanence would be when an infant

    (A) flushes a favorite toy down the toilet

    (B) laughs when an adult makes a silly noise

    (C) looks under a chair for a ball that rolled under it

    (D) looks up in the sky in response to thunder

    (E) counts to ten

21. Which of the following is a sign of secure attachment?

    (A) A strong reluctance to leave mother to play with new toys

    (B) Ignoring mother when she returns to the room

    (C) Crying when mother leaves the room and not being comforted by her return

    (D) Periodically searching for mother after she leaves the room

    (E) Hugging mother's leg when she returns to the room

22. Which of the following best fits the definition of a symbol?

    (A) A cup

    (B) A red traffic light

    (C) The sound of laughter

    (D) Wind chimes

    (E) The bark of a dog

23. The desire to be "good" and to obey the rules characterizes which stage of Kohlberg's theory?

    (A) Postconventional

    (B) Conventional

    (C) Preconventional

    (D) Morality of care

    (E) Morality of justice

24. According to Erikson, psychologically healthy middle-aged adults are likely to

    (A) engage in reflection on their lives in order to come to terms with unresolved conflicts and questions of meaningfulness

    (B) be concerned with personal advancement in their careers

    (C) develop a deep concern about making a contribution to the society, community, and/or family

    (D) focus on the establishment of intimate relationships with others

    (E) focus on their identities

25. Which of the following statements reflects Kohlberg's "conventional morality"?

    (A) "Do your own thing."

    (B) "Scratch my back and I'll scratch yours."

    (C) "Rules were made to be broken."

    (D) "Buckle up. It's the law."

    (E) "All men were created equal."

26. Which sort of reasoning would likely take place in the mind of a preconventional child?

    (A) "Don't hit Jimmy because you should never hurt anyone."

    (B) "Don't hit Jimmy because it's against the rules."

    (C) "Don't hit Jimmy because then the teacher will not like me."

    (D) "Don't hit Jimmy because there are better ways to get what I want."

    (E) "Don't hit Jimmy because he will hit me back."

27. The goals of social development in adolescence include
    (A) identification with mother
    (B) identification with father
    (C) symbiosis
    (D) moral ascendancy
    (E) separation-individuation

28. A child sees a sparrow and says "bird." Then she sees a crow and says "bird." According to Piaget, the child is using the process of
    (A) scheming
    (B) semantic networking
    (C) assimilation
    (D) accommodation
    (E) conditioning

29. If a goat is separated from her kid immediately after delivery, she rejects it when reunited. But if the separation occurs ten minutes after delivery, no rejection occurs. This illustrates the developmental concept called
    (A) critical period
    (B) mother-infant synchrony
    (C) lack of permanence
    (D) individual difference
    (E) maturation

30. Which of the following is an example of erroneous transductive reasoning, according to Piaget?
    (A) Every child I see wears clothes; therefore, all children wear clothing.
    (B) Children who are good get candy; therefore, if I am good, I will get candy.
    (C) If I say I don't understand something, Daddy will explain it to me.
    (D) If you make the room dark, it will cause night to come.
    (E) If I eat a lot of candy, I will feel sick.

31. The evolutionary psychology perspective tries to
    (A) find effective ways to speed up maturation
    (B) understand the historical origins of human behaviors
    (C) understand how nutrition can influence physical growth
    (D) eliminate bad traits from the human gene pool
    (E) discover humans' closest animal relatives

32. In Bronfenbrenner's ecological theory, interactions between children and their parents take place in the child's
    (A) microsystem
    (B) macrosystem
    (C) mesosystem
    (D) exosystem
    (E) endosystem

33. Erikson's approach to development differed from Freud's approach in that Freud
    (A) emphasized social influences on development
    (B) did not discuss intra-psychic conflict
    (C) de-emphasized the role of animal instincts in controlling human behavior
    (D) emphasized the conflict between dreams and wish fulfillment
    (E) considered personality development to be complete in adolescence

34. One weakness of the case study approach to research is
    (A) a possible inability to generalize results to a larger group
    (B) the researcher cannot get the subject's perspective
    (C) the researcher cannot quantify data that is collected from the subject
    (D) it is artificial
    (E) the researcher cannot measure any variables

35. The only research method that can identify cause-and-effect relationships is

    (A) correlational research

    (B) case study research

    (C) experimental research

    (D) observational research

    (E) twin study research

36. Which of the following research designs is considered the best to study development?

    (A) Cross-sectional

    (B) Case study

    (C) Longitudinal

    (D) Experimental

    (E) Correlational

37. Changes in the brain after birth

    (A) rarely, if ever, occur

    (B) mainly occur in the occipital lobe

    (C) include only pruning of connections

    (D) include both pruning and new neural connections

    (E) include cross-sequencing

38. The fact that you and your spouse have brown eyes does not guarantee your offspring will also have brown eyes. This is due to which principle of genetic transmission?

    (A) Dominance

    (B) Recessiveness

    (C) Zygotic

    (D) Dizygotic

    (E) Chromosomal

39. Genetic abnormalities may be detected prenatally using
    (A) fibrosis
    (B) amniocentesis
    (C) fetal blood testing
    (D) X-rays
    (E) RH tests

40. A fertilized egg cell will differentiate into which of the following unless there is a Y sex chromosome present?
    (A) A female
    (B) A male
    (C) Fraternal twins
    (D) Identical twins
    (E) A zygote

41. Selective attention requires the ability to
    (A) focus on multiple stimuli
    (B) ignore irrelevant stimuli
    (C) solve problems
    (D) think
    (E) multitask

42. The information-processing approach to the study of memory argues there are three memory storage systems. These are
    (A) sensory, primary, secondary
    (B) sensory, semantic, long-term
    (C) primary, secondary, tertiary
    (D) primary, semantic, episodic
    (E) sensory, visual, linguistic

43. The most commonly found developmental change in short-term memory is
    (A) an increase in vocabulary
    (B) an increase in the number of items that can be retained in short-term memory
    (C) an increase in the length of time that items can be retained in short-term memory
    (D) a pruning of associations in short-term memory
    (E) an increase in the organization of information in short-term memory

44. In Vygotsky's theory, the term "scaffolding" describes
    (A) the role of maturation in development
    (B) the role of genetics in development
    (C) older members of the community shaping and guiding children's learning
    (D) how perception guides thinking in children
    (E) how knowledge of the physical world develops in children

45. Which of the following terms refers to the basic grammatical rules of a language?
    (A) Phoneme
    (B) Morpheme
    (C) Pragmatic
    (D) Syntax
    (E) Syllable

46. Which of the following statements is true?

    (A) Infants are born with the capacity to produce all of the morphemes of all of the world's languages and retain this ability throughout adulthood.

    (B) Infants are born with the capacity to produce all of the phonemes of all of the world's languages but lose this ability over time.

    (C) Infants are born with the capacity to produce all of the morphemes of all of the world's languages but lose this ability over time.

    (D) Infants are born with the capacity to produce all of the phonemes of all of the world's languages and retain this ability throughout adulthood.

    (E) Infants are born with the capacity to discriminate phonemes and morphemes but lose this ability over time.

47. One form of learning that appears in the newborn is called

    (A) habituation

    (B) perceptual sensitivity

    (C) classification

    (D) apraxia

    (E) disequilibrium

48. Marissa's parents have raised her to respect elders, obey their rules, and not argue with them. They hardly ever ask for her opinions or point of view on matters of discipline and house rules. Based on this description, their parenting style would be classified as

    (A) love-oriented

    (B) authoritarian

    (C) authoritative

    (D) permissive

    (E) democratic

49. The parenting style that has been found to be associated with the best developmental outcomes for children is
    (A) disorganized
    (B) authoritarian
    (C) authoritative
    (D) permissive
    (E) democratic

50. Albert Bandura argued that children learn behaviors
    (A) by just hearing about the behavior, but not seeing it
    (B) by performing the behavior and then receiving reinforcement
    (C) by observing another person perform a behavior
    (D) by trial-and-error
    (E) to avoid punishment

51. Kübler-Ross performed groundbreaking research on the experiences of people who are dying from terminal illnesses. She concluded that
    (A) dying was an individual experience; no general conclusions about how people approach their death can be made
    (B) the way a person deals with his or her impending death depends on the person's gender
    (C) the way a person deals with his or her impending death depends on the person's personality type
    (D) there are stages a terminally ill person progresses through as he or she deals with impending death
    (E) terminally-ill patients are not interested in talking about death

52. The term used to describe personality in young infants is
    (A) attachment style
    (B) temperament
    (C) extroversion
    (D) autism
    (E) respondent type

53. According to Skinner, a classroom teacher who wishes to decrease students' disruptive behaviors should
    (A) ignore disruptive behaviors and reward appropriate classroom behaviors
    (B) harshly punish disruptive behavior
    (C) give children more play time
    (D) give children more tasks to keep them busy
    (E) remove distractions from the classroom

54. Which is NOT one of the factors found to contribute to resilience in at-risk children?
    (A) Personal resources such as intelligence or grit
    (B) Having at least one person who loves them
    (C) Having an easy temperament that adapts to situations
    (D) Being raised in a two-parent family
    (E) Being sociable

55. There are two attribution styles that have been identified in research on personality development. These are
    (A) extroversion versus introversion
    (B) openness versus a lack of openness to experience
    (C) internal versus external locus of control
    (D) sociability versus non-sociability
    (E) feminine versus masculine orientation

56. Which of the following statements is true?
    (A) Gender is the same as biological sex.
    (B) Feminine is to female as masculine is to male.
    (C) Both males and females can be feminine or masculine.
    (D) Gender is determined at birth.
    (E) Androgyny is a myth.

57. Developmental psychologists who are continuity theorists
    (A) argue that development proceeds through a series of qualitatively different stages
    (B) argue that development proceeds through a series of quantitatively different stages
    (C) disagree with each other on the number of stages of development
    (D) agree that development is controlled by genetic inheritance
    (E) argue that development is best described as increases in amount or strength of abilities and not stages or qualitative shifts in abilities

58. Newborns show signs that they can discriminate among the five tastes: bitter, sweet, salty, umami, and sour. The evidence for this ability comes from examining which of the following changes in newborns when flavored liquid is placed on their tongues?
    (A) Heart rate
    (B) Respiration
    (C) Facial expression
    (D) Moro reflex response
    (E) Grasping

59. Which of the following factors might predict that John, who was born with low birth weight into an impoverished family, would develop normally?
    (A) The fact that John has a difficult temperament as an infant.
    (B) The fact that John has above-average intelligence.
    (C) The fact that John's mother is a stay-at-home mom.
    (D) The fact that John is an only child.
    (E) The fact that John is male.

60. Presbyopia refers to

(A) infants' inability to track moving objects

(B) changes in sensitivity to odors that gradually occur with increasing age

(C) increasingly poor near vision that begins in middle age

(D) newborns' preference for looking at faces

(E) increasingly poor taste sensitivity with age

61. Teratogens have

(A) no effect on prenatal development in the last two weeks of pregnancy

(B) different effects on male versus female fetuses

(C) their greatest influence on the development of systems of the body during the second trimester

(D) effects only in nervous system development

(E) their greatest effects in the first two weeks of pregnancy

62. Which of the following is a key element of Darwin's theory?

(A) There is a constant competition for limited resources, like food, among members of a species, so chance mutations can be helpful or harmful to survival.

(B) There is a constant struggle for existence between species. The strongest species survive, and weaker species go extinct.

(C) Members of species who cooperate as a group have a greater chance for survival, regardless of genetics.

(D) All members of a species inherit the same ability to survive.

(E) Humans and animals evolved from different ancestors.

63. Observations of children's language development indicate that

(A) generalization is achieved before discrimination

(B) production develops faster than understanding

(C) understanding develops faster than production

(D) acquisition is achieved before understanding

(E) imitation develops slower than production

64. According to Piaget, the highest level of cognitive functioning is
    (A) sensorimotor intelligence
    (B) formal operations
    (C) concrete operations
    (D) preoperations
    (E) perceptual operations

65. Which developmental psychologist described the importance of language for the development of thought?
    (A) Sigmund Freud
    (B) Lev Vygotsky
    (C) Erik Erikson
    (D) Jean Piaget
    (E) Urie Bronfenbrenner

66. Research on child abuse shows that
    (A) the United States has the lowest rate of child abuse of any country
    (B) parents who abuse their children have low IQs
    (C) parents who abuse their children were abusive to their siblings
    (D) parents who abuse their children experience high emotional arousal in stressful situations
    (E) abusers typically have bipolar disorder

67. A child runs into his house and expects his Daddy to know what happened to him outside. This is an example of
    (A) autistic thinking
    (B) social thinking
    (C) egocentric thinking
    (D) reciprocal thinking
    (E) vicarious thinking

68. One diagnostic feature of autism is the child's

    (A) delayed physical development

    (B) below average intelligence

    (C) aggressive behavior toward others

    (D) lack of interest and responsiveness to others

    (E) impulsive behavior

69. Which of the following statements is true?

    (A) One of the earliest symptoms to appear in Alzheimer's disease is a speech impairment called "word salad."

    (B) One of the earliest symptoms to appear in Alzheimer's disease is impaired motor coordination.

    (C) One of the earliest symptoms to appear in Alzheimer's disease is paranoia.

    (D) One of earliest symptoms to appear in Alzheimer's disease is memory impairment.

    (E) Alzheimer's is curable if diagnosed early enough.

70. According to the information-processing approach, cognitive development can be tracked by measuring

    (A) improvement in logical thinking

    (B) the construction of mental schema

    (C) changes in mental processing speed

    (D) a decrease in metacognition

    (E) adaptation

71. An example of the connection between language and thought is
    (A) Vygotsky noticed that children use language to get what they want.
    (B) the fact that children do not speak their first words until near their second birthday
    (C) the theory that a culture develops language to match its setting and its need for communicating within and about that setting
    (D) the fact that children almost never lie, but adolescents often do because of their increased cognitive abilities
    (E) Piaget observed children talking to themselves as they mastered object permanence

72. A common feature of attention-deficit hyperactivity disorder is
    (A) mood swings
    (B) obsessions
    (C) a lack of impulse control
    (D) antisocial behavior
    (E) negativity

73. Which level of intellectual disability is closest to the normal range of IQ?
    (A) Mild intellectual disability
    (B) Trainable cognitive disability
    (C) Profound cognitive disability
    (D) Severe auditory disability
    (E) Optimal perceptual disability

74. The reinforcement schedule that yields low performance is the
    (A) fixed-praise schedule
    (B) variable-ratio schedule
    (C) fixed-interval schedule
    (D) variable-praise schedule
    (E) intermittent reinforcement schedule

75. The repeated presentation of the CS without the UCS results in

(A) spontaneous recovery

(B) inhibition

(C) extinction

(D) higher-order conditioning

(E) negative reinforcement

76. The Wechsler Intelligence Scale for Children differs from the Revised Stanford Binet test in

(A) the age groups that can be tested

(B) the distribution of verbal and nonverbal tasks

(C) its applicability with psychotic students

(D) its accounting for cultural background differences

(E) its usefulness for predicting creativity

77. People who repeatedly wash their hands even when they are not dirty may be said to be exhibiting

(A) learned helplessness

(B) a conversion reaction

(C) an obsession

(D) a phobia

(E) a compulsion

78. The stage theory that we all experience a series of psychosocial crises throughout our lives was proposed by

(A) Freud

(B) Rogers

(C) Marcia

(D) Erikson

(E) Jung

79. According to Freud, dreaming is filled with symbolism arising out of
    (A) the superego's desire to dominate the id and ego
    (B) the ego's desire to dominate the id and superego
    (C) the transfer of unconscious materials into the superego
    (D) the individual's waking repression of urges from the id
    (E) a desire to regress to a former state

80. According to psychoanalytic thinking, the personality structure consists of
    (A) habits
    (B) drives
    (C) self
    (D) the id, ego, and superego
    (E) consciousness

81. The "master gland" that regulates other glands is
    (A) the gonads
    (B) the adrenal glands
    (C) the thyroid
    (D) the thymus
    (E) the pituitary gland

82. The focusing part of the eye is called the
    (A) lens
    (B) optic nerve
    (C) pupil
    (D) iris
    (E) retina

83. Receptor cells that are very sensitive to color are the

(A) ganglion cells

(B) rods on the pupils

(C) cones on the retina

(D) iris cells

(E) cells of the lens

84. Children who are bilingual have been found to

(A) have more academic difficulties than their monolingual peers

(B) have increased cognitive scores on certain measures

(C) have lower creativity scores than their monolingual peers

(D) have higher levels of self-esteem than their monolingual counterparts

(E) lack an understanding of the grammar of their second language

85. The sensitive period for language acquisition refers to the fact that

(A) humans are not emotionally stable until they can communicate effectively

(B) after a certain age, language skills deteriorate

(C) if a person has not acquired a language by puberty, he or she may never learn to speak appropriately

(D) humans must acquire one language at a time

(E) the brain needs a time frame to develop language centers

86. Intellectually challenged humans frequently show language deficits. Language acquisition of simple statements and sentences is highly unlikely if the measured IQ is below

(A) 120

(B) 90

(C) 70

(D) 50

(E) 20

87. A young child gets help in language development when the mother repeats what the child says, but in a complete sentence. This strategy is called

    (A) expansion

    (B) telegraphic speech

    (C) motherese

    (D) recasting

    (E) holographic speech

88. Morphemes differ from phonemes in that

    (A) morphemes are utterances that have no meaning

    (B) phonemes carry meaning while morphemes do not

    (C) morphemes carry meaning while phonemes do not

    (D) morphemes refer to animal sounds while phonemes are sounds made only by humans

    (E) phonemes refer to speech sounds while morphemes refer to sign language gestures

89. Alfred Binet is famous for developing the first

    (A) item analysis

    (B) intelligence test

    (C) projective test

    (D) fixed alternative test

    (E) infant intelligence test

90. Children are shown a movie of an adult hitting and kicking a rubber doll, then getting scolded for doing so. Later, the children are given access to the doll. Videotapes of the children made with a hidden camera reveal that

    (A) they hit but do not kick the doll.

    (B) some hit and kick the doll, while others do not.

    (C) the boys hit the doll, while the girls play gently with it.

    (D) the children avoid the doll.

    (E) the girls console the doll.

PRACTICE TEST 2

Answer Key

1.	(A)	31.	(B)	61.	(C)
2.	(A)	32.	(A)	62.	(A)
3.	(B)	33.	(E)	63.	(C)
4.	(E)	34.	(A)	64.	(B)
5.	(D)	35.	(C)	65.	(B)
6.	(A)	36.	(C)	66.	(D)
7.	(C)	37.	(D)	67.	(C)
8.	(C)	38.	(B)	68.	(D)
9.	(D)	39.	(B)	69.	(D)
10.	(A)	40.	(A)	70.	(C)
11.	(E)	41.	(B)	71.	(C)
12.	(D)	42.	(A)	72.	(C)
13.	(A)	43.	(B)	73.	(A)
14.	(A)	44.	(C)	74.	(C)
15.	(A)	45.	(D)	75.	(C)
16.	(E)	46.	(B)	76.	(B)
17.	(B)	47.	(A)	77.	(E)
18.	(B)	48.	(B)	78.	(D)
19.	(A)	49.	(C)	79.	(D)
20.	(C)	50.	(C)	80.	(D)
21.	(E)	51.	(D)	81.	(E)
22.	(B)	52.	(B)	82.	(A)
23.	(B)	53.	(A)	83.	(C)
24.	(C)	54.	(D)	84.	(B)
25.	(D)	55.	(C)	85.	(C)
26.	(E)	56.	(C)	86.	(E)
27.	(E)	57.	(E)	87.	(A)
28.	(C)	58.	(C)	88.	(C)
29.	(A)	59.	(B)	89.	(B)
30.	(D)	60.	(C)	90.	(B)

PRACTICE TEST 2

Detailed Explanations of Answers

1. **(A)** Correlational research involves measuring two variables in a group of subjects and determining whether there is a relationship between the two sets of scores. A correlational design could be used to determine whether there is a relationship between depression and age by measuring age and level of depression in a large sample. Both responses (B) and (C) require an examination of differences, not relationships. Response (D) is a question that is best answered using a descriptive research approach like conducting a survey of a sample of 14-year-olds. The question is asking only what 14-year-olds are like. It is not a relationship or cause-and-effect question. Response (E) is a question about cause and effect. Cause-and-effect relationships cannot be identified using the correlational research design. A correlation does not mean causation because no variables are controlled or manipulated in correlational research.

2. **(A)** Freud's theory is unique in that it emphasizes the role of unconscious thoughts and wishes in motivating human behavior. For Freud, the unconscious held innate biological urges that must be channeled into socially appropriate behavior.

3. **(B)** Skinner described a process of learning he called operant conditioning. According to Skinner, learning, defined as changes in overt behavior, is shaped by reinforcement and punishment. Reinforcement (both positive and negative) received after a behavior is emitted will increase the probability that that behavior will be repeated under the same stimulus conditions. Punishment experienced after a behavior is emitted will decrease the probability that the behavior will be repeated again under the same stimulus conditions. Therefore, to increase the number of times your child does the dishes, Skinner would suggest you reinforce the child when she or he does the dishes. A cookie is generally considered a reward and therefore should work as a reinforcer and increase the frequency of the goal behavior.

4. **(E)** John Holland conducted research on the relationship between personality traits and characteristics of different occupations. Based on this research, he developed a system to match personality types with occupational types.

5. **(D)** Adrenalin is a hormone secreted as part of the body's fight-or-flight response. It is also secreted during times of emotional stress. Consistently high levels of adrenalin can negatively impact the body's immune system.

6. **(A)** The supply of oxygen to a fetus can be disrupted during a vaginal delivery if the umbilical cord becomes crimped or if mucus builds up in the baby's throat. The condition of a depleted oxygen supply is called anoxia.

7. **(C)** Kübler-Ross was the first to systematically study terminally ill patients. Based on extensive interviews with people as they progressed through the process of dying, she formulated a stage model of adjustment to death and dying. The stages include denial, anger, bargaining, depression, and finally, acceptance.

8. **(C)** Goleman suggests that another form of intelligence, called emotional intelligence, is a person's ability to understand and adapt to emotion and emotional situations. People with high EQs have an exceptional ability to understand and deal with their own emotions and the emotions expressed by other people. His controversial prediction is that EQ is a better predictor of success in life than IQ.

9. **(D)** Research has shown that, second to sleeping, preschoolers watch television more than engaging in any other activity.

10. **(A)** A blended family has children from the parents' previous marriage(s) plus any children from their current marriage.

11. **(E)** A person who has an internal locus of control attribution style believes that events in his or her life are under his or her control. Therefore, both successes and failures are attributed to personal abilities, traits, or behaviors.

12. **(D)** Teratogens are substances that pass through the semi-permeable membrane of the placenta, enter the fetus's bloodstream, and cause damage to the fetus. Therefore, anything that occurs in the father's body cannot, by definition, be a teratogen.

13. **(A)** The sensorimotor stage is the first stage in Piaget's model of cognitive development. Piaget demonstrated that object permanence was not present at birth and developed during the sensorimotor stage. He believed object permanence is not fully achieved until the end of infancy.

14. **(A)** Habituation is a simple form of learning that appears in newborns. Habituation is defined as decreased attention to a stimulus over time. Therefore, if a newborn habituates to a stimulus, his or her looking time will decrease.

15. **(A)** The Bayley Scales of Infant Intelligence were developed to measure levels of intelligence in infants. Prior research suggested a positive relationship between measures of attention in infants and later IQ scores. Therefore, measures of auditory and visual attention spans are included on the Bayley Scales.

16. **(E)** Cross-cultural research on the adolescent stage of development has shown variations in the length of adolescence as well as the experiences of adolescents. There is some evidence that the biological changes associated with adolescence produce some universals of experiences and stress. However, in some cultures, adolescence is nonexistent or only a brief phase. Some cultures have a ceremonial rite of passage into adulthood so that a child becomes an adult in the same day, whereas in others, the stage is long and stressful. Therefore, adolescence is both biologically and culturally determined.

17. **(B)** "Disequilibrium" is the term used by Piaget to describe the cognitive experience that occurs when assimilation fails. Assimilation is the process of understanding a new experience using already existing cognitive schema. A person is assimilating when she walks into a Burger King for the first time and acts as she has always acted in McDonald's. Disequilibrium would be experienced by the same girl thc first time she went into a fancy restaurant. Disequilibrium is an important process in cognitive development because it is the experience that motivates us to modify our existing schema. We accommodate when we adjust a schema to include new information. The schema that is a result of this process of disequilibrium-accommodation is more mature.

18. **(B)** Attachment behaviors are behaviors exhibited by the members of an attachment relationship, e.g., mother-infant or father-infant, that increase the strength of the attachment bond. As young infants' smiling develops from a reflexive facial response to an intentional, controlled "social smile," they will smile more frequently in the presence of the target of their attachment. In so doing, the infant attracts the attention of the target.

19. **(A)** Piaget argued that children develop understanding about the world through active exploration of objects. Therefore, children would benefit from a teaching approach that gives them concrete objects to manipulate.

20. **(C)** Object permanence is the concept that objects have a permanent and separate existence from our perception of them. A child who has not achieved object permanence will not actively search for a missing toy. Anything that becomes out of sight becomes out of mind for this child. A child who actively looks for a toy that is no longer in view has the concept of object permanence.

21. **(E)** Ainsworth developed a method of measuring the strength of the attachment relationship between child and caregiver called the Ainsworth Strange Situation. Although this method has been criticized by some theorists as creating an artificial situation for the child and caregiver, it is the most widely used method of assessing attachment. In the Strange Situation, a child is separated from the caregiver and his or her reactions are observed. The observers note the child's reactions when the caregiver leaves, as well as when the caregiver returns. Based upon these reactions, the child is judged to be either securely attached or insecurely attached to the caregiver. A child is judged to be securely attached if she or he is upset when the caregiver leaves and reacts positively and seeks proximity to the caregiver upon the caregiver's return. Insecure-avoidant children do not act distressed when the caregiver leaves and avoid the caregiver upon his or her return to the room. An insecure-disorganized/disoriented child reacts in a conflicted way to the caregiver upon his or her return to the room. This child may seek contact and then move away from the caregiver. Insecure-resistant children are very distressed when the caregiver leaves and actively resist contact with the caregiver upon his or her return to the room.

22. **(B)** A symbol is something that represents something else but does not look like or relate in a rationale way to what it represents. The idea that the color red means "stop" is due to the symbolic relationship our society has created between the color and the idea of "stop."

23. **(B)** Kohlberg developed a theory of moral development in which he described a series of stages through which mature moral reasoning develops. In the stage of conventional morality, one makes decisions about right and wrong by applying societal laws created to control behavior. Hence, one would think being "good" means obeying the rules.

24. **(C)** In Erikson's model of personality development, the psychosocial crisis to be resolved in middle adulthood is generativity versus stagnation. Generativity is the positive resolution of this crisis and involves fulfilling one's desire to make a contribution to society and help members of younger generations of that society develop and meet their goals.

25. **(D)** According to Kohlberg's theory of how moral reasoning develops, in the conventional morality stage, decisions about right and wrong are made by applying societal laws. Thus, given the answer choices, (D) is correct because one would think it is right to buckle up because there is a law that says so.

26. **(E)** During Kohlberg's stage of preconventional morality, a child makes decisions about right and wrong based on his or her expectations of the consequences of his or her actions. Therefore, a preconventional reasoner would decide not to hit another child because he would expect to get hit back. He or she would not hit another child in order to avoid being hit back, not because it is the moral thing to do.

27. **(E)** Adolescence is a transition stage of development in which a person moves from being dependent on caregivers as a child, to becoming a separate and independent being.

28. **(C)** Assimilation is the process of understanding something new using already existing cognitive structures or schema. The child's understanding of the crow is achieved by applying a scheme for similar-looking things, i.e., "bird." In Piaget's theory of cognitive development, the process of assimilation has to be in balance with the process of accommodation, which is changing an old scheme to fit new information. A child who overassimilates will not develop more mature and complex schema.

29. **(A)** The concept of critical period was introduced by the ethologists Konrad Lorenz and John Bowlby. A critical period is a restricted range of time for a characteristic or trait to develop. This question illustrates a critical period in development for a mother-infant bond to form between a goat and her kid. In humans, there is greater flexibility to develop characteristics and traits outside of critical windows of time; therefore, psychologists use the term "sensitive period" rather than "critical period" when discussing human development. For example, in human development there appears to be a sensitive period from birth to puberty during which it is easier to learn a language, but that does not mean no one can learn a language once this time period has passed.

30. **(D)** Transductive reasoning is immature reasoning about cause-and-effect relationships.

31. **(B)** Evolutionary psychology is a field that tries to trace the historical roots of human behavior. This perspective is influenced by Darwin's theory of evolution. In this perspective, behaviors in our species' repertoire are believed

to have adaptive value. Evolutionary psychologists study human behavior to understand its adaptive value, as well as study the behavior of less-evolved species, to develop a better understanding of human behavior.

32. **(A)** Bronfenbrenner argued that development should be studied within the contexts in which it occurs. He suggested several such contexts. A context in which a child plays a direct role is called a microsystem. The family and school are examples of microsystems. In the ecosystem, events from different microsystems interact. The exosystem is a social context that indirectly influences the child's development, like Dad's office, and the macrosystem is the cultural context in which all the other systems are embedded.

33. **(E)** A major difference between the psychosocial model of development from Erikson and the psychosexual model of development from Freud is that Erikson's model is a life span approach. Erikson argued that development takes place throughout the entire life span. According to Freud, development was complete at puberty. Hence, Freud's focus was on the impact of early childhood experiences on personality, while Erikson argued experiences throughout our lives continue to shape our personality.

34. **(A)** The case study approach to research has strengths and weaknesses. A strength is that the researcher is able to learn a great deal about an individual case. The description of the case is detailed and deep. This can be especially helpful when the researcher is studying someone who is unique or had a unique experience. On the other hand, the findings from one case study cannot be generalized to a larger group. A goal of psychology is to understand and explain what is common to all people, as well as to understand individual differences. The case study approach does not help in attaining the first goal.

35. **(C)** Experimental research is the only type of research that can identify cause-and-effect relationships. The two key elements of the experimental approach to research are control and manipulation. In a controlled setting, an independent variable, which is the hypothesized cause, is manipulated so that it is present in one condition of the experiment but not present in another condition in the experiment. In this way, an experimenter can determine if the effect occurs if, and only if, the independent variable is present. Without this control and manipulation, researchers can only observe whether or not two variables are related, as in correlational research.

36. **(C)** There are research designs that are particularly useful in developmental research. Two of these are the longitudinal research design and the cross-sectional research design. Longitudinal design is considered the stron-

ger of the two designs. The longitudinal method involves studying a group of participants at several points in time over a long period of time. The researcher measures changes in this group as they age. A cross-sectional study involves studying samples of participants who represent different age groups. A researcher using this design is able to show how different-aged people are different from each other at one point in time, but not how the same people change with age. Also, cross-sectional design confounds age difference with birth cohort differences. Therefore, longitudinal is considered stronger than cross-sectional design.

37. **(D)** Studies of brain development have shown that as the human brain matures, there is a pruning back of neural connections, even while new connections are being made. Neural connections that are frequently used are retained, while neural connections that were present early in development, but are not used, are pruned.

38. **(B)** A recessive trait is a trait that is carried on a recessive gene. Since we inherit gene pairs from our biological parents, it is possible to inherit two recessive genes, two dominant genes, or a dominant gene-recessive gene pair. The trait on a recessive gene will be expressed only if the dominant gene is not present. The gene for blue eyes is a recessive gene. Even if both the mother and father have brown eyes, they both could be carriers of the recessive gene for blue eyes. It is therefore possible that an offspring would inherit two recessive genes and have blue eyes.

39. **(B)** Amniocentesis is one method of prenatal screening used to detect abnormalities in fetal development. Amniotic fluid is removed from the amniotic sac in the uterus and analyzed for markers of genetic diseases and abnormalities.

40. **(A)** The default is for a fertilized egg cell to develop into a female. The presence of the Y chromosome is what stops this default process and causes the fertilized egg cell to differentiate into a male. It is the biological father, therefore, who determines the sex of the offspring. The biological father is the only parent who can pass on a Y chromosome.

41. **(B)** Selective attention is the process in which perceptual energy is directed toward a stimulus target and kept from distracting irrelevant stimuli in the environment. Therefore, selective attention requires the ability to ignore irrelevant stimuli.

42. **(A)** The information-processing approach to studying cognitive development argues that there are three memory storage systems. These are sensory, primary, and secondary memory. Sensory memory is the temporary storage of what registers in a sensory-perceptual system like vision or audition. This is an automatic and very brief record of information lasting only a few seconds. Primary memory, also known as short-term or working memory, is a memory storage system that also holds information temporarily albeit for a longer period of time than sensory memory. Information can be held in primary memory for a longer period of time through the process of rehearsal. Repeating a telephone number to yourself causes the number to be retained in your consciousness. However, any interruption in rehearsal will cause the information to be lost. Secondary or long-term memory is our long-term storage system.

Memories are stored in secondary memory through the process of encoding. Information that is in primary memory that is encoded for long-term retention is moved from primary to secondary memory. Since encoding is done in primary memory, this system is also referred to as working memory. Some psychologists believe that secondary memory is a permanent storage system and that forgetting occurs not because information is lost, but because the information cannot be retrieved. The better the information to be stored is encoded, the more likely the information will be retrieved later. Secondary memory is a highly organized storage system.

43. **(B)** Researchers have studied changes in memory that occur with age. One finding is that the capacity of primary memory increases with age until it reaches full maturity of seven plus or minus two bits of information.

44. **(C)** Vygotsky described cognitive development as the result of interactions between a child and older people in his or her environment. He argued that a child's thinking is supported or "scaffolded" by adults in his or her life like teachers and parents. Working with an older adult, a child can solve more difficult problems than if he or she was working alone.

45. **(D)** "Syntax" is the term used to describe the grammatical rules of a language. Syntax guides how the elements of language are combined.

46. **(B)** A remarkable finding by psycholinguists studying language development is that newborns have the ability to produce all of the sounds or phonemes required to speak any of the world's languages. Further, this ability is lost with age. Infants will continue to form the phonemes required for their native language and lose the ability to produce sounds of non-native languages.

47. **(A)** Habituation is a simple type of learning that appears in newborns. Habituation is a decrease in responding to a stimulus over time. A newborn will look away from a stimulus object after a period of time.

48. **(B)** Baumrind examined the relationship between parenting style and developmental outcomes. The authoritarian parenting style is seen in a parent who values strict obedience from children and uses punishment to change children's behavior. An authoritarian parent does not provide explanations for the household rules, and children do not have a voice in determining those rules. They also show low acceptance/support toward the child. Authoritative parents provide guidelines and rules for behavior, but also show high acceptance/responsiveness toward the child. Harsh punishment is not used. The permissive parent provides little to no guidelines or rules for the child's behavior but shows high acceptance/support toward the child. The uninvolved parenting style is seen in parents who are low in control/demandingness and low in acceptance/support. These parents pay little to no attention to their child. Marissa's parents are authoritarian.

49. **(C)** Authoritative parenting has been associated with the best developmental outcomes. See the explanation for #48.

50. **(C)** Albert Bandura argued that behavior is learned not only through classical and operant conditioning, but is also the result of imitation or observational learning. Bandura reasoned that when we observe a model being positively reinforced for his or her behavior, we are likely to imitate that model.

51. **(D)** Kübler-Ross was the first to systematically study terminally ill patients. Based on extensive interviews with people as they progressed through the process of dying, she formulated a stage model of adjustment to death and dying. The stages in order are denial, anger, bargaining, depression, and acceptance. Critics of her work argue that Kübler-Ross made death and dying a more normative process than it really is. They argue that not all dying people go through all of the stages and that some people never reach the stage of acceptance. Finally, the circumstances surrounding the dying process affect the dying person's experience.

52. **(B)** "Temperament" is the term used for a rudimentary form of personality in infants. Temperament is the typical style or way infants respond to people and stimulation, and their characteristic activity level. There are three temperament types: easy, difficult, and slow-to-warm-up.

53. **(A)** Skinner argued that in order to shape behavior, reinforcing a goal behavior is more effective than punishing inappropriate behavior. Classroom management techniques reflect Skinner's findings. Therefore, a classroom teacher who wishes to shape a student's behavior would be advised by Skinner to ignore problem behaviors and reinforce good behavior. Attention to problem behaviors may result in inadvertently rewarding the behavior.

54. **(D)** Being raised by only one versus two parents has not been shown to influence resilience. All of the other factors have.

55. **(C)** Psychologists have studied the attributions people make for causes of experiences in life. There are two diametrically opposed styles that have emerged from this work. These are the internal locus of control style and the external locus of control style. Internals place the locus of control over events in their lives inside themselves or under their own control. Externals place the locus of control of events in their lives outside or beyond their own control.

56. **(C)** The term "gender" is often misapplied. In colloquial language, gender has become a substitute term for biological sex. Gender, however, is not the same as biological sex. Sex refers to one's biological makeup, i.e., male or female. Gender refers to a social role and these include masculinity, femininity, and androgyny. Biological sex and gender are independent of each other although stereotypically, males are expected to be more masculine than females, and females are expected to be more feminine than males.

57. **(E)** There is a debate among psychologists as to whether development is best described as a series of qualitative shifts or stages, or steady increases in the amount or strength of abilities. Discontinuity theorists argue for the former. Continuity theorists argue for the latter.

58. **(C)** Research on infant taste perception has relied on infants' facial expressions to indicate whether the infant can discriminate tastes. Reliable changes in facial expression appear in newborns presented with different flavored liquids.

59. **(B)** Having average or higher intelligence, an easy temperament, at least one person who loves you unconditionally, and being sociable have been shown to increase infant resilience in the face of risks. These factors are associated with thriving and normal developmental outcomes in at-risk infants. Low birth weight is a risk factor that can lead to developmental problems in infants.

60. **(C)** Presbyopia is a vision problem associated with aging. Presbyopia is caused by a difficulty focusing on near objects. Most middle-aged adults begin to have near vision problems, but most of these problems are corrected with lenses to help properly focus light waves from near objects onto the retina.

61. **(C)** Teratogens are potentially damaging substances that cross the semi-permeable membrane of the placenta and enter the bloodstream of the fetus. Damage from teratogens rarely occurs in the first trimester or the third trimester. Most organs and systems of the body are most susceptible to damage from teratogens during the second trimester.

62. **(A)** There are several key elements to Darwin's theory of the evolution of species by natural selection. One of these is that there is a competition among members of a species for survival. The population growth of a species is always faster than the growth of the food and supplies needed to support the species. Such limited resources produce a struggle among members of a species for survival. Another element is that members of a species inherit chance variations of the traits of the species. Some members inherit variations that increase their chances of surviving, while others inherit variations that make them less likely to survive. Members of the species who survive to maturity reproduce and therefore keep their traits in the species gene pool. Over a very long time period, a species evolves as genes for the chance variations that did not enable survival gradually disappear from the gene pool.

63. **(C)** Children show an understanding of language that surpasses their ability to produce language. For example, an infant can follow verbal directions before uttering his or her first word.

64. **(B)** Formal operational thought is the ability to reason logically about both concrete and abstract concepts. It is therefore the highest level of cognitive development that can be achieved. While a concrete operational thinker is capable of logical thought, he or she can only reason effectively with or about concrete objects.

65. **(B)** Vygotsky concluded that language influences thought. Talking to oneself either out loud (external speech) or not out loud (internal speech) tends to occur during problem solving. Vygotsky observed that young children use external speech when working out problems. External speech occurs with more frequency in early childhood and then goes inward to become internal speech in older children and adults.

66. **(D)** Studies have shown that parents who abuse their children have stronger than normal reactions to stress. Under stressful conditions, they experience higher emotional arousal than normal. It is possible that this high level of arousal triggers aggression.

67. **(C)** Egocentric thinking is believing that what you perceive and experience is the same as what other people perceive and experience. Egocentric thinkers fail to understand that different people have different points of view. Therefore, a child who is egocentric would expect his father to have seen what happened to him, even though the father was not there.

68. **(D)** A feature of autism spectrum disorders is a lack of responsiveness to others. Autistic children do not easily form social relationships and do not respond normally to social cues. They may actively avoid social interaction.

69. **(D)** Memory impairment is one of the early symptoms of Alzheimer's disease. However, impaired memory does not necessarily mean a person has Alzheimer's. Typically, a person in the early stages of this disease will have difficulty retrieving words.

70. **(C)** Information-processing theorists argue that improved cognitive ability is the result of an increase in processing speed in older children. The increasing speed of mental processing allows the older child to perform more mental operations at one time in working memory. Changes in processing speed are also researched in aging adults.

71. **(C)** There are many theoretical and observable examples of the connection between language and thought, especially in the works of Piaget and Vygotsky. However, only one of these choices is factually true. Benjamin Whorf proposed that languages develop based on environment and culture, and the need to communicate in ways that accommodate both of those factors.

72. **(C)** Impulsivity is a common feature of children with attention deficit hyperactivity disorder (ADHD). Poor impulse control means difficulty controlling behavior and thinking before acting.

73. **(A)** Children with mild cognitive disability have IQ scores between 52 and 75. This is the highest range of all the intellectual disability classifications. An IQ score above 75 is considered normal, with a score of 100 being the average.

74. **(C)** In the fixed-interval schedule, reinforcement is given after a fixed period of time no matter how much work is done. This schedule has the lowest yield in terms of performance. However, just before the reinforcement is given, activity increases.

75. **(C)** Extinction of conditioned respondent behavior occurs when the CS is presented without the UCS a number of times. The magnitude of the response elicited by the CS and the percentage of presentations of the CS that elicits responses gradually decreases as the CS continues to be presented without the UCS. If CS presentation continues without the UCS, the CR will decline to at least the level present before the classical conditioning was begun.

76. **(B)** The Stanford Binet test has a heavy emphasis on verbal skills, while the WISC uses verbal and nonverbal tasks equally.

77. **(E)** Repeated handwashing is known as an obsessive-compulsive neurosis, although, as in other obsessive-compulsive disorders, the two components need not exist simultaneously. Repeated handwashing is termed compulsive if the person feels compelled to perform the behavior, thus interfering with more appropriate behavior. Remember that an obsession is a recurring thought, while a compulsion is an uncontrollable behavior. This disorder is thought to arise as a defense against anxiety.

78. **(D)** Erikson determined that there were eight developmental crises in our lives corresponding to the eight developmental periods. These crises in their developmental order are (1) trust vs. mistrust; (2) autonomy vs. shame and doubt; (3) initiative vs. guilt; (4) industry vs. inferiority; (5) identity vs. role confusion; (6) intimacy vs. isolation; (7) generativity vs. stagnation; and (8) ego integrity vs. despair in old age.

79. **(D)** Freud reasoned that the dream is a hallucinatory state that structures events not as they would be in reality, but as the dreamer wishes them to be. When unconscious desires from the id conflict with conscious restraints, repression occurs. However, in dreaming, the individual can symbolically express the wish.

80. **(D)** The personality structure consists of the id, ego, and superego. According to Freud, the id is the most fundamental component of personality and is comprised of drives, needs, and instinctual impulses. It is unable to tolerate tension, is obedient only to the pleasure principle, and is in constant conflict with the superego. The superego develops out of the ego during childhood. It contains values, morals, and basic attitudes as learned from parents and society.

The ego mediates between the id and superego. The ego is sometimes called the executive agency of the personality because it controls actions and decides how needs should be satisfied.

81. **(E)** The pituitary gland produces several hormones. Its secretions control the actions of other glands. Hence, the pituitary is in a sense a master gland that directs the hormone secretions to other glands and organs.

82. **(A)** The lens focuses incoming light rays onto the retina.

83. **(C)** Cones respond differentially to different color wavelengths, providing us not only with color perception but also the ability to sense fine gradations of color.

84. **(B)** Contrary to earlier research on bilingual schoolchildren, which often confounded bilingualism and sociocultural disadvantages, bilingual children have been found to have high verbal and nonverbal intelligence. They do not suffer academically because of being bilingual.

85. **(C)** Humans seem to be born pre-wired to acquire language. However, the environment must provide the stimulation for the brain areas associated with language to develop. Cases of children raised by animals or under conditions of extreme language deprivation (e.g., kept locked in a room and seldom spoken to) show that if humans don't acquire a language by puberty, they will never acquire any reasonable mastery of language, whether they are later provided with extensive remedial language training or not.

86. **(E)** Humans with an IQ of 20 or less barely make reliable contact with their environments and seldom develop abilities beyond those of an infant. Individuals with an IQ of 50 or higher can learn to comprehend and make simple statements.

87. **(A)** Mothers use expansion to demonstrate how a child's telegraphic speech can be put into full syntax. Motherese is a type of speaking that is high-pitched and clearly enunciated. Recasting is a way of correcting grammatical speaking errors.

88. **(C)** Phonemes are the basic sounds that all humans are capable of making. The coos and babbling of a baby are phonemes. Morphemes are the smallest units of speech sounds that carry meaning. Morphemes are whole words as well as prefixes such as "anti-" and suffixes such as "-ing."

89. **(B)** In 1904, the French government asked Alfred Binet to construct a test that would distinguish between normal children and children with severe learning disabilities. Binet conceived of intelligence as the relationship of mental ability and chronological age. For each age up to 15 years, there is a set of characteristic abilities that develop in the normal child. If they developed earlier than average, the child is more intelligent than average; if the abilities develop later, then the child is considered to be of below-average intelligence.

90. **(B)** Children imitate what they see and hear without making value judgments. However, if children see a negative consequence coming to the person they observe, many will not imitate the behavior.

PRACTICE TEST 1

Answer Sheet

1. Ⓐ Ⓑ Ⓒ Ⓓ Ⓔ	31. Ⓐ Ⓑ Ⓒ Ⓓ Ⓔ	61. Ⓐ Ⓑ Ⓒ Ⓓ Ⓔ
2. Ⓐ Ⓑ Ⓒ Ⓓ Ⓔ	32. Ⓐ Ⓑ Ⓒ Ⓓ Ⓔ	62. Ⓐ Ⓑ Ⓒ Ⓓ Ⓔ
3. Ⓐ Ⓑ Ⓒ Ⓓ Ⓔ	33. Ⓐ Ⓑ Ⓒ Ⓓ Ⓔ	63. Ⓐ Ⓑ Ⓒ Ⓓ Ⓔ
4. Ⓐ Ⓑ Ⓒ Ⓓ Ⓔ	34. Ⓐ Ⓑ Ⓒ Ⓓ Ⓔ	64. Ⓐ Ⓑ Ⓒ Ⓓ Ⓔ
5. Ⓐ Ⓑ Ⓒ Ⓓ Ⓔ	35. Ⓐ Ⓑ Ⓒ Ⓓ Ⓔ	65. Ⓐ Ⓑ Ⓒ Ⓓ Ⓔ
6. Ⓐ Ⓑ Ⓒ Ⓓ Ⓔ	36. Ⓐ Ⓑ Ⓒ Ⓓ Ⓔ	66. Ⓐ Ⓑ Ⓒ Ⓓ Ⓔ
7. Ⓐ Ⓑ Ⓒ Ⓓ Ⓔ	37. Ⓐ Ⓑ Ⓒ Ⓓ Ⓔ	67. Ⓐ Ⓑ Ⓒ Ⓓ Ⓔ
8. Ⓐ Ⓑ Ⓒ Ⓓ Ⓔ	38. Ⓐ Ⓑ Ⓒ Ⓓ Ⓔ	68. Ⓐ Ⓑ Ⓒ Ⓓ Ⓔ
9. Ⓐ Ⓑ Ⓒ Ⓓ Ⓔ	39. Ⓐ Ⓑ Ⓒ Ⓓ Ⓔ	69. Ⓐ Ⓑ Ⓒ Ⓓ Ⓔ
10. Ⓐ Ⓑ Ⓒ Ⓓ Ⓔ	40. Ⓐ Ⓑ Ⓒ Ⓓ Ⓔ	70. Ⓐ Ⓑ Ⓒ Ⓓ Ⓔ
11. Ⓐ Ⓑ Ⓒ Ⓓ Ⓔ	41. Ⓐ Ⓑ Ⓒ Ⓓ Ⓔ	71. Ⓐ Ⓑ Ⓒ Ⓓ Ⓔ
12. Ⓐ Ⓑ Ⓒ Ⓓ Ⓔ	42. Ⓐ Ⓑ Ⓒ Ⓓ Ⓔ	72. Ⓐ Ⓑ Ⓒ Ⓓ Ⓔ
13. Ⓐ Ⓑ Ⓒ Ⓓ Ⓔ	43. Ⓐ Ⓑ Ⓒ Ⓓ Ⓔ	73. Ⓐ Ⓑ Ⓒ Ⓓ Ⓔ
14. Ⓐ Ⓑ Ⓒ Ⓓ Ⓔ	44. Ⓐ Ⓑ Ⓒ Ⓓ Ⓔ	74. Ⓐ Ⓑ Ⓒ Ⓓ Ⓔ
15. Ⓐ Ⓑ Ⓒ Ⓓ Ⓔ	45. Ⓐ Ⓑ Ⓒ Ⓓ Ⓔ	75. Ⓐ Ⓑ Ⓒ Ⓓ Ⓔ
16. Ⓐ Ⓑ Ⓒ Ⓓ Ⓔ	46. Ⓐ Ⓑ Ⓒ Ⓓ Ⓔ	76. Ⓐ Ⓑ Ⓒ Ⓓ Ⓔ
17. Ⓐ Ⓑ Ⓒ Ⓓ Ⓔ	47. Ⓐ Ⓑ Ⓒ Ⓓ Ⓔ	77. Ⓐ Ⓑ Ⓒ Ⓓ Ⓔ
18. Ⓐ Ⓑ Ⓒ Ⓓ Ⓔ	48. Ⓐ Ⓑ Ⓒ Ⓓ Ⓔ	78. Ⓐ Ⓑ Ⓒ Ⓓ Ⓔ
19. Ⓐ Ⓑ Ⓒ Ⓓ Ⓔ	49. Ⓐ Ⓑ Ⓒ Ⓓ Ⓔ	79. Ⓐ Ⓑ Ⓒ Ⓓ Ⓔ
20. Ⓐ Ⓑ Ⓒ Ⓓ Ⓔ	50. Ⓐ Ⓑ Ⓒ Ⓓ Ⓔ	80. Ⓐ Ⓑ Ⓒ Ⓓ Ⓔ
21. Ⓐ Ⓑ Ⓒ Ⓓ Ⓔ	51. Ⓐ Ⓑ Ⓒ Ⓓ Ⓔ	81. Ⓐ Ⓑ Ⓒ Ⓓ Ⓔ
22. Ⓐ Ⓑ Ⓒ Ⓓ Ⓔ	52. Ⓐ Ⓑ Ⓒ Ⓓ Ⓔ	82. Ⓐ Ⓑ Ⓒ Ⓓ Ⓔ
23. Ⓐ Ⓑ Ⓒ Ⓓ Ⓔ	53. Ⓐ Ⓑ Ⓒ Ⓓ Ⓔ	83. Ⓐ Ⓑ Ⓒ Ⓓ Ⓔ
24. Ⓐ Ⓑ Ⓒ Ⓓ Ⓔ	54. Ⓐ Ⓑ Ⓒ Ⓓ Ⓔ	84. Ⓐ Ⓑ Ⓒ Ⓓ Ⓔ
25. Ⓐ Ⓑ Ⓒ Ⓓ Ⓔ	55. Ⓐ Ⓑ Ⓒ Ⓓ Ⓔ	85. Ⓐ Ⓑ Ⓒ Ⓓ Ⓔ
26. Ⓐ Ⓑ Ⓒ Ⓓ Ⓔ	56. Ⓐ Ⓑ Ⓒ Ⓓ Ⓔ	86. Ⓐ Ⓑ Ⓒ Ⓓ Ⓔ
27. Ⓐ Ⓑ Ⓒ Ⓓ Ⓔ	57. Ⓐ Ⓑ Ⓒ Ⓓ Ⓔ	87. Ⓐ Ⓑ Ⓒ Ⓓ Ⓔ
28. Ⓐ Ⓑ Ⓒ Ⓓ Ⓔ	58. Ⓐ Ⓑ Ⓒ Ⓓ Ⓔ	88. Ⓐ Ⓑ Ⓒ Ⓓ Ⓔ
29. Ⓐ Ⓑ Ⓒ Ⓓ Ⓔ	59. Ⓐ Ⓑ Ⓒ Ⓓ Ⓔ	89. Ⓐ Ⓑ Ⓒ Ⓓ Ⓔ
30. Ⓐ Ⓑ Ⓒ Ⓓ Ⓔ	60. Ⓐ Ⓑ Ⓒ Ⓓ Ⓔ	90. Ⓐ Ⓑ Ⓒ Ⓓ Ⓔ

PRACTICE TEST 2

Answer Sheet

1.	Ⓐ Ⓑ Ⓒ Ⓓ Ⓔ	31.	Ⓐ Ⓑ Ⓒ Ⓓ Ⓔ	61.	Ⓐ Ⓑ Ⓒ Ⓓ Ⓔ
2.	Ⓐ Ⓑ Ⓒ Ⓓ Ⓔ	32.	Ⓐ Ⓑ Ⓒ Ⓓ Ⓔ	62.	Ⓐ Ⓑ Ⓒ Ⓓ Ⓔ
3.	Ⓐ Ⓑ Ⓒ Ⓓ Ⓔ	33.	Ⓐ Ⓑ Ⓒ Ⓓ Ⓔ	63.	Ⓐ Ⓑ Ⓒ Ⓓ Ⓔ
4.	Ⓐ Ⓑ Ⓒ Ⓓ Ⓔ	34.	Ⓐ Ⓑ Ⓒ Ⓓ Ⓔ	64.	Ⓐ Ⓑ Ⓒ Ⓓ Ⓔ
5.	Ⓐ Ⓑ Ⓒ Ⓓ Ⓔ	35.	Ⓐ Ⓑ Ⓒ Ⓓ Ⓔ	65.	Ⓐ Ⓑ Ⓒ Ⓓ Ⓔ
6.	Ⓐ Ⓑ Ⓒ Ⓓ Ⓔ	36.	Ⓐ Ⓑ Ⓒ Ⓓ Ⓔ	66.	Ⓐ Ⓑ Ⓒ Ⓓ Ⓔ
7.	Ⓐ Ⓑ Ⓒ Ⓓ Ⓔ	37.	Ⓐ Ⓑ Ⓒ Ⓓ Ⓔ	67.	Ⓐ Ⓑ Ⓒ Ⓓ Ⓔ
8.	Ⓐ Ⓑ Ⓒ Ⓓ Ⓔ	38.	Ⓐ Ⓑ Ⓒ Ⓓ Ⓔ	68.	Ⓐ Ⓑ Ⓒ Ⓓ Ⓔ
9.	Ⓐ Ⓑ Ⓒ Ⓓ Ⓔ	39.	Ⓐ Ⓑ Ⓒ Ⓓ Ⓔ	69.	Ⓐ Ⓑ Ⓒ Ⓓ Ⓔ
10.	Ⓐ Ⓑ Ⓒ Ⓓ Ⓔ	40.	Ⓐ Ⓑ Ⓒ Ⓓ Ⓔ	70.	Ⓐ Ⓑ Ⓒ Ⓓ Ⓔ
11.	Ⓐ Ⓑ Ⓒ Ⓓ Ⓔ	41.	Ⓐ Ⓑ Ⓒ Ⓓ Ⓔ	71.	Ⓐ Ⓑ Ⓒ Ⓓ Ⓔ
12.	Ⓐ Ⓑ Ⓒ Ⓓ Ⓔ	42.	Ⓐ Ⓑ Ⓒ Ⓓ Ⓔ	72.	Ⓐ Ⓑ Ⓒ Ⓓ Ⓔ
13.	Ⓐ Ⓑ Ⓒ Ⓓ Ⓔ	43.	Ⓐ Ⓑ Ⓒ Ⓓ Ⓔ	73.	Ⓐ Ⓑ Ⓒ Ⓓ Ⓔ
14.	Ⓐ Ⓑ Ⓒ Ⓓ Ⓔ	44.	Ⓐ Ⓑ Ⓒ Ⓓ Ⓔ	74.	Ⓐ Ⓑ Ⓒ Ⓓ Ⓔ
15.	Ⓐ Ⓑ Ⓒ Ⓓ Ⓔ	45.	Ⓐ Ⓑ Ⓒ Ⓓ Ⓔ	75.	Ⓐ Ⓑ Ⓒ Ⓓ Ⓔ
16.	Ⓐ Ⓑ Ⓒ Ⓓ Ⓔ	46.	Ⓐ Ⓑ Ⓒ Ⓓ Ⓔ	76.	Ⓐ Ⓑ Ⓒ Ⓓ Ⓔ
17.	Ⓐ Ⓑ Ⓒ Ⓓ Ⓔ	47.	Ⓐ Ⓑ Ⓒ Ⓓ Ⓔ	77.	Ⓐ Ⓑ Ⓒ Ⓓ Ⓔ
18.	Ⓐ Ⓑ Ⓒ Ⓓ Ⓔ	48.	Ⓐ Ⓑ Ⓒ Ⓓ Ⓔ	78.	Ⓐ Ⓑ Ⓒ Ⓓ Ⓔ
19.	Ⓐ Ⓑ Ⓒ Ⓓ Ⓔ	49.	Ⓐ Ⓑ Ⓒ Ⓓ Ⓔ	79.	Ⓐ Ⓑ Ⓒ Ⓓ Ⓔ
20.	Ⓐ Ⓑ Ⓒ Ⓓ Ⓔ	50.	Ⓐ Ⓑ Ⓒ Ⓓ Ⓔ	80.	Ⓐ Ⓑ Ⓒ Ⓓ Ⓔ
21.	Ⓐ Ⓑ Ⓒ Ⓓ Ⓔ	51.	Ⓐ Ⓑ Ⓒ Ⓓ Ⓔ	81.	Ⓐ Ⓑ Ⓒ Ⓓ Ⓔ
22.	Ⓐ Ⓑ Ⓒ Ⓓ Ⓔ	52.	Ⓐ Ⓑ Ⓒ Ⓓ Ⓔ	82.	Ⓐ Ⓑ Ⓒ Ⓓ Ⓔ
23.	Ⓐ Ⓑ Ⓒ Ⓓ Ⓔ	53.	Ⓐ Ⓑ Ⓒ Ⓓ Ⓔ	83.	Ⓐ Ⓑ Ⓒ Ⓓ Ⓔ
24.	Ⓐ Ⓑ Ⓒ Ⓓ Ⓔ	54.	Ⓐ Ⓑ Ⓒ Ⓓ Ⓔ	84.	Ⓐ Ⓑ Ⓒ Ⓓ Ⓔ
25.	Ⓐ Ⓑ Ⓒ Ⓓ Ⓔ	55.	Ⓐ Ⓑ Ⓒ Ⓓ Ⓔ	85.	Ⓐ Ⓑ Ⓒ Ⓓ Ⓔ
26.	Ⓐ Ⓑ Ⓒ Ⓓ Ⓔ	56.	Ⓐ Ⓑ Ⓒ Ⓓ Ⓔ	86.	Ⓐ Ⓑ Ⓒ Ⓓ Ⓔ
27.	Ⓐ Ⓑ Ⓒ Ⓓ Ⓔ	57.	Ⓐ Ⓑ Ⓒ Ⓓ Ⓔ	87.	Ⓐ Ⓑ Ⓒ Ⓓ Ⓔ
28.	Ⓐ Ⓑ Ⓒ Ⓓ Ⓔ	58.	Ⓐ Ⓑ Ⓒ Ⓓ Ⓔ	88.	Ⓐ Ⓑ Ⓒ Ⓓ Ⓔ
29.	Ⓐ Ⓑ Ⓒ Ⓓ Ⓔ	59.	Ⓐ Ⓑ Ⓒ Ⓓ Ⓔ	89.	Ⓐ Ⓑ Ⓒ Ⓓ Ⓔ
30.	Ⓐ Ⓑ Ⓒ Ⓓ Ⓔ	60.	Ⓐ Ⓑ Ⓒ Ⓓ Ⓔ	90.	Ⓐ Ⓑ Ⓒ Ⓓ Ⓔ

Glossary

A

Absolute threshold—The minimum intensity of sensory stimulation an observer can perceive.

Acceptance—The fifth and final stage in Elisabeth Kübler-Ross's model of adjustment to death and dying in which the terminally ill patient comes to realize death is imminent and there is nothing that will prevent it. During this stage the dying patient often helps plan for his or her funeral and puts personal affairs in order.

Accommodation—Piaget's term for the process of modifying an existing scheme in order to include a new experience.

Achievement motivation—The drive to be successful at tasks that are attempted and to meet achievement standards.

Activity theory—The social theory of aging that argues the elderly are motivated to remain active and engaged in meaningful activities, but that a decline in their activity may occur as the result of a loss of social roles.

Adaptation—Piaget's term for the process of constructing cognitive schema that aid children's adjustment to the environment using the complementary processes of assimilation and accommodation.

Adrenalin—A hormone secreted by the adrenal gland which is responsible for the body's fight or flight response. Adrenalin helps the body prepare to respond to danger; however, adrenalin is also released when an individual experiences stress. Adrenalin has a negative long-term effect on the immune system of the body and acts as a teratogen in a pregnant woman.

Affective disorders—See **mood disorders**.

Aggression—See **antisocial behavior**.

AIDS (Acquired Immune Deficiency Syndrome)—A fatal disease caused by the HIV virus that results in the deterioration of the body's immune system. Infected women can pass the disease to offspring prenatally through the placenta, during birth if there is an exchange of her blood with the baby, or through breast milk. The transmission of AIDS to newborns has decreased with the use of new medications and prevention techniques.

Ainsworth Strange Situation—The experimental paradigm developed by Ainsworth to measure the quality of the attachment relationship. This method involves observing a child's reactions when his or her caregiver leaves the room and when the caregiver returns. This method has been criticized as creating an artificial situation for the caregiver and child.

Altruism—See **prosocial behavior**.

Alzheimer's disease—A disease, characterized by neurofibrillary tangles and plaques in the brain of some aging individuals, that is the leading cause of dementia. Symptoms include loss of cognitive functioning, impaired judgment, and eventual death.

Amniocentesis—A test used to screen for genetic defects and chromosomal abnormalities in a fetus. The test involves taking a sample of amniotic fluid from the amniotic sac in the uterus.

Anal stage—The second stage in Freud's psychosexual model of personality development which lasts from the age of one until the age of three. Libidinal energy is focused on obtaining gratifying stimulation of the anal area in this stage. The ego appears in this stage and continues to develop throughout the remaining stages.

Androgens—Male sex hormones.

Androgyny—A gender role that combines the positive elements of both the masculine and feminine gender role.

Anger—The second stage in Elisabeth Kübler-Ross's model of adjustment to death and dying in which the terminally ill patient rages against his or her illness and may act out against caregivers and significant others.

Animistic reasoning—Characteristic of the thought of a preoperational child. Children in this stage tend to project human qualities onto inanimate objects.

Anorexia nervosa—An eating disorder characterized by exceptionally low body weight and an unrealistic fear of gaining weight.

Anoxia—A condition caused by a depleted supply of oxygen to the fetus during labor and delivery. This is normally due to a problem with the umbilical cord as the fetus is making its way down the vaginal canal. If not corrected, the lack of oxygen may cause brain damage. The damage will depend on the length of time and the amount of oxygen depravation.

Anticipatory grief—A process of reacting and adjusting to the loss of a terminally ill loved one prior to that person's death.

Antisocial behavior—Aggressive, violent, and/or criminal behavior. Influences from the family, school, and neighborhood environments (particularly low socioeconomic conditions) have been linked to antisocial behavior.

Apgar scale—A scale developed to quickly assess the condition of a neonate immediately after birth and five minutes later.

Artificial insemination—A process of fertilizing ova with sperm cells via injection. This technique can help infertile couples conceive using their own reproductive cells.

Assimilation—Piaget's term for the process of modifying an experience to make it fit into a preexisting scheme.

Associative play—An early form of play in which children are playing next to each other, interact, and may share materials with each other, but do not share a common goal.

Attention deficit hyperactivity disorder—A disorder characterized by attention difficulties, impulsivity, and excessive motor behavior.

Attribution styles—The term used for the characteristic way a person explains his or her own behavior as well as the behavior of other people.

Authoritarian parenting style—One of the parenting styles studied by Diana Baumrind. Parents who adopt this style are strict disciplinarians who often use physical punishment. These parents are high in control/demandingness and low in acceptance/responsiveness. These parents make the household rules and children are given no voice in that process. Respect and strict obedience to adults are highly valued by this type of parent. Children raised with this parenting style tend to be anxious and withdrawn or defiant and aggressive.

Authoritative parenting style—One of the parenting styles studied by Diana Baumrind. Parents who adopt this style have household rules that often have been constructed with children having a voice in the process. Discipline is present but not harsh, and explanations for the rules, as well as the reason for the discipline, are provided to the children. These parents are high in acceptance/responsiveness and high in control/demandingness. Children raised with this parenting style have the best developmental outcomes. They tend to have high self-esteem and self-control, and are typically cooperative and mature.

Autism spectrum disorders—Pervasive developmental disorders characterized by impaired communication, repetitive behavior, and impaired social interaction.

Autonomy versus doubt—The second stage in Erik Erikson's psychosocial model of personality development; it lasts from age one until three years. The positive resolution of the crisis is when a child develops the ability to be independent and self-reliant, rather than timid and dependent on other people.

Autosomes—All of the chromosomes except for the sex chromosomes.

B

Babbling—The second stage of language development. These vocalizations elicit responses from others in the infant's environment which in turn reinforce the child's babbling. The sounds produced during the babbling stage will be shaped into the baby's first words.

Babinski reflex—One of the neonatal reflexes present at birth. If you stimulate the bottom of a newborn's foot, he or she will reflexively spread out his or her toes.

Bandura—Psychologist who created the social learning theory. He also conducted the classic study which showed that children who previously viewed an adult model acting aggressively toward a doll, imitated the adult model when placed in a room with the doll.

Bargaining—The third stage in Elisabeth Kübler-Ross's model of adjustment to death and dying. In this stage, the dying person will try to negotiate for more time as in saying "Just let me live long enough to see my daughter get married."

Baumrind—One of the first psychologists to systematically study parenting styles and the effect of style of parenting on the developing child.

Bayley scales—An intelligence test developed to be used to assess intelligence in infants and young children.

Beanpole family—The term used to describe a household that has multiple generations of the same family living together.

Behavior modification—An application of operant conditioning used in educational and clinical settings. An individual's behavior is shaped using positive reinforcement. This technique has been successful when used with children with autism spectrum disorders and severe intellectual disability.

Behaviorist perspective—A theoretical perspective in psychology that defines development as changes in overt behavior. This perspective underscores the role of the environment in development and describes the developing person as passive in the developmental process. The mind is viewed as being a tabula rasa (blank slate) at birth. This perspective has its roots in the work of Ivan Pavlov, John Watson, and B.F. Skinner.

Bereavement—See **grief**.

Bilingualism—Being fluent in two languages.

Biological aging—The term for the biological and physiological decline that occurs with age that eventually causes death. There are several competing theories of the cause of biological aging, but most experts agree this decline is inevitable even in a relatively healthy and disease-free individual. Evidence for this claim is that there is a maximum length of life for human beings which is approximately 110 years.

Birth cohort—People born in or around the same year.

Birth cohort effects—Differences found between different birth cohorts or generations.

Blended family—See **reconstituted family**.

Bronfenbrenner—The psychologists who created the ecological systems theory of development.

Bulimia nervosa—An eating disorder characterized by binge eating and then purging through vomiting and/or the use of laxatives.

C

Caesarian section—An alternative birthing method which is the surgical removal of the fetus from the uterus. This is used when there is an emergency or a problem that prevents a vaginal delivery.

Case study—A method used in descriptive research to intensively study a unique situation or person.

Cataracts—The term for the clouding of the lens of the eye which causes vision problems and is associated with aging.

Cephalocaudal development—The term used for the general pattern of physical growth progressing from the head and neck down to the feet.

Cerebral palsy—A neurological disorder caused by anoxia during birth that is characterized by a lack of muscle control and coordination.

Child abuse (physical or emotional child abuse)—An assault on a child that causes physical harm (physical abuse) or causes a mental or behavioral disorder (emotional abuse).

Child sexual abuse—Fondling, having intercourse with, exhibiting to, or sexually exploiting a child through pornography or prostitution.

Chomsky—The linguist who argued humans are prepared at birth to acquire language. He argued that the human brain is pre-wired with a "language acquisition device."

Chorionic villus sampling—A prenatal screening test that can be done earlier than amniocentesis. It involves removing and analyzing fetal cells using a tube inserted in the pregnant woman's cervix.

Chromosome—The term for the biological structure in the cell that contains genes. There are 46 in each cell.

Classical conditioning—The learning process discovered by Ivan Pavlov by which a reflexive response is elicited by a new stimulus. This conditioning is accomplished by the new stimulus, called the conditioned stimulus, becoming associated with the unconditioned stimulus which initially controlled the reflex.

Classification—The ability to group items together that share a common characteristic.

Class inclusion—The ability to classify objects in a hierarchical organization with subordinate and superordinate levels.

Climacteric—The end of sexual reproductive capacity. In women this is referred to as menopause.

Clique—A small collection of close friends who spend a substantial amount of time together.

Cognitive-developmental theory—This theory describes and explains changes in thinking that occur with age. Jean Piaget is the most influential theorist within this perspective. Piaget constructed a stage model of cognitive development and he argued that these stages were universal. He suggested that a child constructs schema based on the result of his or her actions in the environment. A scheme is an organized pattern of thought or action. Schema become more logical and organized as the child progresses through the four stages, which are sensorimotor intelligence, preoperations, concrete operations, and formal operations.

Collectivist culture—Name used for cultures that value the common good rather than individual achievement.

Compulsion—A behavior that a person is compelled to perform to prevent anxiety. A person who evidences compulsive behavior often suffers from obsessive thinking and is diagnosed with obsessive-compulsive disorder.

Concrete operations—The third stage in Piaget's theory that lasts from about the age of 7 until age 11 or 12. During this stage, children develop the ability to think logically with concrete objects and concepts. These children, however, fail to reason logically about abstract concepts.

Conditioned response (CR)—The term used in Pavlov's classical conditioning theory for the motor part of a reflex which is elicited by a conditioned stimulus after classical conditioning has taken place.

Conditioned stimulus (CS)—The term used in Pavlov's classical conditioning theory for the stimulus that elicits the conditioned response after it has been repeatedly presented with the unconditioned stimulus (UCS). Pavlov argued that an associative bond forms between the UCS and CS which enables the CS to elicit the reflexive response.

Conformity—Acting the way that other people want you to act or going along with a group.

Conservation—The understanding that even though the perceptual characteristics of matter may change, the amount of it does not change if you do not add or take anything away.

Constructivism—The term used by theorists like Piaget who argue that the developing child actively constructs ideas derived from an active exploration of his or her environment.

Context specific—The principle that developmental changes are influenced by, and therefore are specific to, the sociocultural context in which the individual lives. Development varies across cultures and contexts.

Continuity theory—Any developmental theory that suggests development takes place through a series of small, incremental improvements gradually occurring over time. Development is considered to involve quantitative rather than qualitative change.

Control—The term used for a key characteristic of experiments. The experimenter tries to keep as many extraneous variables as possible constant across the experimental conditions being compared. This allows the experimenter to isolate the influence of the independent variable.

Conventional morality—The second stage in Kohlberg's theory of moral development in which decisions regarding right and wrong are made on the basis of societal laws. Moral behavior is defined as behavior that follows the laws of the society, and immoral behavior is defined as any behavior that violates the laws of society.

Convergent thinking—Thinking that works toward the one best answer to a problem.

Cooing—The first stage of language development. This stage begins with reflexive, spontaneous sounds that elicit caregivers' vocalizations. The caregiver's response reinforces the baby's cooing.

Cooperative play—A more mature form of play in which play is a coordinated and social activity guided by mutually agreed upon rules and shared goals.

Correlation coefficient—A measure of the strength and direction of a relationship between two variables. The coefficient can range from 0 to 1.00, and can be either negative (scores on the two variables tend to go in opposite directions) or positive (scores on the two variables tend to go in the same direction).

Correlational research—Research conducted in order to describe relationships between two variables measured in a large sample of participants.

Creativity—A characteristic of thinking separate from intelligence. Theorists argue a key component of creativity is divergent thinking.

Critical period—A term used by ethologists to describe a narrow window of time in which a trait or behavior must develop.

Cross-sectional design—A research method that involves comparing samples of different-aged people at the same time. This method can measure differences between people of different ages, but confounds age difference with birth cohort differences.

Crowd—A large collection of people from both sexes having something in common.

Crystallized intelligence—Thinking that relies on knowledge which has been acquired through learning and experience. The use of general information like that which is acquired in school.

Culture-fair intelligence test—A goal of the intelligence testing movement is to create an intelligence test that is not biased against any group. The current tests have been shown to be biased against those from the lower socioeconomic class.

Cystic fibrosis—A genetic disease characterized by a buildup of fluid in the lungs leading to difficulty breathing and eventual death. The disease is caused by two recessive genes.

D

Darwin's theory of evolution—The theory that has influenced both evolutionary psychology and ethology. Darwin argued that species evolve slowly over a long period of time through a process of natural selection. There are four elements of Darwin's theory: 1) there is a struggle to survive among members of a species since there is a limited supply of food and other resources, 2) members of a species inherit chance variations of species' traits, 3) some variations of traits increase the chance of survival because they help the individual better adapt in his or her environment, and 4) those members who inherit adaptive traits tend to survive to maturity and reproduce, thus passing on these chance variations to their biological offspring. Those who do not inherit adaptive traits tend not to survive and therefore do not reproduce and pass on their traits. Very gradually, then, species evolve over time.

Defense mechanisms—Freud's term for the strategies used by the ego to reduce anxiety.

Deferred imitation—Piaget's term for the ability to represent another person's action, store this representation, and later retrieve it in order to imitate it. Piaget argued this was a sign that a child had achieved symbolic representation.

Delay of gratification—The ability to wait for an anticipated reward or goal.

Dementia—An impairment in cognitive functioning in aging individuals which can be acute or chronic. There are many causes of dementia including brain disease (chronic dementia) and drug interaction effects (acute dementia).

Denial—The first stage in Elisabeth Kübler-Ross's model of adjustment to terminal illness. She argued that the terminally ill patient at first does not accept his or her prognosis and may believe that there has been a mistake.

Dependent variable—The variable that is measured after the manipulation of an independent variable in an experiment. It is the hypothesized effect in the cause-and-effect relationship being tested.

Depression—The fourth stage in Elisabeth Kübler-Ross's model of adjustment to death and dying in which the terminally ill patient is overwhelmed by sadness and hopelessness.

Depth perception—The ability to see a three-dimensional world or depth of field.

Descriptive research—Research that is conducted in order to describe characteristics of people, places, or things. Methodologies used include case study, naturalistic observation, interview, and survey.

Difficult temperament—This is the temperament label for infants who are upset by stimulation and do not follow regular patterns of sleeping and eating.

Discrimination—The gradual process of conditioning a response to only occur to a specific stimulus, e.g., a bell of a certain tone, rather than a collection of tones that are similar in frequency.

Disengagement theory—The social theory of aging that argues elderly adults are motivated to withdraw from society in anticipation of death.

Disequilibrium—The term used by Piaget to describe the cognitive experience of imbalance that occurs when a child's experience does not fit into preexisting schema. This psychological state is the motivation for developmental change. According to Piaget, the child is motivated to return to a state of mental equilibrium or balance.

Divergent thinking—Believed to be a key component of creativity, this form of thinking involves generating many different possible solutions to a problem that has no one right answer.

Dizygotic twins—Also known as fraternal twins. These are twins that are the result of multiple ova being fertilized by different sperm and implanting in the uterus at the same time. Although they develop together in utero, these twins are similar to biological siblings.

Down's syndrome—A genetic disorder in children who inherit an extra chromosome on the 21st pair that causes intellectual disability. These children also have distinctive facial features and short, stubby limbs.

DSM (Diagnostic and Statistical Manual of Mental Disorders)—The manual used to diagnose psychological disorders.

Dyslexia—A learning disability that affects children's ability to read.

E

Easy temperament—This is the temperament label for infants who eat and sleep on a regular and predictable schedule, and who react well to new people and stimuli.

Ecological systems theory—Uri Bronfenbrenner's theory that child development occurs within multiple sociocultural systems. The child's experiences and interactions with members of these systems contribute to the child's personality, behavior, and thinking. The systems in this theory are depicted as a series of concentric circles beginning in the center with the microsystem (e.g., the family), which is the system the child directly interacts in, then the exosystem within which the child does not directly participate but which nonetheless impacts the child's development (e.g., parent's workplace), to the outermost circle, the macrosystem, which is the larger sociocultural system.

Ego—The part of the personality structure in Freud's psychoanalytic theory that must manage the impulses of the id. The ego develops in toddlerhood and has to manage the id by finding socially acceptable ways of gratifying the id's wishes. The ego develops defense mechanisms to manage anxiety which may result from its failure to adequately control the id and meet the moral standards of the superego.

Egocentric thinking—A form of thinking typical of the preoperational child in which the child can only view the world from his or her own perspective and cannot take the perspective of others.

Electra complex—Freud's name for the unconscious conflict that arises in the phallic stage of his psychosexual model of personality development. Freud argued that a female child in this phase of development is attracted to her father who she chooses as the target of libidinal energy. The child therefore unconsciously desires a sexual relationship with father, but fears reprisal from mother. According to Freud, girls have a more difficult time resolving this conflict because they have to reject their original love object, mother, and have a difficult time doing so.

Embryo—Name used for the developing baby from the third through the eighth week of pregnancy. This is the period of prenatal development called the second trimester.

Emotional intelligence (EQ)—The type of intelligence proposed by Daniel Goleman that is the ability to think about, and adapt to, emotion. People with high EQs have an exceptional ability to understand and deal with their own emotions and the emotions expressed by other people.

Empathy—The ability to feel the emotions that another person is experiencing.

Empiricist theory—An approach to language development which argues that humans are born with a tabula rasa or blank slate and learn language through experience.

Empty nest (launching phase)—The time when adult children leave the home. Historically, this has been described as a period of stress for parents, particularly mothers, but recent survey research indicates it is a positive time of renewal for couples.

Encoding—The process through which information is prepared for storage in long-term memory.

Endocrine system—The physiological system of the body that contains glands which secrete hormones to stimulate growth and control the physiological functions of the body.

Erikson—The psychologist who constructed the psychosocial theory of personality development. He argued that personality develops throughout the life span and his model contains eight stages beginning with birth and ending in old age. During each stage of development the person faces a psychosocial crisis which can be resolved in a positive or negative way. Erikson is also well known for his discussion of identity development in adolescence.

Estrogen—One of the female sex hormones secreted by the ovaries which directs the development of the female reproductive system during prenatal development and during puberty, and also stimulates the release of growth hormone.

Ethology—The term used for the approach of theorists like Konrad Lorenz and John Bowlby. These theorists compare human behavior with that of other species in order to identify the historical origins of human behavior and development. Ethologists coined the term "critical periods."

Euthanasia—The term for actively assisting the death of a terminally ill person.

Evolutionary psychology—The name of the approach in psychology that was derived from Darwin's theory of evolution by natural selection. The goal of this approach is to explain the historical origins of human behavior and how evolution has shaped human behavior and development.

Expansions—A technique observed in caregivers in which the caregiver responds to a child's vocalization by repeating it in a more complex and advanced way.

Experiment—The research method that can identify cause-and-effect relationships between variables. Two elements of an experiment are control and manipulation. An independent variable is manipulated while extraneous variables are controlled. A dependent variable is used to measure the affect of the independent variable manipulation.

External locus of control—An attribution style in which an individual characteristically believes events in his or her life are caused by forces outside of his or her control.

Extinction—Pavlov's term for the process that reverses conditioning in the classical conditioning paradigm. This is accomplished by successively presenting the conditioned stimulus (CS) without the unconditioned stimulus (UCS). Eventually the CS no longer elicits the conditioned response (CR).

F

Failure to thrive—The term for infants who do not develop normally and show signs of depression. These infants may become seriously underweight. Psychologists believe this condition is caused by a lack of comfort care as it generally occurs in children who are neglected, abused, or separated from their attachment figure.

False belief task—A test that determines if a child has a theory of mind. A child who passes this test says, for example, a person will look for a toy in a basket that person *believes* the toy is in, rather than the basket the child knows contains the toy.

Family systems theory—An approach to understanding the family that describes it as a complex whole system having interrelated members playing different interconnected roles. The action of any one member impacts the whole system.

Fast mapping—The process that Susan Carey suggested is used during the rapid vocabulary growth of the second year. Children will connect a word to an underlying meaning after only a brief encounter.

Feminine—The gender role stereotypically associated with females in our society. Stereotypic elements of this role include being caring, nurturing, and compliant.

Fetal alcohol syndrome—A collection of symptoms including facial abnormalities, small head size, and intellectual disability seen in children whose mothers consumed alcohol in large quantities while pregnant.

Fetus—Name used for the developing baby from the ninth week of pregnancy until birth. This is the period of prenatal development called the third trimester.

Field experiment—An experiment conducted in a natural setting rather than in a controlled laboratory setting. It is less artificial than a lab experiment, but also has less control than a lab experiment.

Fine motor skills—Skills that involve small coordinated movements of the hands, fingers, or toes.

First trimester—The name for the first two weeks of prenatal development. The developing zygote is most protected from negative effects of teratogens at this time.

Fixation—Freud's term for the process of remaining focused on a psychosexual crisis of a childhood stage of personality development well past the normal age of resolving that crisis.

Fluid intelligence—Thinking or problem solving that relies on the power of basic intellectual processes.

Formal operations—This is the fourth and final stage in Piaget's theory. The stage generally begins at age 11 or 12. This level of thought involves hypothetico-deductive reasoning. Adolescents develop the ability to reason logically and systematically even about abstract concepts.

Freud—Well-known father of the psychoanalytic theory. He argued that personality development takes place through a series of universal stages beginning with birth and ending in adolescence. He stressed the role of unconscious motivation and drives, such as the libido, in creating psychosexual crises during these stages. He also posed a structure of the personality which included the id, ego, and superego.

Functional play—See **unoccupied play**.

G

Gender constancy—The understanding that a person's biological sex does not change even if that person makes significant changes to his or her appearance.

Gender identity—The internalized view of the self as masculine, feminine, or androgynous.

Gender role—The collection of behaviors and traits that are expected for males and females in a society.

Gender scheme—An organized set of beliefs about gender a child constructs and then uses to process information and guide his or her own behavior.

Gender stability—The understanding that biological sex remains the same throughout life.

Gender stereotypes—Restrictive social views that males and females should adhere to the masculine and feminine gender roles, respectively.

Gender typing—The social process of identifying roles, traits, or objects as more appropriate for one or the other gender.

Gene—The term for the biological structure carried on chromosomes that contains the blueprint for inherited traits.

Generalization—Pavlov's term for when a conditioned response can be elicited by related conditioned stimuli, e.g., similar tone frequencies.

Generativity versus stagnation—The seventh stage in Erik Erikson's psychosocial model of personality development that lasts for the period of middle adulthood from the age of about 40 until about the age of 65. The positive resolution of this crisis is when an adult experiences the gratifying feeling of giving back to society by mentoring younger generations of that society rather than remaining self-preoccupied.

Genetic counseling—Counseling that is available to couples who are planning to have children. Partners have their genes screened for genetic disorders or abnormalities. Couples then decide whether or not they wish to have children based on the probability of their offspring having genetic abnormalities.

Genetic disorders—Disorders that are caused by genetic mutations, chromosomal abnormalities, or genes that carry the disorder.

Genital stage—The fifth and final stage in Freud's psychosexual model of personality development which begins at age 12. According to Freud, libidinal energy is channeled into work and establishing mature sexual relationships in this stage.

Genotype—The term used for the traits that are programmed in the genetic material an offspring inherits from her biological parents.

German measles—See **rubella**.

Giftedness—Unusually high intellectual ability (IQ scores above 130), creativity, or special talent.

Glaucoma—A disease of the eye caused by pressure inside the eyeball from an excess buildup of fluid. If untreated, this results in blindness.

Grasping reflex—One of the neonatal reflexes present at birth. If you stimulate the hand of a newborn, the baby will reflexively grasp and hold onto your finger.

Grief (bereavement)—The distressful response to the death of a loved one. Some psychologists argue that the grief process involves the same stages as in Kübler-Ross's model of death and dying.

Gross motor skills—Skills that involve coordinated movements of the entire body or large parts of the body.

Growth hormone (GH)—The hormone secreted by the pituitary gland which stimulates physical growth. In the absence of GH, an infant will not develop to normal height. GH also stimulates the adolescent growth spurt.

Growth spurt—A time of very rapid physical development. There is a growth spurt during infancy and then again during adolescence.

Guided participation—Vygotsky's term for the process by which cultural values and beliefs are transmitted from adult guides to children.

H

Habituation—The most primitive form of learning. This is the process whereby attention to a stimulus decreases with continued exposure. Newborns look longer at a new stimulus compared to a familiar stimulus.

Harlow—The researcher who investigated the role of feeding in the formation of an attachment relationship. He conducted a classic experiment in which he observed the behavior of monkeys raised with two surrogate mothers, a terry cloth covered mother and a wire mesh mother. Although the monkeys were fed through a bottle in the wire mesh surrogate, they clung to the terry cloth surrogate.

Holophrase—The term for a word that stands for a sentence or more in the early speech of children. A one-word utterance, e.g., "Up," may mean "Grandma, please pick me up!"

HOME (home observation for measurement of the environment)—The method used to assess the amount of cognitive stimulation in the home environment.

Hospice—A comprehensive support program designed to help terminally ill patients die a good death. The goals of this program are to manage the dying person's pain and enable the person to die comfortably while surrounded by loved ones.

Hostile aggression—A form of physical or verbal aggression in which there is an intent to harm another person.

Huntington's disease—A fatal genetic disease carried by a dominant gene on chromosome 4 which results in nervous system deterioration. Symptoms generally do not appear until adulthood and include slurred speech, jerky movements, personality changes, and dementia.

Hypothetico-deductive thinking—A characteristic of formal operational thinking according to Piaget. This is systematic reasoning from general concepts or ideas to specific instances.

I

Id—The part of the personality structure in Freud's psychoanalytic theory that houses unconscious drives, motives, and repressed thoughts. The id is the irrational part of the personality which must be controlled by the ego. The id is the only part of the personality present at birth.

Identification—The term used by Sigmund Freud for the process which resolves the Oedipal and Electra complexes. The child at the end of the phallic stage shifts his or her attention from the opposite sex parent to the parent of the same sex. According to Freud, the child internalizes the behavior and moral standards of the parent of the same sex which develop into the superego.

Identity achievement—The term used by Marcia to describe the identity status of adolescents who have made a commitment to an identity after experiencing an identity crisis and testing out alternative lifestyles and careers.

Identity diffusion—The term used by Marcia to describe the identity status of adolescents who have not experienced an identity crisis and have not made a commitment to an identity.

Identity foreclosure—The term used by Marcia to describe the identity status of adolescents who decide too quickly on an identity, or simply adopt an identity that others have selected for them. These adolescents have made a commitment to an identity, but have not experienced an identity crisis.

Identity versus identity confusion—The fifth stage in Erik Erikson's psychosocial model of personality development which lasts for the period of adolescence. The positive resolution of the crisis is when an adolescent develops a sense of personal identity and the idea of who he or she will be as an adult.

Imprinting—The behavior, recorded by Konrad Lorenz, of baby ducks following their mother duck as long as they are exposed to the mother within a critical time period of development. Lorenz showed that ducks would imprint on any moving object, including himself, to which they were exposed during the critical period.

Independent variable—The variable that is manipulated in an experiment. It is the hypothesized cause in the cause-and-effect relationship being tested.

Individualistic culture—Name used for cultures that value individual achievement and drive rather than the common good.

Industry versus inferiority—The fourth stage in Erik Erikson's psychosocial model of personality development which lasts from age 6 until age 11. The positive resolution of the crisis is when a child develops positive self-esteem and a sense of competence rather than incompetence.

Information processing approach—An approach to studying cognitive development that uses a computer metaphor for the mind. This approach suggests the mind is an information processing system. Developmental changes in information processing are described as being an increase in processing speed and capacity.

Initiative versus guilt—The third stage in Erik Erikson's psychosocial model of personality development which lasts from age three to age six. The positive resolution of the crisis is when a child develops the confidence to try new activities and initiates endeavors versus being self-critical.

Inner speech—Vygotsky's term for how language guides thought in an older child who talks to himself silently while solving a problem. The older child does not have to talk out loud to himself as younger children do when they are using private speech.

Insecure-avoidant attachment—The term for an insecure attachment relationship in which the child does not seek contact with the caregiver and does not show distress when the caregiver leaves.

Insecure-disorganized/disoriented attachment—The term for an insecure attachment relationship in which the child alternatively approaches and avoids the caregiver. A common response seen in abused children.

Insecure-resistant attachment—The term for an insecure attachment relationship in which the child is very difficult to console when separated from the caregiver and then is angry and resists contact with the caregiver upon his or her return.

Instrumental aggression—A form of aggression used to achieve a goal but not intended to harm another person.

Integrity versus despair—The eighth and final stage in Erik Erikson's psychosocial model of personality development; it lasts for the period of late adulthood from about the age of 65 until death. The positive resolution of the crisis is when an older adult experiences the gratifying feeling that he or she has led a good and meaningful life versus experiencing regret.

Intellectual disability— Lower than average intelligence caused by many factors varies in severity and degree of impairment (formerly known as mental retardation in DSM-IV).

Intelligence—The term used for cognitive power or ability.

Intelligence quotient (IQ)—A calculation that quantifies intelligence by dividing mental age by chronological age. The mean score for IQ is 100.

Intermodal perception—A term for the interconnectedness of our perceptual systems. An experiment has shown that neonates will look longer at a nipple which has the shape of a nipple he or she previously sucked on but did not see.

Internal locus of control—An attribution style in which an individual characteristically believes events in his or her life are caused by his or her own abilities and efforts.

Interview—A method used in descriptive research to collect information.

Intimacy versus isolation—The sixth stage in Erik Erikson's psychosocial model of personality development that lasts for the period of early adulthood from age 20 until about the age of 40. The positive resolution of the crisis is when a young adult is able to form an intimate relationship defined by trust and love versus being unconnected or alone.

In vitro fertilization—A process of fertilizing ova with sperm outside of the female body and then implanting fertilized cells into the uterus. This technique can help infertile couples conceive using their own reproductive cells.

K

Klinefelter syndrome—A sex chromosome abnormality in which males inherit an extra X chromosome (XXY). These males are sterile, develop female sex characteristics, and sometimes have lower than average language skills or some degree of intellectual disability.

Kohlberg—The psychologist who studied moral reasoning and suggested a stage model of moral development. This model contains three stages: preconventional moral reasoning, conventional moral reasoning, and postconventional moral reasoning. He presented moral dilemmas to subjects and observed differences in reasoning about these dilemmas across age groups.

Kübler-Ross—The psychologist who created a stage theory of adjustment to one's own death after conducting extensive interviews with terminally ill patients. The stages are denial, anger, bargaining, depression, and acceptance. Her theory has been criticized by psychologists who argue that all people do not go through all of the stages in her model.

L

Lamaze method (prepared childbirth)—An alternative birthing method that involves a couple preparing for a vaginal delivery by learning and practicing breathing and other relaxation techniques to help manage the pain of childbirth without medication.

Language acquisition device—The term Noam Chomsky used for how the human brain is pre-wired for language.

Latchkey children—The term for children who have no adult supervision after school.

Latency—The fourth stage in Sigmund Freud's psychosexual model of personality development which lasts from age 6 until 12. The libido is quite inactive during this stage and there is no psychosexual crisis. According to Freud, children in this stage are focused on same sex peers, school, and play.

Lateralization—The term used to describe the fact that the left and right hemispheres of the brain control different functions. For example, the language center is located in the left cerebral hemisphere.

Launching phase—See **empty nest**.

Learned helplessness—The perception that one cannot alter events in one's life. This syndrome was first demonstrated by Seligman. Seligman placed animals in an experimental situation where they could not escape an electric shock. Eventually, the animals became lethargic and no longer tried to escape.

Learned helplessness orientation—Attributing failures to stable and internal personal traits, and successes to external, changeable, and uncontrollable factors. This leads to a tendency to avoid challenges and a lack of motivation to attempt difficult tasks.

Learning disabilities—Specific difficulties learning new information believed to be due to a problem in brain functioning. Children with learning disabilities often do poorly in school despite having average or higher intelligence.

Learning styles—Individual differences in the way information is processed. Some people are visual, auditory, or kinesthetic learners. Each type of learner will acquire information easier if the information is presented in a modality that matches their learning style.

Learning theory—This is the theory of language development derived from the behaviorist perspective in psychology. Language development is described as being continuous and gradual. Development is believed to be the result of experience. Language is defined as verbal behavior which is conditioned or shaped.

Libido—The term for the sexual instinct or drive in Freud's theory of psychoanalysis.

Life expectancy—The average length of life that can be expected for a birth cohort.

Life-span perspective—Contemporary approach to development suggesting development occurs throughout the entire life span. Historically, developmental theories have suggested development is complete at adolescence. This perspective changes the view that childhood experiences shape who we become.

Living will—A legal document that outlines an individual's wishes regarding end-of-life care and treatment. Often the document will dictate that no extreme measures to revive or sustain life under hopeless conditions are to be used. Examples of extreme measures are resuscitation, ventilation, or use of a feeding tube.

Longitudinal design—A research method that involves studying a sample of people over a long period of time in order to measure changes that occur with age.

Long-term memory—See **secondary memory**.

M

Manipulation—A key characteristic of experiments. The experimenter varies the independent variable so that it is present under one condition in the experiment but not present in the other condition(s). The experimental group receives the independent variable but the control group does not.

Masculine—The gender role stereotypically associated with males in our society. Stereotypic elements of this role include being aggressive, dominant, and competitive.

Maslow, Abraham—American psychologist who created the Hierarchy of Needs, a five-tier model of human needs. He was one of the earliest psychologists to focus attention on personal well-being and fulfillment rather than on psychopathology.

Mastery-oriented attributions—Attributing successes to stable and internal personal traits or abilities, and failures to external, changeable, and uncontrollable factors. This leads to a tendency to step up to challenges and persevere through difficult tasks.

Maturation—The term used to describe biological/physical changes that occur with age.

Menarche—The first menstruation in females.

Mental age—An age assigned to a person as a result of comparing that person's intelligence test performance with norms for different age groups. This age represents that person's level of functioning.

Metacognition—Being consciously aware of one's own cognitive processing.

Middle generation sandwich—The term for the stress experienced by middle-aged adults who are both caring for their own children as well as their aging parents.

Mindblindness—A condition which is likened to autism, which is characterized as being unable to understand the behaviors of others, or read their emotions—even when obvious such as crying.

Mirror test of self-recognition—This is the technique used by Lewis and Brooks-Gunn to test for self-recognition in infants. Infants, at least 18 months of age, who have rouge surreptitiously put on their nose, will rub their nose when they look at themselves in a mirror, rather than rub the mirror, as younger infants do.

Modeling—See **social learning theory**.

Monozygotic twins—Also known as identical twins. These are twins that are the result of an extra division of a fertilized ovum. These twins share the exact same genetic material.

Mood disorders (Affective disorders)—Disorders characterized by abnormal affect or emotion. Examples include major depression and bipolar disorder.

Morality of care—The term used by Carol Gilligan for the style of moral reasoning found generally in females. She found that women think about other people's needs and how decisions affect interpersonal relationships when deliberating about moral dilemmas. Moral reasoning is contextualized in people with this style.

Morality of justice—The term used by Carol Gilligan for the style of moral reasoning found generally in males. Males tend to make decisions about right and wrong by applying general, universal, immutable principles of justice.

Moratorium period—The term used for a period of time given to children and adolescents to explore different identities and prepare for adulthood.

Moratorium status—The term used by Marcia to describe an adolescent who is currently experiencing an identity crisis and is testing out alternatives.

Moro reflex—One of the neonatal reflexes present at birth. This is a startle response a newborn will emit if they suddenly lose physical support.

Morpheme—The term for the basic unit of meaning in a language.

Multiple intelligences—The theory of intelligence offered by Howard Gardner that argues intelligence is not one general factor but eight different cognitive abilities. This approach to intelligence defines intelligence more broadly compared to the traditional view of intelligence.

N

Nativist theory—An approach to language development that argues humans are innately predisposed to acquire a language.

Naturalistic observation—A method used in descriptive research to collect information about a person or event. Overt behavior is observed and recorded in a natural setting.

Natural selection—The name Charles Darwin used for the process through which species evolve over time.

Nature-versus-nurture controversy—A debate regarding the relative influence of heredity versus experience/the environment on development. While some developmental theorists underscore one over the other, both nature and nurture influence development.

Negative reinforcement—In Skinner's operant conditioning theory, this is the term for a reward that involves removing a noxious stimulus or condition after a goal behavior is emitted. This term is formally defined by Skinner as the removal of a noxious stimulus after a behavior is emitted that increases the probability the behavior will be repeated under similar stimulus conditions.

Neglect—A parent's failure to protect a child from harm and/or meet the basic biological and medical needs of a child.

Neonate—Term used to refer to the newborn from birth to about one month of age.

Neonate preferences—Neonates come with preferences for what they look at, listen to, and taste. For example, neonates will look at the edges of an object more than the interior details.

Neurofibrillary tangles—Abnormal neural structures found in the brains of people with Alzheimer's disease.

O

Obesity—Weighing more than 20 percent than the average weight for one's age, sex, and body type.

Object permanence—A concept that develops during sensorimotor intelligence. This is the understanding that physical objects have a separate existence from the perceiver.

Observational learning—See **social learning theory**.

Obsession—A disturbing thought or pattern of thought that a person has difficulty controlling. People who have an obsession often develop compulsive behavior and are diagnosed with obsessive-compulsive disorder.

Oedipal complex—Freud's name for the unconscious conflict that arises in the phallic stage of his psychosexual model of personality development. Freud argued a male child in this phase of development unconsciously desires a sexual relationship with his mother but fears reprisal from his father. The resolution of this conflict occurs by the child identifying with his father.

Onlooker play—A form of play in which the child is an observer of the play activities of other children, but does not participate.

Operant conditioning—A type of learning, described by B.F. Skinner, in which behavior is shaped through the use of reinforcement and punishment. A behavior which is followed by reinforcement will tend to be repeated and a behavior followed by punishment will tend not to be repeated.

Oral stage—The first stage in Sigmund Freud's psychosexual model of personality development which lasts from birth until one year. Libidinal energy is focused on obtaining gratifying stimulation of the mouth in this stage.

Osteoporosis—The term for a bone disease which is the result of a calcium deficiency in the body. Bones become very brittle and may spontaneously fracture. Osteoporosis correlates with age.

Overregularization—This is the term for applying syntactic rules as if there were no exceptions to these rules. For example, children may say "goed" instead of "went" because they are applying the rule that says "To make a verb past tense, add *-ed*."

Ovum—The term for the female reproductive cell found in the ovaries.

P

Parallel play—An early form of play in which children who are playing share the same physical space, but are engaged in individual play activities and do not interact with each other very much.

Pavlov—The behavioral psychologist who created the classical conditioning theory within the learning theory approach. Pavlov discovered that a previously reflexive response could be conditioned to be emitted in response to a novel stimulus. He discovered classical conditioning serendipitously while conducting experiences on the salivary reflex in dogs.

Perception—The process of assigning meaning to a sensation.

Perceptual constancies—First described by the Gestalt psychologists, these are the perceptual phenomena of size constancy, shape constancy, lightness constancy, and color constancy. These involve maintaining the same percept even when the information reaching the eye has significantly changed. In size constancy, for example, an observer perceives a dog to be the same size when it stands 20 or 200 feet away.

Permissive parenting style—One of the parenting styles studied by Diana Baumrind. Parents who adopt this style are overindulgent and lenient. Children are free to make their own decisions. These parents are high in acceptance/responsiveness and low in control/demandingness. Children raised with this style tend to be non-achievers who are dependent, impulsive, and disobedient.

Phallic stage—The third stage in Sigmund Freud's psychosexual model of personality development which lasts from the age of three until age six. Libidinal energy is focused on obtaining gratifying stimulation of the genital area in this stage. It is during this stage that the Oedipal and Electra crises arise and are resolved through identification with the same sex parent. The superego develops in this stage.

Phenotype—The term used for the traits that are actually expressed in the individual rather than the sum total of inherited genetic material.

Phenylketonuria (PKU)—A genetic disorder characterized by an inability to metabolize phenylalanine. Without treatment, a child with PKU will become intellectually disabled and hyperactive.

Phobia—An abnormally intense fear of an object or situation.

Phonemes—The term for the basic units of sound in a language that are needed to form meaningful units.

Phonics approach—An approach to reading instruction that teaches reading by emphasizing the connection between letters and sounds.

Piaget—Theorist who constructed a stage model of cognitive development and who argued that cognitive development is the result of the child constructing schema based on his or her activity with objects in the environment. His theory is a discontinuity theory of development which emphasizes universals in development.

Pituitary gland—Called the "master gland," this gland controls other glands in the endocrine system and secretes growth hormone (GH).

Placenta—The semi-permeable membrane that supports the developing embryo. It is the source of blood and nutrients for the baby. It also allows some harmful substances (teratogens) to pass through to the baby's bloodstream.

Plaques—Abnormal masses of toxic neural material in the brains of people with Alzheimer's disease.

Population—The entire set of people, animals, events, or things that make up the group to which a researcher is interested in applying the results of her research.

Positive reinforcement—In Skinner's operant conditioning theory, this is a type of reinforcement used to shape behavior. Positive reinforcement is presenting a reward to a person or animal after the goal behavior is emitted. This term is formally defined by Skinner as any thing that is given to a subject after a behavior is emitted that increases the probability the behavior will be repeated under the same stimulus conditions.

Postconventional morality—The third and final stage in Kohlberg's theory of moral development. People at this level make decisions about right and wrong using universal principles of justice.

Post-traumatic stress disorder (PTSD)—A psychological disorder characterized by flashbacks to a traumatic event, and feelings of anxiety and helplessness. This is often experienced in victims of crime, sexual abuse, as well as those who have experienced military combat.

Pragmatics—The practical rules of language use.

Preconventional morality—The first stage in Kohlberg's theory of moral development. Decisions regarding right and wrong are made on the basis of expected consequences for actions, i.e., whether or not the actor will be punished for his or her actions.

Preoperations—The second stage in Piaget's theory that lasts from about two years of age until about age seven. The child in this stage can use symbolic representations but cannot think logically.

Prepared childbirth—See **Lamaze method**.

Presbyopia—The term for loss of visual acuity for near objects that is associated with aging.

Pretend play—A form of play that Piaget believed signaled the development of symbolic representation. Children pretending can use an object to take the place of another absent object.

Preterm babies—The term used for fetuses born before 36 weeks' gestation.

Primary memory—See **working memory**.

Private speech (Egocentric speech)—Vygotsky's term for how language guides thinking in young children. He argued that children talk out loud to themselves while problem solving because such speech guides their problem-solving activity.

Progesterone—One of the female sex hormones secreted by the ovaries which directs the development of the female sex system during prenatal development and during puberty, and stimulates the release of growth hormone.

Project Head Start—A federal program created to help prepare economically disadvantaged children for school. The program combines preschool education with nutritional and health care services and parental involvement in the children's education.

Prosocial behavior (altruism)—Behavior that is intended to be for the good of others and without any expectation of reward or personal gain.

Proximodistal development—Term used for the general pattern of physical growth progressing from the center of the body outward to the extremities.

Psychosexual crisis—The basic motivation for personality development in Sigmund Freud's model. A sequence of four crises occurs caused by the interacting forces of the child's sexual instinct in the id and society's expectations for behavior.

Psychosocial crisis—The basic motivation for personality development in Erik Erikson's model. Eight crises occur in each of the eight stages from birth to death. Each crisis is the result of the interacting forces of the child's own physical and cognitive growth and society's expectations for the child's behavior.

Puberty—The term for the phase of development in which males and females reach sexual maturity.

Punishment—A term from Skinner's operant conditioning theory. It is anything a subject experiences after a behavior that reduces the probability the behavior will be repeated under similar stimulus conditions.

R

Random sample—The term used for a sample of the target population that has been drawn using a sampling technique that gave every member of the target population an equal and independent chance of being selected. It is therefore a representative sample of the target population rather than a biased sample.

Recall—The process of retrieving information using a general clue only.

Recasts—A technique observed in caregivers in which the caregiver repeats a child's verbalization after correcting the child's mistakes.

Reciprocal determinism—The principle that suggests development is the result of the bidirectional relationship between the person and the environment.

Recognition—The process of retrieving information by matching stored information with information presented at the time of the test. This produces the feeling of having experienced the information before.

Reconstituted family (blended family)—The term used for families that are the result of remarriages.

Regression—The term used by Freud for the process the ego uses to displace anxiety-provoking thoughts from consciousness.

Rehearsal—The process used to maintain information in working/primary memory.

Rejected children—The term used for children who are disliked and not accepted by their peers. Some are rejected-aggressive children and others are rejected-withdrawn children.

Relational aggression—A form of hostile aggression, like gossiping, which is aimed at damaging another person's social relationships.

Resilience—The term used by developmental psychologists for the characteristic in some children that enables them to overcome early obstacles and develop normally.

Retrieval—The process of finding information in long-term memory and bringing it to consciousness.

Reversibility—The ability to mentally rewind a thought pattern.

Rh factor—A factor in blood that is present or absent in people. Those who do not have the Rh factor are called Rh-negative and those who do have the factor are called Rh-positive. If a pregnant woman and her fetus are not compatible (both Rh-negative or both Rh-positive), the mother's immune system will attack the fetus as it would any foreign body. In the past this was a common cause of intellectual disability, but damage to the fetus is prevented today by an inoculation given to a pregnant woman to prevent the immune response.

Rooting reflex—One of the neonatal reflexes present at birth. If you stimulate the cheek of a newborn, he or she will turn toward the source of the stimulation.

Rubella (German measles)—A disease that if contracted by a pregnant woman, particularly in the first 3 to 4 months of pregnancy, causes birth defects including blindness, deafness, and intellectual disability.

S

Sample—A subset of the target population who participate in a research study.

Scaffolding—Vygotsky's term for the amount of teaching support given a child as he or she moves from being less to more competent at a task.

Schema—Piaget's term for the organized patterns of thought or action that the child constructs as a result of interacting with objects in the environment. These schema become more logical and organized with age.

Second trimester—The name for the phase of prenatal development from the third through the eighth week of pregnancy. The embryo is most susceptible to the effects of teratogens during this period. Most organ systems and body parts develop during this time.

Secondary memory (long-term memory)—The third memory storage system in the Information Processing Approach. Information that is encoded in working memory will be stored in this organized memory system. Some theorists argue that this is a permanent memory storage system and that forgetting is the result of failure to retrieve rather than a loss of the information.

Secure attachment—The term for a healthy relationship between a child and a primary caregiver. This relationship is characterized by a strong emotional bond between the caregiver and child, a dislike of separations, and proximity seeking. The target of a secure attachment is a source of comfort when an individual is stressed.

Selective attention—A cognitive control process that enables observers to maintain a focus on a target while ignoring other sensory information.

Selective looking—A term used to describe the preferences for looking that appear in neonates.

Self-concept—The term psychologists use for the perception a person has of himself or herself.

Self-esteem—The term psychologists use for the evaluative judgment a person makes about who he or she is.

Self-recognition—A child's ability to recognize himself or herself in a mirror.

Semantic overextension—This is the term for applying a category label, e.g., "ball," to things that are not members of the category, but share some similar characteristic(s), e.g., globe.

Semantics—The system of meaning of a language.

Sensation—The registration of information in a sense organ.

Sensitive caregiving—According to developmental psychologists, this is one requirement for a secure attachment relationship to form. This caregiving style is consistent, prompt, and appropriate responding to the child's needs.

Sensitive period—A modification of the term "critical period" to communicate the fact that humans show a greater flexibility to acquire behaviors or traits outside of a critical period of time. While a trait or behavior may be acquired more quickly or more easily during the critical period for its development, it is not impossible for it to be acquired outside of this time frame. The term "sensitive period" connotes the time frame within which a behavior or trait is more readily acquired.

Sensorimotor intelligence—The first stage in Piaget's theory of cognitive development which lasts from birth to about two years of age. Infants who are in this stage are not capable of logical reasoning, but develop object permanence and symbolic representation during this stage. Schema from this stage are organized patterns of action only.

Sensory memory—The first memory storage system in the Information Processing Approach. This storage system automatically holds information that has registered in a sensory system. This storage is very brief, and information will be lost unless it is transferred to working memory via the process of attention.

Sequential design—A research method that combines the cross-sectional and longitudinal designs. This method can measure changes that occur with age, differences between people who are different ages at one point in time, and can also quantify birth cohort effects.

Seriation—The ability to rank-order objects on one attribute or dimension.

Sex chromosomes—The chromosomes (X and Y) that carry the blueprint for the offspring's biological sex. A female has an XX pair and a male has an XY pair of sex chromosomes.

Sex-linked dominant trait—A trait that is carried by a gene on a sex chromosome (X or Y) that will always appear. Someone who has this trait may have also inherited the gene for the recessive trait and would therefore be called a "carrier." An individual with the dominant trait could have inherited instead two dominant trait genes.

Sex-linked recessive trait—A trait that is carried by a gene on a sex chromosome (X or Y) that only appears in the absence of the gene for the dominant trait. Someone who has this trait did not inherit the dominant gene.

Sexual orientation—Whether a person is sexually and romantically attracted to members of the same or opposite sex.

Shaping—Skinner's term for the process of learning whereby a new behavior is conditioned. Shaping is accomplished by systematically reinforcing successive approximations of the goal behavior. Skinner created the Skinner box or operant chamber, which is the apparatus used to shape behavior. A hungry or thirsty animal is placed in the Skinner box and successively rewarded with food or water, respectively, for closer and closer approximations of the goal behavior.

Short-term memory—See **working memory**.

Sibling rivalry—The term for jealousy and competition for the attention and affection from parents that occurs between siblings.

Sickle cell anemia—A genetic disorder of the red blood cells inherited mostly by people of African and Latino descent.

Skinner—The behavioral psychologist who created the operant conditioning theory within the learning theory approach. Skinner argued that behavior is shaped through reinforcement and punishment. If a behavior is reinforced, the probability increases that it will occur again in the same stimulus conditions. Punishment, on the other hand, reduces the probability that a behavior will be repeated. Skinner's approach has been very influential in classroom management as well as in clinical approaches to treating disorders.

Slow-to-warm-up temperament—This is the temperament label for infants who are relatively less responsive to people and other stimuli in the environment.

Small-for-date babies—The term used for neonates born after the full 36-week gestation who have lower than normal birth weight, and to premature babies who have exceptionally low birth weight.

Social cognition—Reasoning about social situations and social relationships.

Social comparison—The process of comparing one's own abilities and characteristics to those of his or her peers.

Social learning theory (observational learning)—A contemporary modification of traditional learning theory. Social learning theorists argue that changes occur in behavior as a result of modeling the behavior of others. In this way, new behaviors are acquired not through the process of shaping and direct reinforcement and punishment, but through vicarious reinforcement. Albert Bandura formulated the social learning theory. The social learning theory suggests that our cognitions about the behavior of others we observe influence our own behavior.

Sociocultural theory—This theory describes the influence of social and cultural forces on human development. Lev Vygotsky formulated this approach and argued that an individual's cognitive development occurs within a context of interaction between the individual and other members of the individual's culture. Hence, sociocultural values and beliefs are transmitted to younger generations in a society.

Sperm—The term for the male reproductive cell found in the testes.

Stage theory—Also known as discontinuity theory. Any developmental theory that suggests development occurs through a series of qualitatively different stages or phases. Stages are usually described as having to occur in a specific order and as being universal across contexts and/or cultures.

Stranger anxiety—A negative emotional reaction to unfamiliar people that appears in normal development beginning around the age of six months and lasts through the second year.

Sucking reflex—One of the neonatal reflexes present at birth. If you stimulate the lips of a newborn, he or she will begin to suck.

Sudden Infant Death Syndrome (SIDS)—The death of an infant during the first year from respiratory failure that has no identifiable cause and usually occurs when the infant is sleeping. Research has identified a correlation with maternal smoking.

Superego—The part of the personality structure in Freud's psychoanalytic theory that develops in middle childhood. It is the part of the psyche that contains moral standards of behavior. These moral standards are internalized during the resolution of the Oedipal and Electra complexes of the phallic stage of development. The superego is the source of moral anxiety and guilt.

Survey research—A method used in descriptive research to collect a lot of information from a large sample of participants.

Symbolic representation—The cognitive ability to use one thing to stand for or mean something other than itself. A word is an example of a symbol. This ability comes in at the end of sensorimotor intelligence.

Syntax—The grammatical rules of a language.

Syphilis—A sexually transmitted disease that is easily treatable with penicillin. Syphilis organisms can pass through the placenta of an infected pregnant woman after 18 weeks gestation and cause the fetus to be infected, miscarried, or stillborn.

T

Tabula rasa—The term used by the ancient Greek philosopher Aristotle and the British philosopher John Locke to describe the mind as being blank at birth. This is an extreme nurture view in the nature-versus-nurture controversy.

Tay-Sachs disease—A fatal genetic disease caused by a pair of recessive genes which cause nervous system degeneration. Children with this disease normally do not live beyond childhood and typically can trace their ancestry to Jewish relatives from Eastern Europe or French Canadians.

Telegraphic speech—The term for the abbreviated speech of young children in which two or three word combinations stand in place of complex sentences. In this way the speech is economical.

Temperament—The term used for the characteristic way an infant responds to people and the environment. It is viewed as an early form of personality. The three infant temperaments are slow-to-warm-up, easy, and difficult.

Teratogen—A substance that can pass from a pregnant mother to the fetus and cause harmful effects.

Terminal drop—A term for the precipitous drop in cognitive functioning occurring just prior to death.

Test bias—Traditional intelligence tests have been shown to be biased against those from the lower socioeconomic class. It is theorized that this is because test items are drawn from the experience of members of the middle and upper classes.

Testosterone—The male sex hormone that is secreted by the testes and that directs the development of the male reproductive system during prenatal development and puberty. It, along with other androgens, stimulates the growth of secondary sex characteristics during puberty and stimulates the secretion of growth hormone (GH) which triggers the adolescent growth spurt.

Thalidomide—A prescription drug used by many women in the 1950s to control nausea during pregnancy. The drug caused birth defects in limbs, feet, hands, or ears depending on when the drug was used during pregnancy.

Theory of mind—The understanding that people have states of mind and what takes place in the mind of others is responsible for guiding their reactions.

Third trimester—The name for the phase of prenatal development from the ninth week through birth. The fetus is less susceptible to the effects of teratogens at this time.

Time out—A method of discipline that is based on the operant conditioning model. Children given time out are removed from the situation in which undesirable behavior is occurring in order to remove what is reinforcing the behavior.

Tracking—A perceptual ability to follow a moving stimulus.

Transductive reasoning—A characteristic of the illogical reasoning of the preoperational child. This is inaccurate thinking about cause and effect in which the child believes that events that have simply occurred together are causally related.

Triarchic theory of intelligence—A theory of intelligence proposed by Robert Sternberg that argues there are three types of intelligence: analytic intelligence, creative intelligence, and practical intelligence.

Trust versus mistrust—The first stage in Erik Erikson's psychosocial model of personality development; this stage lasts from birth until age one. The positive resolution of this psychosocial crisis is when a child develops a sense of basic trust in people and in the world. The negative resolution is a sense of mistrust in oneself and other people.

Turner syndrome—A sex chromosome abnormality in which females inherit only one X chromosome (XO). These females do not develop secondary sex characteristics, cannot reproduce, and often have specific cognitive deficiencies or some degree of intellectual disability.

Twin studies—A research technique originated by Frances Galton to investigate the nature-versus-nurture controversy. Concordance rates for traits in monozygotic and dizygotic twins are assessed. If a trait is controlled by heredity, there should be greater concordance for the trait among monozygotic twins than dizygotic twins, biological siblings, and unrelated people. Examining concordance rates between monozygotic twins separated at birth and raised apart represents the best test of the nature-versus-nurture question.

U

Umbilical cord—The structure that connects the embryo with the placenta during prenatal development.

Unconditioned response (UCR)—This is the term in Pavlov's classical conditioning theory for the motor response part of a reflex.

Unconditioned stimulus (UCS)—This is the stimulus that elicits a reflexive response in Pavlov's classical conditioning theory.

Unconscious—The part of the psyche that Freud suggested contained innate drives and impulses. These instincts are described as animalistic and irrational. One instinct Freud underscored in his system was the libido or sexual instinct. The unconscious also is a receptacle for repressed thoughts. Thoughts that are unacceptable to the ego and superego are pushed into the unconscious to reduce anxiety. It is these repressed thoughts, however, that can lead to neuroses.

Uninvolved parenting style—One of the parenting styles studied by Diana Baumrind. Parents who adopt this style do not pay attention to the child or care for the child's needs. There are no rules of the household and no discipline. These parents are low in control/demandingness and low in acceptance/responsiveness. Children raised with this parenting style tend to engage in antisocial behavior.

Universality—The principle that developmental changes occur in all people across all cultures.

Unoccupied play (functional play)—An early form of play in which the child repeats movements like rolling a car back and forth, but the activity does not appear to be directed toward any particular goal.

V

Vicarious reinforcement—The term for the control over an individual's behavior that is a consequence of observing a model being reinforced. Social learning theorists argue an individual is more likely to imitate a model's behavior if he or she observes that behavior being rewarded.

Visual acuity—The degree to which an observer can perceive details in a stimulus.

Visual cliff experiment—Eleanor Gibson's classic experiment done to test whether depth perception is learned or innate. She created a visual cliff using a box with a checkerboard pattern on the floor with a clear glass top. Half of the box had a raised checkerboard piece and the other half had the checkerboard pattern on the floor. There appeared to be a drop-off at the halfway point of the glass top. She tested seven-month-olds and found the majority would not crawl across the visual cliff.

Vygotsky—The Russian theorist who created the sociocultural theory of development.

W

Wechsler Adult Intelligence Scale (WAIS)—A popular measure of intelligence in adults that measures verbal and non-verbal intelligence.

Whole language approach—An approach to reading instruction that de-emphasizes phonics and keeps reading instruction similar to the natural process of language learning.

Wisdom—A term that means a wealth of practical knowledge and insight into life's challenges that is a result of lived experience. While wisdom normally correlates with age, it is not found only in the elderly.

Working memory (primary memory; short-term memory)—The second memory storage system in the Information Processing Approach. Memories are stored here for a brief period of time, up to a few minutes, unless one uses rehearsal. Information is worked on and encoded in this system in order to be transferred from short-term to long-term memory.

Z

Zone of proximal development—Vygotsky's term for the range of a child's competence from what she can do working alone at a task, to what she can do working with someone who is cognitively advanced.

Zygote—Name used for the fertilized ovum when it is still only one cell.

Index

H

I

M

N

Q

R

T

U

V

W

Z

Notes

Notes

Notes

Notes

Notes

Notes